The Fundamentals of Good Writing

Thomas E. Pearsall
University of Minnesota
Donald H. Cunningham
Texas Tech University

The Fundamentals

of Good Writing

Macmillan Publishing Company
New York
Collier Macmillan Publishers
London

Printed in the United States of America

Macmillan Publishing Company
866 Third Avenue, New York, New York 10022
Collier Macmillan Canada, Inc.

Library of Congress Cataloging-in-Publication Data

Pearsall, Thomas E.
The fundamentals of good writing.
Bibliography: p.
Includes index.
1. English language—Rhetoric. I. Cunningham,
Donald H. II. Title.
PE1408.P38 1988 808'.042 87-14044
ISBN 0-02-477100-7

Printing: 1 2 3 4 5 6 7 Year: 8 9 0 1 2 3 4

ISBN 0-02-477100-7

Preface

For the Teacher

Richard Young has pointed out that teachers of the "new rhetoric" are divided into two camps: one camp he designates as *new romanticism*, the other as *new classicism*.[1] By Young's definition, a major tenet of new romanticism is that writing is a mystery that at its center is unconscious and irrational. The teacher cannot "teach" writing but can only provide "occasions that stimulate the creative process."[2] New classicists, on the other hand, believe that writing is teachable, that actions that lead to good writing can be perceived, isolated, and taught. At the center of new classicism would be the attitude expressed by Aristotle:

> It is the sign of a man who knows and of the man who does not know, that the former can teach, and therefore we think art more truly knowledge than experience is; for artists can teach, and men of mere experience cannot.[3]

We agree with Professor Young. However, we also suspect that few new classicists or new romanticists exist in pure form. Some of the difficulty springs from conflicting ideas about the goals of a class in writing. Some teachers view the primary goal of a writing class as allowing students to explore their own experiences and values, producing what James Britton has termed "expressive writing."[4] For their resources, the students look mainly inward. When expressive writing produced in such classes becomes public, it will do so largely in a literary form. The creation of expressive and literary writing does often lie shrouded in mystery. One can learn, or be taught, the forms of novels, short stories, and poems, but the creation of them often does seem to spring from the unconscious and irrational parts of the mind. The process is typified by William Faulkner's description of how he came to write *The Sound and the Fury*:

> It began with the picture of the little girl's muddy drawers, climbing that tree to look in the parlor window with her brothers that didn't have the courage to climb the tree waiting to see what she saw. And I tried first to tell it with one brother, and that wasn't enough. That was Section One. I tried with another brother, and that wasn't enough. That was Section Two. I tried the third brother, because Caddy was still to me too beautiful and moving to reduce her to telling what was going on, that it would be more passionate to see her through somebody else's eyes, I thought. And that failed and I tried myself—the fourth section—to tell what happened, and I still failed.[5]

Teachers who direct their students inward to subjective writing are likely to tend toward new romanticism.

Other teachers believe that the primary goal of a writing course is to teach students how to produce writing that takes the student not inward but outward to the world at large. Teachers so oriented want to teach students how to achieve and strengthen analytical skills and how to articulate abstract concepts by clothing them in reality. While recognizing the role of intuition in writing, such teachers believe that there are conscious acts in producing writing that can be taught. Many also believe that the type of writing best suited to these goals and to a conscious process is referential writing—writing designed to inform, defend hypotheses, evaluate, and recommend.[6] It is writing that takes students outward to a world of ideas and experience. Teachers with these views are likely to tend toward new classicism.

Our beliefs place us on the classical end of the scale. We believe that general composition courses can best serve the needs of most students by having them work largely with referential writing. We have several reasons for this position.

The goals of a writing class should mirror the goals of a liberal education. The world that waits for college graduates expects that a liberal education (or the liberal components of a technical education) should teach students how to think analytically, how to deal with abstractions and integrate them with relevant examples, how to test hypotheses and evaluate evidence, and how to articulate and communicate the results of such thinking in writing and in speech. Such expectations of the educated have been a part of our civilization from the ancient Greeks to the present.[7]

A liberal education takes students outside themselves to deal with the world in all its aspects, social, political, cultural, and technological. A liberal education must accomplish something paradoxical: At the same time that it must teach students to think independently, it must also teach them to understand the assumptions and to assess the values upon which our civilization is based. A writing class restricted to inner exploration misses the opportunity to tie in with these major concerns of a liberal education.

Referential writing is the kind of writing that most students will need in college and in their work after college. Students have to research, plan, and write reports in their disciplines. They have to write the answers to examination questions. At work someday, our graduates will need to use their analytical and communication skills to write correspondence and reports that inform, analyze, evaluate, persuade, and that justify decisions and recommendations.

Finally, referential writing helps to make clear the distinction between exploring a topic and presenting that topic to an audience. In exploring a topic, a writer needs both logic and intuition. A prepared and well-stocked mind can make correct choices and reach correct conclusions in ways that seem outside conventional logic. But the presentation of conclusions, whether logically or intuitively reached, needs rhetorical skills that can be taught and consciously applied. A writing class that focuses too sharply on subjective writing is not likely to give rhetoric its due. By its very nature, referential writing forces the writer to make conscious choices to adapt to purpose, audience, and occasion.

Because we believe strongly in the values of referential writing, this is a book for teachers who plan to have their students write referential reports based upon library research as well as upon observation and experience. It is designed for use in writing classes and in writing-across-the-curriculum programs where such activities go on. The scope of the book is explained in the next section, "For the Student."

For the Student

As you will see in Chapter 1, "Discovery: The Beginning of the Writing Process," we tell you that the writing process begins with the writer thinking about the occasion, purpose, topic, and audience for a piece of writing. Perhaps a good beginning for your acquaintance with this book and our thinking is to tell you about our discovery process for the book.

The occasion of our coming together to write a composition book was prompted by several things. We are good friends who have collaborated on another book and have enjoyed working as a team. We enjoy the problem solving involved in writing. Together, we have over fifty years of experience in writing and teaching writing and feel we have something to say on the subject. That "something to say" involves a deeply held belief that a major goal of education is to take students outside themselves, to connect them to the world at large, with its diversity of ideas, cultures, literatures, political philosophies, sciences, and technologies. We firmly believe that exploring that world through writing, both in writing classes and in the classes of the various college disciplines, plays a major role in your development as a participant in your civilization. We also believe that actions that lead to good writing can be taught.

The occasion led in a natural way to our purpose: to write a book that would, as our title states, teach students the fundamentals of good writing. We visualized a book that would be both complete and concise. The purpose so simply stated led us into the complexity of exploring the topics involved. From the very beginning, we knew we needed to discuss the writing process itself. That is, how does a writer mentally, and even physically, approach the writing act? We asked ourselves questions: What is the purpose of that act? How is the act carried out? Who writes? What do people write? Why do people write? When and where do they write?

In our exploration of ideas, we realized early on that writing involves more than just process. Like any person working at a craft, writers need tools. That idea possessed us for weeks. What were a writer's tools? In one sense, the tools are paper, pencil, ink, typewriters, and word processors. We could maybe have something to say about such things, but we sensed they weren't really what we meant by tools. Finally another set of tools began to emerge in our thinking:

the words, sentences, and paragraphs that writers use. That seemed right to us. With more thought we added grammar and format to the list. Chapters, 6, 7, 8, 9, and 10, "Words," "Grammar," "Sentences," "Paragraphs," and "Format," respectively, which now seem rather obvious to us when lined up in such neat order, took weeks of debate to evolve, not to mention the months it took to compose and edit them.

Writing has conventions, such as punctuation, use of abbreviations, and capitalization, that are not a concern in speaking. We knew that in order to write a complete book about writing we would have to cover such conventions.

Interspersed with thinking about occasion, purpose, and topic, we thought about you, our eventual audience. We don't know you, of course, but we do know the thousands of students we have had in our classes. Thinking about them helped us to visualize you. We saw you as an average to above-average student with a decent high school background and an interest in learning and applying that learning. You have at least average reading skills but perhaps haven't read as much as you should have. You are probably more interested in one branch of learning than another—perhaps in the humanities or the physical sciences, for example—and you are serious about what interests you. At the moment, you probably have, at best, only a mild interest in writing. You may even fear becoming involved in a writing class. You are intelligent but lack knowledge about the writing process and the concepts and terminology used in a writing classroom.

We are quite aware that all students do not match our description of you. But we couldn't be all things to all people, and the student we have just described represents the potential student audience we felt we could reach with our book.

And so the discovery process went. Sometimes we plodded for weeks nudging our ideas forward one step at a time. At other times we would arrive quickly at concepts that would guide us throughout the writing of our book. In time, the discovery process gave way to the composing of the book—the actual planning, writing, and revising of the text you have before you. A final stage involved editing to make sure that our book was accurate and well presented in all aspects. The book that finally emerged was guided by our original discovery process but changed by additional discoveries we made along the way. Our final revision was also guided by the comments made about our manuscript by several reviewers. We thank them now but absolve them of any responsibility for the faults our work may contain. They are Arthur E. Walzer, University of Minnesota; Kathleen L. Bell, Old Dominion University; George Miller, University of Delaware; John O'Connor, George Mason University; David Stacey, University of Louisville; and Judith Stanford.

The book in its final form is divided into three parts. Part I describes the writing process and consists of five chapters. Chapter 1, "Discovery: The Beginning of the Writing Process," details the beginning of the writing process. In it we provide you with ways, such as brainstorming, to draw from within yourself knowledge about your occasion, purpose, topic, and audience.

Chapter 2, "Discovery: Using the Library," takes you outside yourself to the library. At college, we learn how to learn. The library plays a major role in learning, and we tell you how to use it efficiently.

Chapter 3, "Composing: Using Logic and Rhetoric," puts down the foundation for the composing process that follows discovery. *Logic*, as we define and use the term, is the thinking process that underlies writing. It employs thinking skills, such as generalization, classification, comparison, and contrast, that you have been developing and using for most of your life and are still developing. It is partly rational and partly intuitive. *Rhetoric* is also thinking, but it is thinking about how best to present the results of your logic: for example, how best to present a persuasive argument, or how best to define a term so that your audience will readily grasp it.

Chapter 4, "Composing: Planning, Writing, and Revising," takes you step by step through the actual composing process.

Chapter 5, "Editing," describes the final preparation of a paper, its editing for accuracy, good format, and acceptable English.

The process we describe in Part I is one that can be followed over the weeks that it might take you to write a term paper. But it can also be compressed into the 30 minutes you might have to answer an examination question. The time spent will be less, but the steps of discovery, composing, and editing will remain essentially the same.

The five chapters of Part II describe the writer's tools: words, grammar, sentences, paragraphs, and format. Successful artists and craftspeople know their tools thoroughly. Master carpenters possess a complete vocabulary to describe the tools of their craft. They know a screwdriver from its head to its tip. They know the difference between a cabinet tip, a keystone tip, and a Phillips head tip. They can describe a handsaw completely from its handle to its saw teeth. They know what configuration of backs, points, faces, and gullets in the teeth will provide the kerf (cut) they need. Whether you as a writer consider yourself to be an artist or a craftsperson, you should know your tools as well as does a carpenter. The chapters of Part II provide such knowledge. We think it's important, for example, that you understand that grammar is much more than the few prescriptive rules you have learned in school. Therefore, we tell you in Chapter 7 what grammar really is, its importance, and how you acquired it without even realizing what you were doing.

Part III is our handbook. By definition, a handbook is a small reference book that provides specific guidance to some activity. Our handbook is a succinct guide to the style and conventions of writing. We include in it a glossary of terms that will be useful to you in discussing writing. The list of proofreading marks inside the back cover is your best guide to what is available in the handbook.

Writing is hard work. It can also be an exciting exploration of what you and others know. We have not slighted the work in our book, but we hope we have also pointed the way to the exploration. We wish you good writing in school and in the rest of your life.

T.E.P.

D.H.C.

Brief Contents

III

Handbook 201

Detailed Contents

I The Writer's Process 1

II

The Writer's Tools 101

1

The Writer's Process

1

Discovery: The Beginning of the Writing Process

Reruns of the television series "The Honeymooners," starring Jackie Gleason as Ralph Kramden and Art Carney as Ed Norton, occasionally show Norton attempting to write something. Invariably he sits at the Kramden's kitchen table, poised to write, with pencil in hand and a blank sheet of paper in front of him. There is always a long pause as Norton gets ready to write. Then he begins flexing the wrist of his writing hand, moves his arms and shoulders to loosen up, flicks an imaginary speck of dust off the paper, pushes up his shirtsleeves, tentatively attempts the first stroke of a letter, adjusts the position of the paper, examines the point of the pencil—until Kramden (who has been staring his patented wide-eyed glare) screams "AWRIGHT! GIVE ME THAT!"

When inexperienced writers sit down to write, they may find, as Norton and many others have found, that the first few words don't come easily. Staring at a blank sheet of paper or an empty computer screen, they may feel that their thoughts are so deeply buried that they will never haul them to the surface of their mind and express them.

The problem seems to arise from an effort to do too much too soon or too much at one time. They may be trying to define their subject in a single sentence, they may be attempting to get the opening sentence or paragraph exactly right, or they may be trying to remember how to spell *achievement* or to recall the plural of *octopus* or some other word that they plan to use. They may be wondering if they know enough about the subject to say anything interesting and significant. If they know the subject well, they may be trying to keep their general ideas and the supporting details straight while deciding on a title for the paper.

Many inexperienced writers worry so much about what they are going to write that they put off the ordeal until the night before the paper is due. Then they must hurriedly dash off something. They are, in a way, trying to run a four-minute mile without proper preparation.

Overview of the Writing Process

In this chapter we discuss how to get started on a piece of writing. Before going into detail on how to start, however, let's look at the writing process in its entirety. We'll begin by being honest and saying that there is no one mechanical, perfectly formulated writing process. The process followed depends on many factors, including, for instance, the following:

- Time available for the work.
- Level of difficulty of the work.
- Your temperament, style, and ability.
- The kind of writing—for example, fiction, poetry, research report, personal reminiscence, newspaper article, and so forth.
- Purpose of writing—for example, to clarify a point, press home an argument, define a term, record an interesting experience, and so forth.

Such variables will frequently cause even the same writer to use somewhat different processes on different occasions. However, despite such variables and differences, there does seem to be a process that can be described. It is a process that is partly rational, partly intuitive, partly hard work, partly inspiration. Your authors, who have between them written ten books and numerous articles, can discern the working of the process in themselves. The process can be discerned in the discussions of other writers who describe how they write.[1] To some extent, the process has been spelled out in the work of writing theorists.[2] What we know about the process is encapsulated in Figure 1-1. Look at it now; study it for a moment.

As you can see, we have broken the process into three major parts: *Discovery, Composing*, and *Editing*. The solid arrows in the diagram indicate the major movement of the process. The dotted arrow between *Discovery* and *Composing* indicates the possibility, the likelihood in many cases, of the writer having to turn back in the process. The process in all but the simplest writing is a recursive one, not a linear one; that is, writers frequently have to rethink their

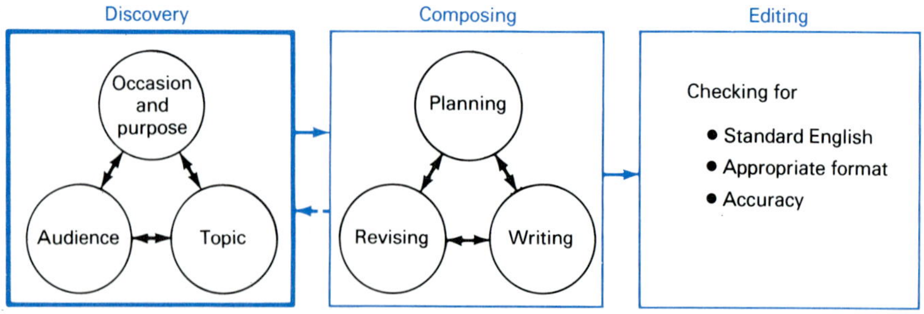

Figure 1-1 *The Writing Process.*

purpose, analyze their audience more carefully, and discover more information. But, obviously, if the work is to get done, the major thrust has to be in the direction of the solid arrows.

Briefly described, the process goes like this:

- *Discovery* is at least a three-part process. You have to analyze your writing problem in a preliminary way by thinking about the occasion and purpose for the writing, the material you will use, and the audience who will read it. Notice that the arrows between the circles for these three components are double headed. We draw them so to indicate to you that there is no set order in which to approach the components. On different occasions you may start at different points, and certainly you'll move freely back and forth among all three components while you are in the discovery part of the process.
- *Composing,* like discovery, is a three-part process. It involves planning the paper, writing the paper, and revising the paper. Notice once again that the arrows are double headed, indicating that composing, like discovery, is a flexible process. For example, you, as the writer, might begin by jotting down a simple organizational plan and then begin to write. Or you may sometimes choose to begin by writing a rough draft of the paper and then use the thoughts generated by that draft to help organize the paper. Revision may include much more than smoothing out style. It may involve additional planning and considerable rewriting. If the composing simply won't go, it's likely that you'll have to return to the discovery process to rethink your purpose or to generate or gather more material.
- *Editing* is perhaps the one stage in the process that is somewhat linear. By editing we mean making sure that your work is expressed in acceptable standard English, that it is formatted appropriately, and that your facts, calculations, and graphs are accurate. You should not enter this stage until you are reasonably sure that there is no time or no need for any turning back in the process.

In the remainder of this chapter, we discuss discovery. In Chapter 2 we discuss the use of the library when that is necessary as part of the discovery process. In Chapters 3 and 4, we discuss composing, and in Chapter 5, editing.

Occasion and Purpose

Occasion, as we use the term, refers to the situation that brings about a piece of writing. *Purpose* refers to the goals that the writer has for the piece of writing itself.

Occasion

Most of your writing in college will be done as class assignments. Teachers often regard writing assignments as a way to give students an opportunity to learn more about a subject or as a test to see if students understand the subject matter of their courses. They may also have as goals giving you the chance to think critically or to use the conventional formats and styles of their disciplines. So you are often required to research and report on some topic or problem in the discipline.

You might be asked to define some key terms in genetic engineering for your microbiology teacher. You might be asked to look into the literature concerning research done to determine if there is any correlation between being left-handed and being color-blind and report your findings to your posessor of experimental psychology. You might choose after consultation with your history professor to research and write a term report tracing the migratory patterns of German emigrants following the German revolution of 1848.

In many of these instances, you will not be writing to provide information to the teacher. After all, he or she knows the subject matter well, whereas you are still attempting to understand it. Sometimes, though, you might write as a possessor of knowledge and will write to inform teachers. For instance, the teacher may ask you to write a paper on how better to teach students to distinguish between concepts that students tend to confuse, such as the differences between *meiosis* and *mitosis* or *adsorption* and *absorption* or *fission* and *fusion*. Teachers, as you will learn, do not know *everything*. Students majoring in public health administration probably know more than their sociology or English teachers about the comparative health risks of cigarette smoking, skipping an annual physical checkup, working in certain occupations, being overweight, and driving twenty miles or more to work each day. On some occasion you might write a proposal for a term research project to inform your teacher of the topic or problem you wish to investigate, of the techniques you plan to use for gathering information, and of your qualifications to undertake the project. Or you might write a progress report to inform the teacher of your work toward completing a research project.

In addition to writing for teachers, there are also occasions for writing outside the classroom. Even before you became a college student, you might have been required to write an autobiographical essay and a statement of your academic intentions and professional ambitions. Such writing is sometimes required in applying for a scholarship or for admission to college, to professional programs in law, dentistry, medicine, and veterinary science, or to graduate school. As a student, you are also part of the larger campus community, and you may want to express your views in the campus newspaper on topics about which you are concerned. As an officer in a fraternity, sorority, or co-op, you might write to the city zoning board requesting that a project receive an exemption from a zoning ordinance. As a member of some other campus organization, you might produce a brochure or newsletter or write a report required by the dean.

You may write for yourself, perhaps for sheer enjoyment. Writing for yourself is also an excellent way to grasp a concept or work through a personal problem. Writing is a way to explore a subject. The discipline of putting your thoughts on paper forces you to be more exact in your thinking than you are likely to be when you merely reflect on the subject in your mind. Because it is indeed true that we often don't know what we think until we have written it, writing is a form of learning.

After graduation, you will discover that as a professional you will be providing information to persons inside and outside your workplace. You will, on occasion, be required to write about your work or to report on special tasks that you have been assigned. Sometimes you may choose to write memos and reports to inform others of things you think they should know or to offer recommendations. As a college graduate, you will encounter many occasions when you are expected to demonstrate in writing your critical and analytical skills. You should use the occasions for writing while you are in college to prepare yourself to meet such professional expectations.

Purpose

In college and later in your professional life, the purpose of most writing is to present and analyze reality in an understandable way. Such writing has been termed referential writing. In general the specific purposes of referential writing are these:[3]

- To present and explain knowledge you possess or to define terms.
- To explain and defend a thesis.
- To present an evaluation of something—for example, a movie, a process, a governmental policy.
- To present and support a recommendation that something be done—for example, that the movie should be seen, the process should be changed, the policy should be accepted.

The four purposes are listed in increasing order of difficulty. Also, each succeeding purpose will normally include the previous purposes. To defend a thesis, you have to present and explain knowledge. An evaluation normally contains one or more theses: *This was a good movie because the flying scenes were so realistic.* A recommendation will not stand without a thorough evaluation of the situation: *Our process for painting cars on the assembly line is expensive, inefficient, and hazardous. It should be changed by using current technology available to us.*

When, as it usually does, your occasion for writing calls for referential writing, you should frame your purpose in terms of one of the four presented here. For example, we have earlier presented three typical college assignments: defining some terms in genetic engineering, reporting research on color blindness, and tracing the migratory patterns of German emigrants that followed the German revolution of 1848. The genetic engineering paper is an easy one. It has a well-stated purpose—*definition*—and definition is one of the easier purposes to satisfy. The teachers who made the other two assignments may have purposely presented no further guidance. You can avoid writing a vague, insubstantial paper if you decide on a purpose and write your paper around that purpose, as in these suggested possibilities:

- Report and explain the current research concerning the relationship between color-blindness and left-handedness, just as a journalist might do.
- State and defend or attack the thesis that a correlation exists between color-blindness and left-handedness.
- Evaluate the research that exists concerning correlation between left-handedness and color-blindness and reach some conclusion about its effectiveness.

Each succeeding purpose is more difficult than the preceding one. Which one you choose might depend on your own strengths in the area and on which purpose you think would best satisfy the assignment. The assignment concerning German emigration could be handled similarly.

At some point in the discovery part of the writing process, you should decide on the purpose that will become a significant controlling factor in your paper. When the purpose is part of the assignment, the decision is made for you. When the purpose is missing, you will simplify your task by choosing an appropriate one for yourself.

Investigation of a Topic

Whatever the writing task, the writing has to be about something, some topic. Sometimes, the topic may be spelled out fairly specifically for you as part of the assignment or exam: "Defend or attack this statement: 'Understanding Hamlet's relationship with his mother is the key to understanding the play.'" Or "Discuss the role of television in influencing public policy. Give examples to illustrate your discussion." At other times, you will have only a broad and general area to deal with: nuclear power, the Middle East, free will, diplomatic history, or personal experience. At such times you will need to generate a specific topic for yourself. Before focusing in on your topic, you may have, as we have seen, some idea of purpose. It too may be quite specific, as in "define several key terms in genetic engineering," or somewhat vague, as in "Explain why you have come to college."

In any case—specific or general topic, specific or general purpose—most writing begins with a period of focusing in on a topic, a time spent in inventorying information already held and generating ideas about what to do with such information. Much of the intellectual adventure of writing, certainly much of the learning, is created by discovering what you know and what you don't know. You have to deal with a paradox at the beginning of any writing task. If you focus in too quickly or too tightly on a topic, you may needlessly restrict yourself and overlook much that would be worth remembering, learning, and saying. But if you focus in too slowly or too fuzzily, you may not generate enough pertinent information or ideas to support the development of your paper when you come to the composing stage. To help you in this critical stage, we present three methods of focusing in—*brainstorming, asking questions,* and *developing a hypothesis*—that are flexible enough to help you uncover a good deal of information and yet structured enough to move you toward your goal of a worthwhile paper.

Brainstorming

Brainstorming is an effort to generate as many ideas as possible about a problem or topic, without concern for judging or organizing the idea. It is based upon the association of ideas—the process by which one idea calls up another one, so it is imperative that the generation of ideas is not interrupted until there are no ideas left. The goal of brainstorming is to compile a list of ideas: quantity, not quality, is the immediate concern. The ideas can be evaluated later.

You have probably used some form of branstorming as part of a group problem-solving effort, such as to come up with possible sites for a Christmas dinner, or with projects for raising money, or with ways to honor an admired person, or with solutions to a parking problem, or with a theme for a party. The success of group brainstorming depends on four key activities:

- Writing down every idea that comes up.
- Not evaluating any idea—no matter how far-fetched it seems.
- Encouraging people to build upon ideas previously stated.
- Allowing plenty of time for everybody to contribute ideas.

Even though brainstorming was originally designed for small-group activities, you can use a similar version of brainstorming to focus on a topic. But until you get used to doing it yourself, you might find the process a bit difficult. At first, you might find it hard to postpone judgment of an idea and probably will have an aversion to jotting down an idea that appears to be a little off-the-wall. Just remember that the goal is to generate as many ideas as possible. Later, you can develop criteria for evaluating the ideas and keep the good ones and discard the less appropriate ones.

Brainstorming is an important resource for writers, because it can be used to discover ideas about anything. It can be used to generate very specific ideas or very general topics.

Let's suppose, for example, that you have either been assigned or have chosen to write a term paper on some aspect of nuclear energy. It's not a totally unfamiliar subject to you; you've heard quite a bit about it during the last few years: its potential as the energy source of the future after fossil fuels have been depleted. . . . the distinctive shape of nuclear reactors and cooling towers. . . . concern about leaks of radioactive material. . . . demonstrations against power plants on the West Coast, in New Hampshire, and somewhere in England. . . . the Three Mile Island accident. . . . nuclear-powered submarines. . . . the Chernobyl accident. But you might feel that you know comparatively little about these things and might be overwhelmed by the task of choosing a topic.

A student faced with such a task produced three pages of ideas in about thirty minutes. When she was finished, she had several topics to choose from to write a paper: advantages of nuclear power over other forms of energy, security of nuclear power plants, press and media coverage of nuclear power accidents, actual dangers versus perceived dangers of commercial uses of nuclear power, beneficial uses of radiation in materials testing, medicine, agriculture, crime detection, and so on.

A page full of jottings from brainstorming is not an orderly sight. There are likely to be misspellings, unparallel lists, and repetitions of earlier ideas. But you will have a list of potential topics when the sheet is full. You will know better what you only half knew before and will have discovered things you didn't know you knew. You will also probably become aware of additional things you can pursue with another round of brainstorming. We encourage this kind of messy appearance at this point, because the jottings result from rapid-fire thinking that helps you overcome the belief that you don't have any ideas about the topic.

Once you stop brainstorming, go through the list looking for related words and for topics that might interest you. Some people will naturally be interested in pursuing particular lines of thought and topics. Somebody studying environmental science might have high interest in pollution problems; a business major might be interested in the costs of nuclear power plants or the cost/benefit ratio of safety devices; a pre-med student in the short- and long-term effects of radiation exposure and links to genetic defects, cancer, and other forms of radiation illness. A political science major is probably more interested in the political rather than the technical aspects of the topic—the role of government regulatory agencies, federal, state, and local laws and ordinances pertaining to nuclear power plants, or to the role of public opinion in developing nuclear energy policy. Any one of these topics could be chosen as the topic for a paper.

After making your choice, you may be ready for a second round of brainstorming in which the focus will be tighter than in the first. The second round of brainstorming should produce both information for your paper and ideas on how to deal with the material. Likely also, further brainstorming may reveal a revised purpose for your project.

Asking Questions

Another powerful, but more orderly, method of generating information and topics is to use the well-known and widely used journalistic questions *what?*

who? where? when? how? and *why?* This method is often an effective second stage after an initial round of brainstorming has clarified your topic and purpose for you.

Suppose, for example, you decide to write about the nuclear accident at Three Mile Island in 1979. Asking these six questions and finding answers to them would give you lots of information about the event.

What?	What is Three Mile Island?
	What actually happened?
	What could have happened?
	What could have been done to prevent it?
	What has been done to prevent its reoccurrence?
	What should be done to prevent its reoccurrence?
	What caused the accident?
	What has been the cost of cleaning up the accident?
	What effects has the accident had on the nuclear power industry?
	What effects has the accident had on government regulations concerning nuclear energy?
	What has been public opinion concerning the accident?
	What incidents of radiation sickness have been reported?
	What has been done to study the effects on the health of nearby residents?
Who?	Who owns Three Mile Island?
	Who was in the plant when the accident happened?
	Who, if anybody, is responsible for the accident?
	Who was directly affected by the accident?
	Who else was affected by the accident?
	Who decides when the plant can be reactivated?
Where?	Where is Three Mile Island?
	Where have other nuclear accidents occurred?
	Where was the problem first noticed?
When?	When did the accident occur?
	When was the accident announced?
	When were the full details of the accident disclosed?
	When will Three Mile Island be reactivated?
	When have other nuclear accidents occurred?
How?	How did the accident happen?
	How close did the accident come to being a full-scale meltdown?
	How could the accident have been avoided?
	How can the accident be prevented from reoccurring?
	How much radiation leaked?
	How did the media cover the accident?
	How did people living near Three Mile Island react?

How do people living near Three Mile Island feel about reactivating the plant?
How has the accident affected the nuclear power industry?
How have similar accidents occurred?
How many other nuclear accidents have occurred?

Why? Why did the accident occur?
Why has the accident so affected public policy?
Why, despite the accident, have some scientists continued to support nuclear power?
Why do people continue to live in the vicinity of nuclear power plants?
Why has the accident become such an emotional issue?

The questions you can ask are virtually endless. Each question might have a number of answers, and you can probe each answer by some or all of the same six questions. Any of these questions might suggest a specific topic focused enough for your paper. Some questions will reveal sharply to you those areas in which you already have sufficient information and those areas that will require additional research. Such questions can also be a basis for future research and for the future development of your paper.

Some of the questions may be more important than others, depending upon your familiarity with the subject matter or on the scope of the topic. If you are thoroughly familiar with information about the Three Mile Island accident, the new material you need can be elicited by more speculative questions such as, "What might have happened?" "What could have been done to prevent the accident?" "What has been public opinion concerning the accident?" or "When will Three Mile Island be reactivated?" If you are not very familiar with the accident, then you have to get the facts as well.

Selecting a specific topic involves ignoring most of the questions and developing just one or two. For example, if you choose to develop a topic about the future of Three Mile Island you might concentrate on those questions that relate to reactivating the power plant and what can be done to prevent a reoccurrence of the accident.

Developing a Hypothesis

Late in your investigation of your topic you may feel the need to rethink your purpose and focus it more narrowly than you did when you began. Often, a useful guide at this point is to form a hypothesis—a supposition or conjecture put forth to explain the facts and to serve as a basis for collecting and analyzing additional data (see also pages 32–33).

The most important thing to remember about a hypothesis is that it is an *unproven* theory. Here are five sample hypotheses:

- Polygraph tests should not be used in screening job applicants because such tests are often inaccurate.
- Shakespeare's *Hamlet* is based on a now-lost play by Thomas Kyd.
- Defects in the design of the Titanic contributed to the ship sinking so rapidly.
- If General McClellan had followed up the Union victory at Antietam by pursuing General Lee's army, he could have gained a decisive victory that would have ended the American Civil War in 1862.
- The accident at Three Mile Island created enough public anxiety and controversy to affect seriously the public nuclear policy of the United States government.

These statements may or may not be true, but each serves as a working hypothesis to be tested. In testing a hypothesis, you should follow these principles:

- Form your hypothesis as a declarative statement, not as a question, so that you are forced either to defend it or refute it.
- Give as much consideration to evidence that does not support your hypothesis as to that which supports it.
- Do not suppress evidence that contradicts your hypothesis.
- Be willing to modify or abandon your hypothesis if the evidence doesn't support it.
- Do not cling to your hypothesis if it is inconsistent with the facts.

You should retain a hypothesis as long as the facts support it. The more evidence that supports a hypothesis, the more likely the hypothesis is accurate. Still, we can never be absolutely certain that a hypothesis is unassailably true. Does this apply to every hypothesis? Yes. An admirer of Albert Einstein once congratulated him on the results of an experiment predicted by his theory of relativity: "It must give you a great deal of satisfaction to have been proven right." Einstein responded: "No amount of experimentation will ever prove me completely right, but one new fact can prove me completely wrong."[4] So always be prepared for that one fact that cannot be reconciled with the rest of the evidence. However, if—after a rigorous examination of the facts—you are convinced that the evidence supports your hypothesis, you are ready to regard it as your thesis, a proposition you are prepared to defend. And, of course, your thesis could be the refutation of a hypothesis—yours or someone else's.

What should be the results of your topic investigation? You should have a fairly specific topic. You should have either enough information to pursue the topic or some idea of what information you will need to gather to pursue it. You should have a focused purpose. At this point you are almost ready to move on, either to the composing stage described in Chapter 3 or to the information-gathering stage described in Chapter 2. However, before you move on, it may benefit you to think, at least in a preliminary way, about that other factor in the writing process, the audience.

Audience

When you investigate a topic and develop and test a hypothesis, you are engaged in discovering bits and pieces of information, synthesizing them into a coherent whole, adding to your store of knowledge, relating new ideas to the ones you already have, creating and clarifying your own thoughts, and getting in touch with your own feelings about the topic. You are, to a lesser or greater degree, achieving new knowledge and becoming a new person. And while you are wrestling with these changes and taking measure of your changing self, you are very much in your own private world. However, before you begin to communicate your ideas to others, you must think about the size and makeup of the audience with whom you will share your thoughts and feelings.

Audience in writing is similar to audience in speaking. You speak to your friends and relatives in a different way than you speak to strangers. You speak to close friends and relatives differently from the way you speak to casual acquaintances and distant relatives. You adjust your language and content depending on your listeners, and you do the same thing when you write.

There is, however, a significant difference between speaking to an audience and writing to readers. When you speak, real listeners give you a sense of the reality of the communication situation and provide you with immediate feedback. Because your reader is not before you when you write, that reality is difficult to achieve when you are writing. Writing to somebody you know very well, such as family and close friends, is similar to speaking to them. You know pretty much their knowledge and feelings about the topic you are discussing, and you can adapt your writing to their background, attitudes, and needs.

The audience you write for most in college will be professors, classmates, and other members of the campus community. You won't know them as well as you know family and close friends, but you can safely assume that they have expectations that you must respect.

- Your readers will expect you to know your subject. Even when you're writing about your own experiences, explore them deeply enough so that you understand them thoroughly. When additional information is needed, research your subject until you have a stockpile of data, including facts, ideas, details, and apt quotations. You won't use every piece of information you dredge up, but you should have enough solid data to allow you to pick and choose from among them.
- Your readers will expect you to present your information in a reasonable and logical manner. They will be put off by overstatements and exaggerations, unsubstantiated opinions, gross oversimplifications, and either-or thinking. They will expect you to be openminded enough to recognize and consider with respect ideas that oppose yours.
- Your readers will expect your writing to have a beginning, middle, and end. They will not respond favorably to what they perceive as a random set of

statements thrown together. Your writing should have a beginning that states your subject and thesis and piques readers' interests, a middle that provides all the information readers need, and an end that tells readers that the piece of writing is coming to an end.

- Your readers will expect you to be sensitive to their needs and their egos. They will appreciate honesty but not rudeness. They will expect your tone to be appropriate—serious when need be, light and humorous when called for.
- Your readers will expect you to follow acceptable conventions of grammar, punctuation, spelling, paragraphing, and formatting.
- Many readers will expect your out-of-class papers and reports to be well typed or printed. Others may accept neat pen-and-ink copy. However, we advise you to get in the habit of typing or word processing papers. The professional look achieved that way enhances your work.

The more you depart from these expectations, the less easy your papers become to read and the less acceptable you become to readers. The more you satisfy these expectations, the more likely most of your readers—even if they may not agree with everything you say—will be willing to hear you out.

But knowing these universal expectations is only part of the job. For specific writing situations, you also must assess how well informed your readers are about your subject and what their attitudes are. Such knowledge, at the composing stage, will help you decide what material to use and what strategies will be effective.

In writing for audiences not well informed about your subject, you will have to be prepared to furnish sufficient general background information and definitions for them to understand what is for them new and strange material. Ordinarily, in writing for a well-informed audience, the reverse is true. You would not furnish definitions of words already known. You would limit the background information you present, giving only enough to bring the reader up-to-date on the specific subject being discussed. In college, however, the occasion for the piece of writing may sometimes call for a different approach.

In college, your audience is frequently a professor who knows more about the subject than you do, who already possesses the necessary vocabulary and background. But sometimes the professor may be trying to find out if *you* know the necessary background and if *you* can define key words. At other times, the professor genuinely may not know the necessary background or vocabulary, perhaps because you are working in a related field. Therefore, you'll need on such occasions to provide background and definitions. Sometimes the need for such information is obvious from the way the assignment or test question is phrased. At other times, the need is not clear. When such is the case, if possible, clarify the matter with the professor.

You must also think of your reader's attitude about your subject and the way you treat it. In most cases, professors will be fairly objective. But they may not always be; they are human, after all, and may hold some opinions fairly strongly. And if you are writing for some forum outside of class, such as a letter to the campus newspaper, you can depend on your readers not being totally objective on all issues.

In writing on hot social and political issues (such as gun-control legislation, abortion, or commercial use of nuclear power) or on local campus issues (such as the quality of campus-cafeteria food, the adequacy of parking space for students, or the adequacy of computer facilities), you will face readers who favor one side or the other. You need to be aware of these attitudes.

It is difficult to write well on a subject about which feelings run high. Chances are that some polarization has already occurred and that many readers will already have firm opinions.

You can assume that readers who agree with your position will be inclined to receive your ideas favorably. They are reading to gather more information that supports their views. Your greatest service to them is to provide strong arguments that are supported well. You might summarize the beliefs you share and then proceed to offer additional, newer, arguments. If you don't have newer, stronger arguments to offer, you contribute little to the discussion except where you stand on a particular topic. Perhaps that is enough. But this is probably not the case, for you will not have exposed readers to new ideas.

Writing to readers who disagree with you presents a different situation. You can assume that your readers will not accept your ideas at face value and that they will be looking for any mistakes you might make. Although it is possible to change some of your opponents' minds, it is more realistic to assume that readers won't convert solely on the basis of a single argument. Such conversion is particularly unlikely when changing one's mind involves abandoning cherished beliefs and lines of reasoning that have strengthened over time. Your greatest service to your opponents (and to yourself) is to get them to understand your position and to examine the evidence you offer in support of your beliefs. It does little good to confront opponents until you demonstrate that you understand and respect their beliefs. Then you must back up your main points by supplying the data that will make the truth of your statements evident to everybody. If you can succeed in getting opponents to see that you have a coherent argument, you have succeeded in keeping the debate open.

Most people regard themselves as sincere, competent, and objective, and they are usually willing to consider the ideas of those they think share those same qualities. Readers quickly form an impression of a writer, and when they sense that he or she is sincere in purpose, is well informed about the subject, and is scrupulously honest and fair in arguing, most are willing to consider new ideas.

For example, even most advocates and opponents of nuclear energy will listen to each other. After all, both sides share several characteristics. They are concerned about their own health and the health of the nation; they are interested in making the best decisions possible concerning the nation's future nuclear power policies. Of course, there are always some who are informed and reasonable and some who are misinformed and shrill. If you enter the controversy—either as an advocate or an opponent of nuclear power—you want to be regarded as sincere, competent, and objective, not as arrogant, narrowminded, and intolerant. Achieving these goals requires the right kind of preparation.

Being sincere will involve using language your readers will understand. If you think your readers won't understand the concept of the half-life of elements, you will need to explain it simply and clearly. If you state that no nuclear plant can explode like a nuclear bomb, you will need to explain why. Being competent means being right and being able to demonstrate it. If you state that no commercial breeder reactors are operating in the United States, check to make sure you are right. Substantiate every point with the best available evidence possible. Being objective means that you will present your evidence without exaggerating the strength or underestimating the weaknesses of your case. If your research shows that nobody knows precisely the effects of low-level radiation over long periods of time, you should admit it. If you oppose storing nuclear waste in salt domes or granite foundations, you should admit that these kinds of geologic formations have remained stable for hundreds of millions of years. Then, and only then, will you have the right to go on to explain why you are concerned about this particular method of nuclear waste deposit.

Making yourself understandable is not enough. You must also give your audience a basis for believing and trusting you. Unless you are a publicly acknowledged expert on a subject, you must earn your credibility by the way you write. You certainly don't become credible by claiming that you are right and that everybody who disagrees with you is wrong. You become credible by exploring all sides of a topic and by admitting when the opposition has a point. Nearly 2,300 years ago, Aristotle wrote that being worthy of belief is the most powerful means to persuasion. Time has not dispelled that statement.

Now we return to the image with which we opened this chapter. When you have a writing task, don't sit down and, like poor Ed Norton, twiddle aimlessly. Approach the task with a process. To some degree that process will reflect your own abilities and temperament. However, because effective writing requires attention to occasion and purpose, topic, and audience, consideration of these elements is an excellent beginning.

Exercises

1. Write a short essay describing the way you have begun writing tasks in the past. Compare your approach to the approach described in this chapter. Are there similarities? What are the differences?

2. As a class, consider as an essay topic the subject of cigarette smoking. The essay when written will appear as an article in the campus newspaper. Its purpose will be to speculate about why people who smoke continue the habit in the face of increasing evidence that it is hazardous to their health. With someone taking notes on the blackboard, brainstorm the topic. (Remember that to *brainstorm* means to put down as much information on a topic as fast as possible without any attempt to criticize or organize the information as it occurs.)

Such a brainstorming session will produce a mass of information about smoking. Following the brainstorming, ask *who, what, when, where, why,* and *how* questions about smoking. After the questions have been asked, answered, and discussed, the class should divide into groups of four or five. Each group will select one member to be a recorder for the group; this person will record the material generated from this point forward. Each group will generate a hypothesis about why people smoke; using that as its basis, the group will select material relevant to the hypothesis from the material generated during the brainstorming and question exercises. Groups should not hesitate to use additional material that thinking about the hypothesis generates. How much of the available material can be used as is? How much will require additional research in the library?

Each group will consider the audience for whom the article will be written. Will they already be somewhat informed about the subject? What new information can the group offer them? Will there be any background or vocabulary problems involved? Will there be any attitude problems?

When the exercise is completed to everyone's satisfaction, the class should come back together. The recorders should report to the entire class the results of the exercise within their groups. The class should discuss the effectiveness of the exercise. Where did it run smoothly? Where did it run into problems? Was useful material generated? If the teacher wishes, the recorders' notes will be preserved to serve as a basis for future work.

3. Find a news article and an editorial on the same subject. Write a short essay that compares and contrasts them. How do they differ in purpose and in the way they approach the topic and the audience? Which is more factual and objective? Which is more argumentative? Support your statements with evidence drawn from the article and the editorial. Also, attach them to your essay. Be prepared to discuss your essay in class.

2

Discovery: Using the Library

As you saw in Chapter 1, the investigation of a topic begins with an inventory of the information you have in your head about a subject. In your inventory, you use such techniques as brainstorming and asking questions. If, when your inventory is complete, you do not have enough knowledge to enable you to move on to composing, you have to look elsewhere for information. You can gather and generate information in many ways—for example, by interviews, questionnaires, observation, and experimentation. Some disciplines emphasize one method over another. Social scientists do a good deal of their research with interviews and questionnaires. Physical scientists rely heavily on laboratory equipment and techniques. As you progress in your discipline, you'll learn the needed information gathering methodologies. However, central to all disciplines is the gathering of information from the library. Knowing how to use the library puts you in touch with information and knowledge already in existence.

Teaching you how to use the library in an efficient way is our goal in this chapter. We show you how to explore a library and describe a process for gathering information from it. We want to teach you the process, not overburden you with long lists of library resources. As the old saying goes, we don't want to give you a fish, but to teach you to fish for yourself. However, we realize that some people in our audience may have little familiarity with the resources of a library or the vocabulary needed if they are to work successfully in a library. Therefore, we end our library chapter with an alphabetical glossary of library terms. (See pages 49–52.) Even if you are already familiar with the library, you might want to browse through the glossary to see if there is some useful information new to you there. If you are innocent of much library knowledge, you ought to read the glossary with some care before you read the rest of this chapter.

Also, throughout this chapter, we have italicized and marked with an asterisk all the terms explained in the glossary. If you come across an unfamiliar term marked with an asterisk, you'll know where to find its meaning.

Exploring the Library

The first step in learning to use the library is to spend an afternoon exploring one. We describe a leisurely program for you that in a few hours will allow you to learn more about the library than a great many seniors know. Start your exploration through the library at the *circulation desk**. Check on library rules and hours. Ask for any available brochures or booklets that explain the use of the library. Find out if your library has *closed stacks** or *open stacks**. Ask about the library's *catalog**. Find out if you will be working with a *card catalog**, a *COM catalog**, a *book catalog**, or even an *online catalog**. In some libraries you may be working with some combination of two or more of these. If you will be working with a COM or an online catalog, ask for instruction in using the mechanical equipment involved.

Look through the catalog. Look up a few books by subject, title, or author. For help with subject headings, use the *Library of Congress Subject Headings** (LCSH). This red, two-volume set of books will most likely be located somewhere convenient to the catalog. Using the subject headings suggested by the LCSH, locate a few books in the catalog from a discipline that interests you. Jot down their *call numbers**. Note whether the call numbers begin with a number, something like 575.4, or letters—for example, QA365. If you discover a number, your library uses the *Dewey Decimal Classification System**. If you find letters, you're working with the *Library of Congress Classification System**.

Near the catalog, you'll find charts and maps explaining the library's system and showing where you can find different elements of the library's *collection**. Notice the location of the books of the discipline that interests you. If your library has *open stacks**, go to that location next. Walk along the shelves, noticing the book titles and the *call numbers**. Find the books with the call numbers you took from the catalog. Take them and other books in the same vicinity from the shelves. Look through them, particularly noticing the information in their tables of contents and indexes. In a leisurely way, you'll be introducing yourself to some of the ideas and vocabulary of the discipline. If you have time, read the introductions to several of the books. Perhaps one will interest you enough so that you will want to take it along with you. Check it out through the *circulation desk** before you leave the library.

Your next stop is the *reference section**. Here will be gathered the various reference books that will be so useful to you in your lifetime: *almanacs**, *atlases**, *indexes**, *dictionaries**, *encyclopedias**, *reference guides**, and so forth. Introduce yourself to the reference librarian on duty. Ask for some guidance in using the reference section and finding things in it. Often, help is available in the form of a printed guide. Often, too, the reference section will have a catalog of its own that will help you locate specific reference works. In any case, familiarize yourself with what is available and where key items are located. For example, find the *Readers' Guide to Periodical Literature** and some of the general guides, such as Sheehy's *Guide to Reference Books**.

Take Sheehy's off the shelf. Read its introduction and table of contents. Look through its section on general reference works. Note the hundreds of books available to answer almost any reference question you might have. You'll not remember all these books, of course, but you will remember where to look when you need to find them. While you have Sheehy's open, find the section, perhaps under humanities or the pure and applied sciences, that lists the reference books and *periodicals** in a discipline that interests you. Read this section with some care. Jot down the names of some of the books and periodicals. Before you leave the reference section, find some of the books and scan through them to see what they contain.

When you're through with Sheehy's, look into *Ulrich's International Guide to Periodicals**. Read its introduction and table of contents. Find the section in it that corresponds to your discipline of interest. Record the names of several periodicals that strike you as being useful. Notice those periodicals that are also listed in Sheehy's. Notice, too, that *Ulrich's* lists the *indexes** and *abstracting journals** that allow you to locate information in the periodicals it covers. Some of the indexes and abstracting journals listed may be the same ones you found in Sheehy's. Those periodicals and reference books listed in both places are likely to be the ones most useful to you as you pursue your discipline.

When you have finished your tour of the reference section, stop by the catalog again to look up the periodicals that you noted as being important to you. (Some libraries list periodicals in their regular catalog. Others list them in a separate catalog or in a computer printout. If in doubt, ask a librarian how to find out which periodicals your library holds.) Check the map to locate the periodical section; then go to it. Again walk the stacks, noticing the tremendous variety of titles available to you. There will be commercial magazines, trade and professional journals, and scholarly journals, all shelved together in alphabetical order. Using that alphabetical sequence to guide you, find the periodicals you have noted in *Ulrich's,* Sheehy's, and the catalog. Take them off the shelves and browse through them. See if you can understand the articles you read. You are beginning your education in what may become your major field.

Periodicals are tremendously useful to you. In them, you'll find the latest general information and also the latest information in specialized disciplines and professions. In scholarly journals and professional magazines, you'll be able to trace the progress of research in a specific area or trends in some business or profession. Indeed, much of your real learning in college and after will be based upon your ability to go beyond textbooks to the periodicals that provide most of the material you find condensed and interpreted in textbooks.

All this walking around and browsing takes time; perhaps you will need to devote a full afternoon. It is time well spent. Done thoroughly, it can save you many hours of time and frustration as you begin to use the library in a serious way.

One more thing. Check to see if your library has any special collections, perhaps of audio and video tapes. If such items are available, check one out, put it into a tape deck or a VCR, sit back, and enjoy it. You've earned the right.

Using the Library

Some of your research tasks are really what librarians call "ready reference questions." That is, you simply need a few pieces of information that are easily obtainable and easily recorded. Other research tasks are truly problems. They may require you to research through a wide variety of *reference guides**, books, and *periodicals**. Because you will, in such tasks, be gathering, recording, and synthesizing a large body of material, you will need a system to do it efficiently. We deal with the ready reference task first and the research problem second.

Ready Reference

Countless ready reference questions will pop up during your college career, and, indeed, your lifetime. Some are questions important in your work. Others are simply interesting, a kind of "trivial pursuit," if you will. In any case, millions of such questions can be answered if you utilize even a small *reference section**. If you have read carefully to this point and explored your library, you can probably find the answers to many such questions with no further help. As you grow more proficient in your use of the library, you will probably develop favorites among the reference books, simply because you know they contain the kinds of information you need. As a quick review of the ready reference task, let's ask and answer several questions.

• *Who won the Olympic gold medal for the men's marathon in 1984?* The answer to this question is factual, general knowledge, and is fairly current information. That combination should suggest one ready reference source, an *almanac**.

In the general index of *The World Almanac and Book of Facts*, we find a reference to "Olympic Games, Summer." Consulting the referenced pages, we find that Carlos Lopes of Portugal won the men's marathon. Perhaps for a story or essay we are doing we wish to refer to the event and want to mention the colors of Portugal's flag waving above the gold medal ceremony. Again, *The World Almanac* seems the right source to find a description of this nation's flag. Looking under "Portugal" produces a good deal of information but nothing about its flag. We try a different tack and look under "flag." There we find "Flags, World." At the referenced pages, among many flags, we find a picture of Portugal's flag, and note that its colors are green, red, gold, and blue.

• *When was Louis Pasteur born? When did he die? What were his major accomplishments?* Here we are dealing with biographical information about a well-known historical figure. We could go to *biographies**, but his stature suggests that *dictionaries** and *encyclopedias** would also contain material about him. Such is the case. *The American Heritage Dictionary* tells us that his dates were 1822–1895, and that he was a French chemist who made discoveries in immunology and microbiology. Directly below the entry for Pasteur we find "pasteurization" and "Pasteur treatment." The first, we learn, is the "process of destroying most disease-producing microorganisms and limiting fermentation in milk, beer, and other liquids by partial or complete sterilization." The "Pasteur treatment" is a treatment for rabies.

If we need more, the entry for Pasteur in *The New Columbia Encyclopedia* gives us additional information about his research and teaching and refers the reader to several biographies about him.

- *What are the job prospects for foresters?* This is a more difficult question than the previous two. Here we are dealing with information that almost certainly someone has gathered, but its source may not be immediately obvious. In such a case, turning to Sheehy's *Guide to Reference Books** is a good idea. We look into the index in the back of Sheehy's. We try "forester" and "forestry" but find nothing to answer our question. Forestry is a "profession," so we try that and again get nothing useful. When you are trying to find things by subject in an index, you have to try to outguess the people who compiled the index. You have to use your imagination. A "profession" is also an "occupation." With that we hit paydirt. "Occupation" in the index leads us to the *Occupational Outlook Handbook,* published by the U.S. Department of Labor.

In the *Handbook* we find information about most of the various trades, professions, and occupations followed in the United States—information about education and skills needed, job prospects, work conditions, salary ranges, and so forth. In the 1984–85 edition, we find that "Employment of foresters and conservationists is expected to grow more slowly than the average for all occupations through the mid-1990's." Also, we find that the average starting salary in forestry in 1983 was a little over $13,000 a year, and that the average federal forester made about $27,900 yearly.

We could produce more examples, but we hope you have now got the point. Somebody, somewhere, has probably gathered the answers to most of the questions you might think of. The problem is finding those answers. With a working knowledge of the library and some imagination, you can find many of the answers by yourself. If you are weak in ready reference work, we recommend that you read our glossary entries for *Almanacs**, *Atlases**, *Bibliographies**, *Biographies**, *Dictionaries**, *Encyclopedias**, *Handbooks and Manuals**, *Reference Guides**, and *Yearbooks**.

If you do get stuck, don't hesitate to ask the reference librarian for help. But remember that you'll get your answer much more quickly if you have thought out your question carefully before approaching the librarian.

Research Problem: Analysis of the Problem

In Chapter 1, we describe the beginning of the writing process as a discovery of your occasion and purpose for writing, your material, and your audience. Most of the discovery techniques still apply, when you prepare to deal with a research problem in the library.

Suppose that you are a beginning student in political science with a fair knowledge of current events. Suppose further that you have a term paper assignment in a class in public policy. The assignment reads as follows:

> It is often difficult to tell when public opinion affects governmental policy. Find a situation that has occurred in the last fifty years that has produced considerable public interest and controversy. Argue either pro or con on this statement: In this situation, public opinion had a significant effect on governmental policy.

Let's analyze this occasion. You are dealing with a term paper that will have a significant effect on your grade. The reader will be someone who knows far more about public policy making than you do. However, her knowledge of the specific situation you choose to discuss may be incomplete and perhaps even quite sketchy. You worry about the length of the paper. When the class questions the professor about length, she is evasive, and she responds by saying, "Your paper should be as long as it needs to be to make a convincing case." However, after further questioning, she concedes that term papers in this class average about 1,500 words. That gives you room to develop a topic, but not room to be terribly expansive. It's a tough assignment.

Remember that in Chapter 1 we suggest brainstorming as a way to begin thinking about a writing project. You brainstorm this assignment and make a list of situations that might make an interesting paper for you. You list such things as the Viet Nam war, the trade deficit, social security, civil rights, tax reform, and the hostage crisis in Iran. Late in your brainstorming, the notion of nuclear power plants comes to mind. You remember that in a high school physics class, your teacher said that the 1979 nuclear accident at Three Mile Island in Pennsylvania had soured public opinion on nuclear power and maybe ended the method's chances of ever being a major source of power in the United States. You think over that subject and decide to consider it for your term paper. You decide to go to the library and do a preliminary study to see if it is a good subject for you.

But before you go, some further thought on what you are seeking in the library might be in order. We suggest you consider the following questions:[1]

- *How familiar are you with the subject?* If you are quite familiar, you will need to seek little background information. You can proceed more directly to the heart of the problem. If you are not familiar with the topic, you will need to spend some time absorbing background information from sources you can understand. You may later choose not to use all or any of the background information in your paper, but the iceberg theory applies here. Just as most of an iceberg remains out of sight under water, much of the knowledge you gather for a paper may not make it into the paper. But the knowledge will support and enrich your paper because you will not be straining to work in every last bit of information you have on a subject and because you will have a better understanding of what you do write. For your power plant problem, you realize you need a fair amount of background.

• *How much material will you need?* You have discovered that you need enough material for about a 1,500 word paper. That does not mean that you gather 1,500 words of notes and quit. But it does give you a reasonable idea of the quantity of material you can present. A 1,500-word paper had better have a narrower scope than a book containing 100,000 words.

• *What level of material will you need?* You must consider at least two factors in answering this question. First and foremost is what level of material can you handle? If you are a novice, you'll need to deal with general sources: such things as encyclopedias, commercial magazines, and newspapers.

Second, how technical and expert must your coverage be to suit your audience? If your audience requires highly technical material, you'll have to find such material in, for example, scholarly journals and books. If you cannot handle such material, you had better rethink your problem and come up with a different subject.

In this instance, you realize that you have enough knowledge of physics and government to handle the subject at the level of an intelligent layperson. You are capable of dealing with fairly complex accounts of the nuclear power problem that might appear in high-level magazines and even some trade journals. But you would not be able to handle technical material written by physicists for other physicists. You realize that your reader probably shares your background as far as nuclear power plants are concerned. You now have a good idea of the level of material you need.

• *In what disciplines will you conduct research?* Some research projects may take you into the humanities; others will lead you to the social sciences, history, or science and technology. Some will cut across several boundaries. Such things as *indexes** and *abstracting journals** are often discipline-related, so you'll save time if through reference *guides** like Sheehy's *Guide to Reference Books** you seek reference help, *periodicals**, and books in the right disciplines.

• *What kinds of reference sources will help you?* The answer to this question depends upon your answers to earlier questions. If, for example, you need and can handle technical material, you perhaps need scholarly journals. Your starting points for such publications might be *Ulrich's International Periodical Directory** and Sheehy's *Guide to Reference Books**. These guides are largely organized by discipline, so your knowledge of the disciplines involved is important here. In our example problem, you have several disciplines as starting points, such as atomic power, environmental safety, public policy, and physics. That suggests a diversified index such as the *Applied Science and Technology Index*. If your interest is in contemporary accounts of news events, the *Readers' Guide** will point you to accounts in news magazines. The *National Newspaper Index* and *The New York Times Index* will indicate newspaper accounts. *Facts on File** will give you objective news summaries. The more you know about reference sources, the less time your search will take.

• *How much time will all this take?* Be totally realistic about the time you have to work with a research problem. But also plan enough time to do a respectable job, and stick to your plan. Library research and writing are time-consuming. Suppose you have eight weeks to complete your research and your paper. You realize that you can budget about four hours a week for the project, thirty-two hours in total. You figure that planning, writing, and revising the paper will take about twelve hours. That leaves twenty hours for your research. That's the equivalent of two and a half working days. The time should be comfortable if you promptly begin the research and stick to your plan.

As you grow skilled in using the library, you'll be able to mount a search with only limited help from reference librarians. But when you do need help, you'll find that having thought through the answers to the questions we have posed here will speed the process greatly. You'll be able to approach the librarian with sharper, more relevant questions than if you simply throw yourself on the librarian's mercy with a request like, "I need some stuff on nuclear power, you know, atomic plants and stuff."

Once you have thought through your problem, it's time to go to the library and begin your literature search.

Research Problem: Searching the Literature

Your first step is to learn how much and what kind of material your library has available on your subject. You have decided that you need material suitable for an intelligent layperson. You have also decided that the situation created by the Three Mile Island (TMI) accident is likely to be the focal point of your paper. You have even created a tentative hypothesis:

> The TMI accident created enough public anxiety and controversy to affect seriously the public nuclear policy of the United States government.

Remember that a hypothesis is simply a statement subject to proof; it is not necessarily true or false. You will approach it scientifically, being as happy to demonstrate it wrong as correct. The facts you find and your interpretation of these facts will decide the issue. Used properly, the hypothesis will sharpen the focus of your research.

You need background on the TMI accident. The sensible starting point seems to be contemporary accounts. The accident occurred in 1979. Because news magazines are familiar to you and easy to work with, you go to the *Readers' Guide to Periodical Literature** and take the 1979 edition off the shelf. After trying several subject headings, you find numerous relevant articles under headings such as "atomic power plants" and "atomic power industry." Looking into the 1980 and later *Readers' Guides,* you find a steady stream of articles on TMI. You breathe a sigh of relief. There will be no shortage of material.

You have to record the citations to these articles. How will you do that?

At this preliminary stage of your search, a notebook will probably be sufficient. Be sure to record enough information from any index you use to enable you to find what you are seeking. In your notebook you record a working bibliography, a portion of which looks like this:

> "Atomic Mishap; Setback for Nuclear Power; Three Mile Island Nuclear Power Plant." *U.S. News & World Report.* 86:23, April 9, 1979.
>
> "Three Mile Island; a Hot Attraction." S. L. Begley and M. Lord. *Newsweek* 94:12+, Oct. 1, 1979.
>
> "Global Shock Wave; Samplings of Worldwide Reaction to Three Mile Island Accident." *Atlas World Press Review* 26:39–41, June 1979.

In your preliminary analysis, you decided that you would want some material from a level higher than is found in news magazines. Also, you realize that you might get a more complex analysis in specialized magazines. To pursue such material, you turn to the *Applied Science and Technology Index* for 1979 and beyond. Under the heading "atomic power," you find many promising articles. You add more items to your working bibliography, including these:

> "Lessons from Three Mile Island." J. Edwards. *New Scientist* 97:79–84, Jan. 13, 1983.
>
> "Nuclear Power Outlook Dim, Report Concludes." *Chemical and Engineering News* 62:5, Feb. 13, 1984.

While you are in the reference section, you decide to look into Sheehy's *Guide to Reference Books** to see if it may have some leads for you. You find that Sheehy's lists some sources under the heading of "Nuclear Engineering." Under that heading you find, among other things, that the U.S. Atomic Energy Commission publishes *Nuclear Science Abstracts*. Sheehy's says that *Nuclear Science Abstracts* covers government reports, reports from universities and research organizations, and conference proceedings. This strikes you as a useful reference, and you jot down the name for future use. You also take note of two dictionaries of nuclear terms and several handbooks. These may come in handy later, and you record their names in your notebook as well.

As you look up from Sheehy's, the reference librarian comes by. A question occurs to you. You ask the librarian if there are any encyclopedias that give a more technical account of atomic power plants than you would find in a general encyclopedia.

"You might try the *McGraw-Hill Encyclopedia of Science and Technology,*" he answers. "It's on the wall over there, to the right."

Finding the encyclopedia, you glance through several volumes. Under "nuclear power" you find a ten-page article, written at a level you can understand and profusely illustrated with pictures and schematics detailing how nuclear power plants work. There is also a section on the regulatory agencies and laws that govern such plants. You spend thirty minutes reading for background and make a note to return to the encyclopedia if you later run into concepts you do not understand.

You already have a working bibliography that will keep you busy, but you decide to check the *catalog** before you begin. For new acquisitions your library uses a *COM catalog**. You go to a *microfiche** reader and insert a microfiche that includes coverage of "atomic." There you find, under "atomic power plants," useful looking books that, noting their *call numbers**, you add to your working bibliography:

Nuclear Energy Prospects to 2000: A Joint Report by the Secretariats of the OECD–Nuclear Energy Agency and the International Energy Agency. Washington, D.C.: OECD Publications and Information Center, 1982. (TK 9145 .N828)

Before It's Too Late: A Scientist's Case for Nuclear Energy. Bernard L. Cohen. New York: Plenum Press, 1983. (TK 9145 .C576)

You also note in the catalog entries other subject headings where you can pursue additional information at a later time. "Energy policy" and "government policy" look especially promising.

You look at your watch and realize that you have been at your search for over two hours. It's time to call it a day. You pick up your notebook with its working bibliography and other reference notes. You feel well satisfied and plan to get back in a few days to continue your search.

Research Problem: Recording the Literature

Before you return to the library for further research, we suggest you stop by the bookstore and buy a pack of cards that are at least four-by-six inches in size. From here on, you will record your bibliographic notes and your informational notes on the cards. Why should you abandon your notebook or, perhaps, your yellow pad as a recording device? The answer lies in ease of organizing. Notes taken on notebook pages, pages ripped from pads, and old envelopes are notoriously hard to organize. Notes taken on cards are simple and easy to organize in any order you wish: alphabetical, chronological, argumentative, whatever. The notebook is satisfactory, as we have seen, for recording items you *may* use. It is really inadequate for taking notes from items that you *do* use. As you continue your research, you will create two sets of cards, one with bibliographic information, the other with informational notes from your sources.

Bibliographic cards. As soon as you know you are going to record information from a source, create a bibliographic card for it. Write down on the card *all* the information you may need later on to create a bibliographical or reference note for the item (see pages 181–190). Failing to take all the information when you first have the item in your hand often leads to time-wasting, frustrating, last-minute trips back to the library late in the writing of your paper. Figures 2-1 and 2-2 illustrate bibliography cards, one for a book, one for an article. It is not necessary that the information on the card be exactly in the form it will take as a note, but it helps if it bears some resemblance to that form. Note that the book entry in Figure 2-1 includes the *call number** (TK 9145 .C576). The article entry in Figure 2-2 includes the volume number (51), issue number (10), date (March 1, 1985), and inclusive page numbers (309–12).

In the upper, right-hand corner of the bibliographic card, place a brief phrase or name that will identify the source for you: "Before It's Too Late" for the book and "Weaver" for the article in our figures. As you'll see when we

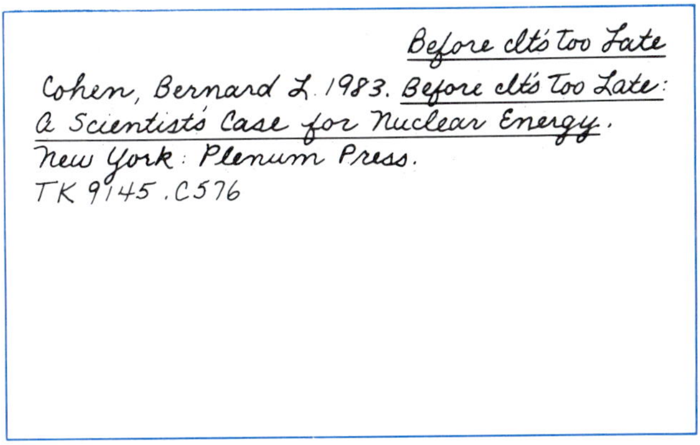

Before It's Too Late

Cohen, Bernard L. 1983. Before It's Too Late: A Scientist's Case for Nuclear Energy. New York: Plenum Press. TK 9145 .C576

Figure 2-1 *Bibliographic Card: Book.*

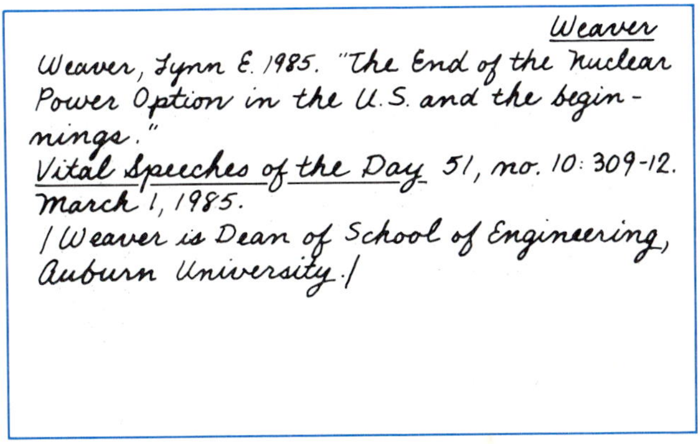

Weaver

Weaver, Lynn E. 1985. "The End of the Nuclear Power Option in the U.S. and the beginnings." Vital Speeches of the Day 51, no. 10: 309-12. March 1, 1985.
/Weaver is Dean of School of Engineering, Auburn University./

Figure 2-2 *Bibliographic Card: Article.*

discuss note cards, these source identifiers will save you a good deal of time. As illustrated in Figure 2-2, you can also put notes about the source on the bibliographic card.

Note cards. Figures 2-3 to 2-5 illustrate various kinds of note cards. We have annotated Figure 2-3 to make discussing it easier. Look at it before reading on.

In the upper left-hand corner of a note card, you write the topic identifier, a short phrase that identifies the topic the note concerns. The topic identifier enables you easily to find the cards you have on a given topic, but its value goes beyond that. Creating the topic identifier forces you to begin thinking about the topics and subtopics your paper will contain. Additionally, as you later review and organize your material, the sorting of your note cards into different packs according to topic identifiers is likely to be an important step in organizing your paper.

In the upper right-hand corner, write your source identifier, the short phrase you created to identify the source on a bibliographic card. The source identifier keys you back to the bibliographic card and saves you from having to write out the full documentation on each note card.

The main body of the card is the note itself. Be sure to make only one note per card. If you crowd cards with several notes, you'll destroy the ease of sorting the cards. Compared to your time, note cards are cheap. Also, we suggest that you take your notes in ink. Pencil will smudge and become difficult to read in time. Some people, though, do like to put the topic identifier in pencil, so they can easily change the wording as their organization becomes clearer to them. We also suggest that you use only one side on each card. It's much easier to

Not to keep you in suspense, let me jump ahead to my conclusion: No, nuclear power is not a viable energy source in the United States—not yet. In 1984 the concept of nuclear energy as a realistic source of new supplies of electric power was officially pronounced dead. Yet at the same time seeds were being planted that could well lead to its revival before the end of the '80s.

The announcement of nuclear power's demise came not from its critics, but from its own trade association, the Atomic Industrial Forum. A major report on "Nuclear Power in America's Future" produced by a senior SIF study group began with this historic lead sentence: "Nuclear power cannot at this time be considered a viable option on which to base new electric generating capacity in the U.S." Thus the nuclear industry itself was declaring the nuclear option dead.

Even though the source of that statement may have been a shock, no one who has followed for fortunes of nuclear power

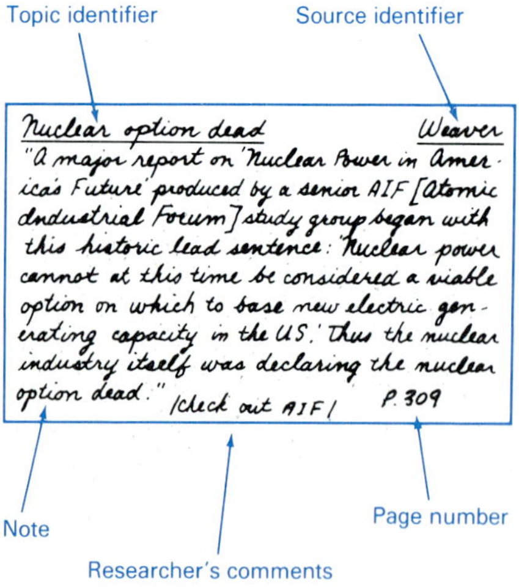

Figure 2-3 *Note Card: Verbatim Quote.*

read them when you review your material and write your draft. If you do use both sides, write a big *OVER* on your card to remind yourself to look on the other side.

Under your note, put the page number or numbers where the material can be found. If you are taking a verbatim quotation that comes from two pages, it is a good idea to indicate in your note where the page break comes.

Finally, at the bottom of the card you may have your own comments or ideas that have been stimulated by the material you are reading. Place slashes around such comments, so that you'll know they are your own material and not from the source.

When you take notes, they are either verbatim quotes, paraphrases, or summaries of the material you are working with. The verbatim quotation is illustrated in Figure 2-3. You may wish to use the verbatim quote when the source so clearly and economically makes a point that you see no reason to recast it. You may also use verbatim quotes from authorities in the field as a way of strengthening your paper. However, too many verbatim quotes will suggest that you have not synthesized your material, that you have not understood it fully. Use verbatim quotes sparingly.

When you do use verbatim quotes, use them exactly. Do not misquote. You may eliminate material you don't need as long as you don't change the intent of the author. If you do omit material, indicate the omission with the ellipsis: three spaced dots, four at the end of a sentence (see pages 252–253). If you add material to a quote, as in Figure 2-3, perhaps to clarify a date or to straighten out sentence order, enclose the added material in brackets. Do not use parentheses for such additions (see page 238). If there are already quotation marks within the material you are quoting, as in Figure 2-3, use single quotation marks to indicate them (see page 267). Finally, put bold quotation marks around the quotation so that no doubt will exist in your mind at some future date that the material is quoted.

Sometimes instead of quoting, you will paraphrase or summarize the material. In a paraphrase, you restate the material in your own words, but do not shorten it particularly. In a summary you condense the material. In either case, you must exercise particular care not to use the phrasing of the original. While you may well and legitimately use a few of the key words of the original, merely changing a few prepositions or adjectives is not enough. You must truly restate the material. *You plagiarize if you use the exact words and sentence structures of other people as your own or even if you use too close paraphrases.* Plagiarism in school can result in a failed paper, a failed course, or worse. In life beyond school, it can result in law suits. Plagiarism is both unethical and illegal.

In the note-taking process, we recommend that you extract your material in a condensed way as often as possible. It helps when extracting material to avoid using complete sentence structures. In that way, when you reconstruct the material into complete sentences for your paper, you are much more likely to use your own words and phrases.

Figure 2-4 illustrates a paraphrase, Figure 2-5 a summary.

Utilities are still building 30 nuclear plants that they hope to have in operation by the end of the decade—and every one of those projects was ordered in 1973, or before. The average construction period for U.S. nuclear plants has doubled since the early 1970s, from 6 years to 12. This can be compared to nuclear plants that have recently been completed in France, Japan, Sweden, Taiwan and other countries in only five to six years—often, plants that are virtually identical to U.S. projects and that are even designed and constructed by the same U.S. suppliers. A recent study has shown that nuclear generating costs would be 40 percent lower than coal generating costs if the construction time for nuclear plants was comparable to that in France or Japan.

> Construction time — Weaver
>
> - 30 nuclear plants still under construction.
> - Planned completion dates for 1990.
> - All ordered in 1973 or earlier.
> - Completion times: early 1970s 6 years, now 12 years.
>
> P. 310
>
> /Tie this increase in construction time in with the increase in government regulation./

Figure 2-4 *Note Card: Paraphrase.*

Historically investors have bought utility stock—not for any get-rich-quick ambitions, but for security. Utility investors have in effect, traded the opportunity for high returns in exchange for a minimal risk: They felt confident that, if a utility sold stock to help finance a new power plant, that plant would indeed begin producing power—and begin earning money to repay their investment—roughly on the schedule that had been laid out.

That is no longer the case. Regulatory and management problems have delayed plants for years and contributed to costs that have gone up as much as a factor of 10. After a decade of construction and billions of dollars of expense, some new plants are not being allowed entirely in the "rate base" by regulatory commissions, where they can repay their investment costs. At least in the case of Shoreham, a plant is not being allowed to operate at all because of local government opposition. Today it appears that investors in utility construction programs are accepting a limited return—but are being saddled with a sizable, open-ended risk. Investors in several utilities have seen their dividends cut, or totally eliminated, and some have even had to explore the ramifications of a utility bankruptcy.

> Effect on investment — Weaver
>
> Utility stocks formerly a safe investment, though with low returns. Now a risky investment, but still low return.
> Why? Excessive costs from delays caused by problems in management and government regulation
>
> P. 310

Figure 2-5 *Note Card: Summary.*

Research Problem: Thinking and Reviewing

As you proceed with your research problem, take time periodically to review what you have and to think about what you still need. As you gather your material, relate it to your audience and purpose. Consider questions like these: Are you answering your main research questions? Is the material you are gathering and synthesizing suitable to your audience and purpose? Do some of the answers you're getting raise new questions? Are there leads you have that need to be followed up? Does the evidence you are gathering support or refute your hypothesis? Do you have enough material in a given area to satisfy your requirements? Does the material you have gathered suggest a change in the original tentative hypothesis?

After you have been investigating the nuclear power problem for a few weeks, a review might reveal the following to you:

- You have sufficient evidence to show that the nuclear accident at TMI was a serious one with long-lasting effects. You have a sufficient understanding of what happened to be able to relate it in lay terms in your paper. You do not need any more information in this area.
- You have learned that some nuclear experts think there are different kinds of atomic power plants that are safer alternatives to current models. You need to explore that avenue a bit because the growth of safer alternatives could affect public opinion and public policy.
- You realize that for years following the TMI accident a steady flow of articles about TMI has appeared in newspapers, magazines, and trade and professional journals. This constant interest by itself is an excellent measure of public concern and reaction. You wonder if anybody has done an actual count or if it would be worth your time to do a year-by-year count, say in the listings of the *Readers' Guide** and the *Applied Science and Technology Index*.
- The Nuclear Regulatory Commission (NRC) has increased its staff since TMI and at the same time drastically reduced the number of atomic power plant operating licences it has issued. It has issued no new construction permits at all. This certainly indicates a change in public policy. In fact, you know that some advocates of nuclear power think the NRC is a bureaucracy run rampant and more of a threat to the development of safe atomic power than TMI. Regardless of who is right on that issue, the tightening up indicates a change in public policy.

And so on. As you continue to review your material at regular intervals, you'll see increasing amounts of information in many areas. You'll begin to feel confident in your grasp of the material. A plan for your paper will begin to form in your head as discovery moves quite naturally into composing. In fact, thinking about the plan of your paper will guide your research as you realize you need more or less information in certain areas. Conversely, waiting too long to plan your paper may reveal large holes in your information at a time when it is too late to fill them.

At some point, your research will be done. We hope it will be because you have gathered everything you need and not because you have run out of time. When your research is done, you must compose your paper. The strategies and tasks of composing are the subjects of our next two chapters.

Glossary of Library Terms

Abstracting Journals An abstracting journal is closely related to an *index**. It is a guide to finding *periodical** articles. Like an index, the abstracting journal allows you to search for an article under the headings of either author or subject. Like an index, the abstracting journal will locate the article for you on a specific

THE SILENT SCREAM: PATTERNS OF HORROR IN THE WORKS OF HENRY JAMES

DEFREN, JUDITH, PH.D. *The University of Manitoba (Canada)*, 1984.

This study explores the patterns of horror in the novels and stories of Henry James. It traces the recurring motif of crises that shake the foundations of the characters' belief in themselves, in others and in their society. Although critics have alluded to Jamesian horror, they have not treated it as a vital component in the development of character and as a necessary ingredient for self knowledge. Horror, a central element in James's fiction, acts as a catalyst. It is defined as the realization by the characters of those destructive elements that lurk behind and beneath the fragile fabric of a carefully built and mannered society. In the confrontation between the Jamesian character and cultured civilization, the confrontation with horror bring awareness and, although revelation brings pain, the consequences of the moment often heighten the sensibilities and the imagination of the sensitive; the characters can never again be as they were. The protagonists who can delve into and remain with the emotions that are aroused by the horror approach their lives transformed and with greater strength to endure. The confrontation, though sometimes fatal, is still positive and live-affirming. In James's fiction, horror illuminates; revelation is life, action and knowledge.

The themes of confrontation, recognition and revelation used by James fall into five patterns of horror: the death of innocence and the victimization of the young; the depotism of the family; the well-intentioned destroyer; the betrayal in marriage; and the horror within. This study comments on the principal texts that assert the patterns, illustrating how the patterns of horror reverberate through them.

Figure 2-6 *An Abstract. (From* Dissertation Abstracts International *46, no. 1 (1985), 151-A.)*

page in a specific periodical. But, in addition, the abstracting journal provides an abstract—that is, a short summary of the article. For an example, see Figure 2-6. The abstract will usually allow you to decide whether you need to read the article. Sometimes the abstract itself may contain all the information you need. Abstracting journals are available in most disciplines. See, for example, *Psychological Abstracts, Abstracts of Popular Culture, Historical Abstracts,* and *Chemical Abstracts*.

For information on how to find an abstracting journal useful in your discipline, see *Indexes** and *Reference Guides**.

Almanacs For ready reference information and quick access to a multitude of miscellaneous facts, nothing can be more useful than an almanac. In an almanac, such as *The World Almanac and Book of Facts,* published annually, you can find complete copies of the Declaration of Independence and the Constitution; Olympic Games information, such as records and winners of the events; weather, income, and employment statistics for all major U.S. metropolitan areas; zip and area codes; and so on. *The World Almanac's* Quick Reference Index reproduced in Figure 2-7 will give you some idea of the information you can find. To use any almanac, consult such a quick reference or the more complete general index. For more complete coverage on Great Britain and Europe, consult *Whitaker's Almanac,* published in London. See also *Reference Guides**.

Atlases Geographic information is the special province of atlases. General-purpose atlases, such as Rand-McNally's *Cosmopolitan World Atlas,* the *National Geographic Atlas of the World,* and *The National Atlas of the United States of America,* provide hundreds of maps and indexes to the maps. In general-purpose

QUICK REFERENCE INDEX

Figure 2-7 *Quick Reference Index. (From* The World Almanac and Book of Facts, *1985 edition, copyright © Newspaper Enterprise Association, Inc., 1984, New York, NY 10166.)*

atlases, you can find information on the location, size, topography, population, resources, climate, and geology of the major areas of the world.

In addition to the general-purpose atlases, there are many specialized ones that deal specifically with such topics as soils, mineral resources, manufacturing, crops, history, trade, literature, economics, and so forth. One example of such is the *Commercial Atlas and Marketing Guide,* which contains information on business, trade, transportation, and manufacturing. Another is *The Times Atlas of World History,* which, through maps, charts, and incisive essays, traces humankind from the age of hunters and gatherers through modern times. See also *Reference Guides**.

Bibliographies A bibliography is a list of books and articles in a given subject matter area or located in a specific place. The *catalog** in your library is the bibliography for your library. It lists all the books (but not the articles) held in your library's *collection**. Bibliographies appear in book form and at the end of articles in *encyclopedias** and *periodicals**. To find such bibliographies, see the *Bibliographic Index,* an annual guide to such sources.

Useful general bibliographies are *Books in Print* and *Subject Guide to Books in Print.* These multivolume bibliographies list by title, author, and subject all the books printed in the United States that are currently available "in print." This means that they are available as new books. The *Cumulative Book Index* lists books printed in English anywhere in the world.

Specialized bibliographies also exist. Examples of such are the *MLA International Bibliography of Books and Articles in the Modern Languages and Literatures, International Bibliography of Social and Cultural Anthropology, Social Science Reference Sources, Current Information Sources in Mathematics,* and *Guide to the Literature of the Life Sciences.* See also *Reference Guides**.

Biographies For short reference sources to well-known people, you can look under their names in collegiate *dictionaries** and general *encyclopedias**. For longer references, and for people less well known, you'll have to turn to books that specialize in biographies. Some of the most useful are the various *Who's Who* books: *Who's Who in America, Who's Who in American Art, Who's Who in Rock Music,* and so forth. Most major fields have a specialized biographical source, with either a *Who's Who* title or a title such as *American Men and Women of Science.* Other useful biographical sources of a more general nature are *Current Biography, Dictionary of American Biography, Dictionary of National Biography* (for the British), and *McGraw-Hill Encyclopedia of World Biography.* See also *Reference Guides**.

Book Catalog See *Catalog**.

Call Number Every book in your library's *collection** has a call number printed on its spine; that is, on the back of the book that you see as you scan the shelves. The call number is the book's identifier. Think of it as the book's address. It is also found on the entry in the library's *catalog** for the book (see *Catalog** and Figure 2-8). With the call number, you can find the book on the shelves or request it at the *circulation desk**.

Card Catalog See *Catalog**.

Catalog The catalog is the library's bibliography (see *Bibliographies**). It lists all the books in the library's *collection**. You are very likely familiar with the file cabinets with their rows of alphabetically marked drawers that comprise the typical card catalog. You search through the card catalog either by the name of the author, title of the book, or a subject identifier. Every book in the card catalog will have one card for the author, one for the title, and one or more for the subject, depending on how the book is cross-referenced. The *call number** displayed on each card is your key to finding the book you're after.

Look at Figures 2-8 through 2-10, which display four cards for a particular edition of Charles Darwin's *On the Origin of Species.* Notice that all four cards

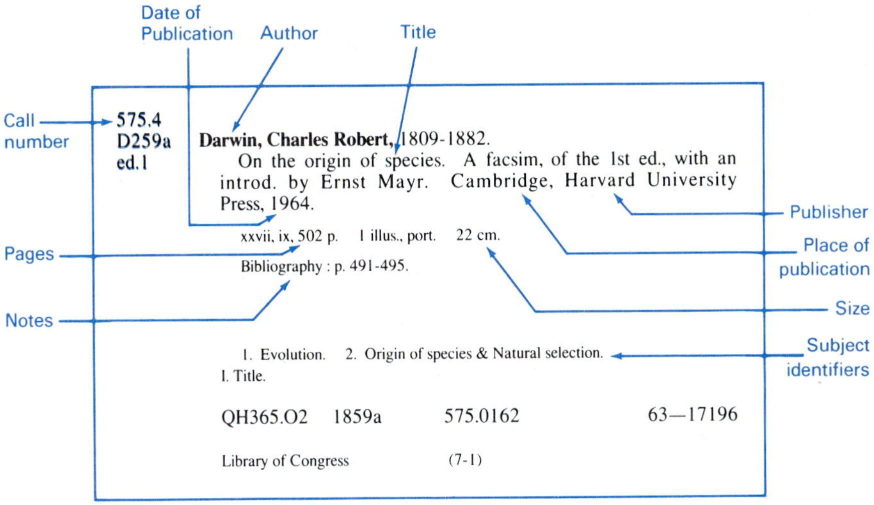

Figure 2-8 Author Card.

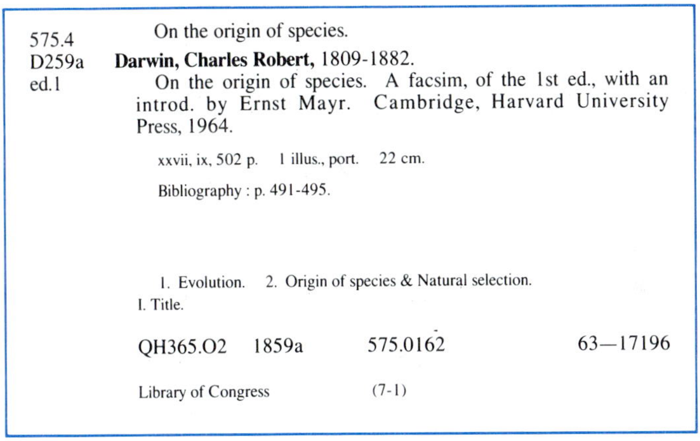

575.4
D259a
ed.1

On the origin of species.

Darwin, Charles Robert, 1809-1882.

On the origin of species. A facsim, of the 1st ed., with an introd. by Ernst Mayr. Cambridge, Harvard University Press, 1964.

xxvii, ix, 502 p. 1 illus., port. 22 cm.

Bibliography : p. 491-495.

1. Evolution. 2. Origin of species & Natural selection.
I. Title.

QH365.O2 1859a 575.0162 63—17196

Library of Congress (7-1)

Figure 2-9 Title Card.

are identical except for the top line. Figure 2-8 is an author card; therefore, the author's name is on the top line. Figure 2-9 is a title card; it displays the title on top. Figure 2-10 illustrates subject cards with the subject on top.

If you have an author's name or a title to begin your search, your job is easy. You go through the alphabetical listings on the file drawers until you find the one that corresponds with the spelling of the name or title. Open that drawer and thumb through the cards until you find the card you want. Keep in mind that in titles the words *a, an,* and *the* are not considered in the alphabetizing of an entry. For example, *The Chicago Manual of Style* is found under the *c's* and not the *t's*.

575.4 Natural selection.
D259a **Darwin, Charles Robert,** 1809-1882.
ed.1 On the origin of species. A facsim. of the 1st ed., with an introd. by Ernst Mayr. Cambridge, Harvard University Press, 1964.

xxvii, ix, 502 p. 1 illus., port. 22 cm.

Bibliography : p. 491-495.

1. Evolution. 2. Origin of species & Natural selection.
I. Title.

QH365.O2 1859a 575.0162 63—17196

Library of Congress (7-1)

(a)

575.4 Evolution.
D259a **Darwin, Charles Robert,** 1809-1882.
ed.1 On the origin of species. A facsim. of the 1st ed., with an introd. by Ernst Mayr. Cambridge, Harvard University Press, 1964.

xxvii, ix, 502 p. 1 illus., port. 22 cm.

Bibliography : p. 491-495.

1. Evolution. 2. Origin of species & Natural selection.
I. Title.

QH365.O2 1859a 575.0162 63—17196

Library of Congress (7-1)

(b)

Figure 2-10 *Subject Cards.*

If you are searching for a book by subject, you need to be more creative. Try to be as specific about the subject as you can be. Notice that although Darwin's book is about biological subject matter, *biology* used as a subject identifier would not have found the book for you. In this case, *biology* is too broad a term. When you are having difficulty focusing in on a narrow subject, try the *Library of Congress Subject Headings* (LCSH), a red, two-volume set of books, which, as the title implies, lists the subject headings used by the Library of Congress.

If you check the LCSH section on *biology,* you will find listed as subheadings such terms as *anatomy, botany, cytology, embryology, evolution, genetics, microbiology,* and *seashore biology*. It is likely that *evolution* would ring a bell for you, and as we see on Figure 2-10, *evolution* is one of the subject headings used. Were you to look under *evolution* in the LCSH, you would find a further list of subject headings, including such terms as *adaptation, living fossils, natural selection, ontogeny, origin of species, phylogeny,* and *teleology*. Both *natural selection* and *origin of species* are terms that would also have helped you to find Darwin's book. Thus, by using the LCSH, you can both widen your search by having more terms to work with and tighten your search by working with more specific terms.

Most libraries place the LCSH near the card catalog. Look for it. If it fails to be a useful subject identifier for you, ask a reference librarian for assistance.

Once found, the catalog card holds a good deal of information for you. We have annotated Figure 2-8 for you. Because this is an author card, Darwin's name is on top, followed by the years of his birth and death. The next line gives the title of the book. It is customary in catalog cards for only the first word and proper nouns to be capitalized; therefore, do not be confused by the lack of capitals. Following the title will be a good deal of information about the book. In this case, you will discover the fact that the book is a facsimile of the first edition and that it has an introduction by Ernest Mayr. The book was published by Harvard University Press in Cambridge in 1964. The little Roman numerals refer to the prefatory pages in the book, such things as introductions, prefaces, and tables of content. The text itself has 502 pages and a bibliography on pages 491–495. The book has one illustration, a portrait, and is twenty-two centimeters (about nine inches) high. If you have trouble deciphering abbreviations, such as *port.*, on catalog cards, look them up at the reference desk in the *Librarians' Glossary and Reference Book*.

Near the bottom of the card, you see the subject identifiers for the book, *Evolution, Origin of Species,* and *Natural Selection*. These identifiers help you in two ways. They give you additional information about the book's subject matter and, also, give you additional places to find other books in the same subject areas.

The additional information at the bottom of the card is for librarians and is not needed by you. However, the number at the top left, the *call number**, is your key to finding the book. If you library has *open stacks**, consult the map near the card catalog. It will display the layout of the library, and will show you where to find books of particular numbers. If your library has *closed stacks**, you will need to fill out a request slip, using the call number, to turn in at the *circulation desk**. In either case, the call number is your key to obtaining the book.

Modern libraries may have several variations to the card catalog: the COM catalog, the book catalog, and the online catalog.

COM catalog COM stands for *computer output microform,* which means the entries are computer generated and are displayed on *microform**, either microfilm or microfiche. The entries to the COM are usually author, title, and subject, as in the card catalog. Figure 2-11 shows a typical COM entry, in this case a title entry. Notice that it contains the same information as a card in essentially the same order. One difference is that, in this instance, the call number, 573.2 Ar29, appears at the end of the entry. Using microform requires special equipment. You may need to check with your librarian about its use.

African genesis
Ardrey, Robert.
African genesis: a personal investigation into the animal origins and nature of man. Drawings by Berdine Ardrey. [1st American ed.] New York, Atheneum, 1961.
380 p. illus. 25 cm.
1. Man - Origin. 2. Human evolution. 3. Psychology, Comparative. I. Title.
573.2 Ar29

Figure 2-11 *COM Entry.*

Book catalog Some libraries use their computer to print out book catalogs instead of or to supplement the COM catalog. These book catalogs may be cheaply printed and placed in many strategic places in the library, including in the stacks themselves. They are a convenience to library users. Entries in them look like those in COM catalogs. Check with your librarian about their existence and use in your library.

Online catalog The online catalog represents the ultimate in library cataloging. Through a computer terminal, consisting of a keyboard and a monitor, you can gain access to the library's computerized catalog. No standardized online system exists as yet; however, those that do exist generally use the familiar author, title and subject as entry points. Figure 2-12 shows a series of screens you might get on one such system, the series initiated by the user's call for HELP.

Some libraries are introducing online systems for their new acquisitions, while keeping their older books listed in the card catalog. If your library has an online system, check with your librarian regarding its coverage and use.

Circulation Desk The circulation desk is where you check out books from the library. It is also a good information source about the library's organization, services, and hours. Many circulation desks, in fact, provide free printed guides to the library.

Closed Stacks See *Collection**.

Collection Basically, a library collects two things—books and *periodicals**. The books may be novels, histories, biographies, scientific texts, or anything else someone thought important enough to give a book-length treatment. The book collection will represent all the various disciplines and categories of knowledge human beings have invented for themselves in order to understand the world. Topics will include anthropology, sociology, law, literature, religion, music, and the physical sciences. *Periodicals** are chiefly magazines, journals, and newspapers.

The collection will be housed on shelves, commonly called "stacks." If your library allows you access to the stacks, they are known as "open stacks." If you are not allowed access, they are "closed stacks."

A collection of anything as large as a library collection needs a classification scheme of some sort. (See also pages 57–58.) Libraries use one of two systems:

```
Search type? A)uthor, T)itle, S)ubject or O)ther: H

I'm sorry you are having trouble. I'll try to HELP. If you can tell
me what's wrong or what you don't understand, I may be able to give
you a better explanation.

To begin, let's review the procedures for telling the computer what you
want to do. To issue a command, press the RED key followed by:
S:  To start searching,
P:  To list search results,
X:  To get special list options,
D:  To display previously executed search statements,
H:  To get Help!,
E:  To get explanations of how the system works,
L:  To logoff and reset the system for the next user,
Q:  To logoff and sign off the system for the day.

Then press the RETURN key.

If you need more information about how the system works, there are lots
of topics I can EXPLAIN for you. If you'd like to see
some, please give the EXPLAIN command (RED key followed by E) and then
press the RETURN key.

Please tell the system what you want to do next by giving one of these
commands now. Press the RED key followed by S,P,X,D,H,E,L, or Q and
then press the RETURN key.

If you are still in doubt, please call X2574.


Search type? A)uthor, T)itle, S)ubject, or O)ther: A
Search statement: commoner
Checking terms. . .
Do you want to add more to your search statement?
     Y or N: Y
Search type? A)uthor, T)itle, S)ubject, or O)ther: T
Search statement: poverty of power
Checking terms. . .
Do you want to add more to your search statement?
     Y or N: N
(COMMONER).ME,AE. AND (POVERTY WITH POWER).TI.
Do you want to execute this search (Y or N)? Y
Searching. . .

       Result 1
       1
LO DRBU.
       GF75-C65-1974
ME Commoner, Barry, 1917–.
TI  The closing circle: nature, man, & technology / Barry Commoner.
IM  New York: Bantam Books c1974.
CO viii, 343 p. 19 cm.
SU Pollution.
NT Includes bibliographical references and index.

R0601 * END OF DOCUMENTS IN LIST
```

Figure 2-12 Online Catalog Screens. (Reprinted with permission of Neal-Schuman Publishers, Inc. Copyright © 1983 by Neal-Schuman Publishers, Inc.)

000	General works
100	Philosophy and related disciplines
200	Religion
300	Social sciences
400	Language
500	Pure science
600	Technology (Applied sciences)
700	The arts
800	Literature
900	General geography and history

Figure 2-13 *Dewey Decimal Classification System.*

the Dewey Decimal Classification System or the Library of Congress Classification System. See Figure 2-13 for the general breakdown of the Dewey System and Figure 2-14 for the Library of Congress System. As you might expect, each system is capable of further classification. For example, in the Library of Congress system, the subject of Science—Q,—breaks down further into QA (mathematics) QB (astronomy) QC (physics) and so forth. These subdivisions divide still further. The Dewey system has similar divisions and subdivisions. In a library with *open stacks** will be a chart, usually near the *card catalog**, that shows which system the library uses and a map that shows the layout of the library. If you learn the system your library uses, particularly for areas of major interest to you, you will be able to browse in open stacks with some idea of what you are doing.

Modern libraries collect things other than books and periodicals. They also contain films, audio- and videocassettes, and records. Such material can be quite useful to you. For instance, hearing Robert Frost read one of his own poems may give you an insight into the poem that your reading of the printed page might not provide. Most libraries devise their own ways of storing and cataloging such nonbook material. Check with your local librarian to find out what is available and how to get to it. Check also with your librarian for any guides the library provides to its collection. Most libraries provide such guides that explain the collection, how it is shelved, and how to gain access to it.

COM Catalog See *Catalog**.

Dewey Decimal Classification System See *Collection**.

Dictionaries You are no doubt familiar with a collegiate dictionary, and you probably own one. Such a general-purpose dictionary is used chiefly for checking the spelling, pronunciation, and meaning of words. However, many dictionaries are also useful ready reference tools. For example, well-known people will be listed with a bit of biographical data, as in this entry from the *American Heritage Dictionary of the English Language:* "Darwin, Charles Robert. 1809–1882. British naturalist; expounded theory of evolution by natural selection in *On the Origin of Species* (1859); grandson of Erasmus Darwin; father of Sir George Darwin." You can also use dictionaries to find geographical information, such as the source and length of rivers or the location and population of countries and cities. In the dictionary, you can discover that Mercury, the planet, is 36.2 million miles from the sun; Mercury, the mythical god, was a messenger for the other gods; and mercury, the element, has an atomic number of 80 and an atomic weight of 200.59. The amount of information you can find in an ordinary collegiate dictionary is really quite amazing.

For information on the English language, the most complete dictionary is *The Oxford English Dictionary* (OED). The multivolume OED with its supplements attempts, as it says in its introduction, "to present in alphabetical series the words that have formed the English vocabulary from the time of the earliest records down to the present day, with all the relevant facts concerning their form,

A	General Works
B–BJ	Philosophy. Psychology
BL–BX	Religion
C	Auxiliary Sciences of History
D	History: General and Old World (Eastern Hemisphere)
E–F	History: America (Western Hemisphere)
G	Geography. Anthropology. Recreation
H	Social Sciences
J	Political Science
KD	Law of the United Kingdom and Ireland
KF	Law of the United States
L	Education
M	Music. Books on Music
N	Fine Arts
P–PA	General Philology and Linguistics. Classical Languages and Literatures
PA Supplement	Byzantine and Modern Greek Literature. Medieval and Modern Latin Literature
PB–PH	Modern European Languages
PG	Russian Literature
PJ–PM	Languages and Literatures of Asia, Africa, Oceania. American Indian Languages. Artificial Languages
P–PM Supplement	Index to Languages and Dialects
PN, PR, PS, PZ	General Literature. English and American Literature. Fiction in English. Juvenile Literature
PQ, Part 1	French Literature
PQ, Part 2	Italian, Spanish, and Portuguese Literatures
PT, Part 1	German Literature
PT, Part 2	Dutch and Scandinavian Literatures
Q	Science
R	Medicine
S	Agriculture
T	Technology
U	Military Science
V	Naval Science
Z	Bibliography. Library Science

Figure 2-14 *Library of Congress Classification System.*

sense-history, pronunciation, and etymology." The OED uses almost two million quotations to show the historical uses of the words it lists, thus allowing its readers to trace the changes in a word's usage. See the sample entries in Figure 2-15. Time spent with the OED is time well spent. See also our references to the OED in our discussion of words in Chapter 6 (pages 100 ff).

You can find many specialized dictionaries in the library, such as *Chamber's Dictionary of Science and Technology,* the *Dictionary of Technical Terms,* the *McGraw-Hill Dictionary of the Life Sciences,* the *Dictionary of World Mythology,* and *The Penguin Dictionary of Architecture*. There is even a *Dictionary of American slang* that will inform you that the word *gutbucket* began life in 1890 as a pail for carrying food, became a pail for collecting donations, then a cheap saloon, and finally a suggestive style of jazz, as in Louie Armstrong "blew it good and right, gutbucket." See also *Reference Guides**.

Directories You are familiar with at least two directories: the White Pages and Yellow Pages published by your telephone company. The White Pages provide an alphabetical listing of the telephone subscribers in a given area. The Yellow Pages are organized by type of business: Automobile Body Repairing and Painting; Automobile Body Shop Equipment and Supplies; Automobile Dealers—New Cars; and so forth. The business divisions are then further divided alphabetically. Most directories, and there are thousands, are organized in similar ways. One company, Polk, publishes over eight hundred city directories, with titles such as *Minneapolis City Directory*. In each of them you can look up people and businesses by name, street, phone number, or business. Salespersons, journalists, bankers, and others find such directories extremely useful. Some of the many specialized directories available are *Literary Market Place, Thomas' Register of American Manufacturers, Ethnic Information Sources of the United States,* and *Best Doctors in the U.S*. See also *Reference Guides**.

Encyclopedias You have almost certainly been familiar with encyclopedias from early school days. Encyclopedias are useful tools at any stage of your education and life. They always provide a good starting point for research in an unfamiliar area. They give basic information on thousands of subjects and people and provide, as well, bibliographies to guide you to more detailed information. Most libraries will shelve several sets of general encyclopedias, such as *Colliers Encyclopedia, Encyclopedia Americana,* and the *New Encyclopedia Britannica*.

Specialized encyclopedias are available in almost all fields. The *McGraw-Hill Encyclopedia of Science and Technology* is an excellent reference source for those who need and can understand more scientific information than general encyclopedias provide. For yet more advanced needs, there are sources such as the *Encyclopedia of Chemical Technology* and the *Encyclopedia of Polymer Science and Technology: Plastics, Resins, Rubbers, Fibers*. Art, literature, history, the social sciences—all have their own encyclopedias. See also *Reference Guides**.

Facts on File See *Periodicals**.

Guide to Reference Books see *Reference Guides**.

PEPPER.

Pepper (pe·pəɹ), *sb.* Forms: 1 **pipor, piper,** 4 **peopur,** 4–5 **pepir,** (5 **pepyr(e, -ur, pepre),** 4–6 **piper,** 4–8 **peper,** 6– **pepper.** [OE. *pipor* = OLG. **pipar*, MLG., MDu. *pēper* (LG. and Du. *peper*), OHG. *pfeffar*, MHG. and Ger. *pfeffer*, ON. *piparr* (Norw. *pipar*, Sw. *peppar*, ODa. *piberr*, Da. *peber*); Com. WGer. a. L. *piper* = Gr. *πέπερι*, of Oriental origin: cf. Skt. *pippalī* long-pepper. The condiment must have become known to the Germanic peoples with its Latin name before the 4th c. From OE. *pipor*, through **piopor*, **peopor*, came ME. *peopur*, *pepur*, *peper*.

(L. *piper* gave Pr. *pebre*, OF. and AF. *peivre*, F. *poivre*.)]

1. A pungent aromatic condiment, derived from species of *Piper* and allied genera (see 2), used from ancient times for flavouring, and acting as a digestive stimulant and carminative; *esp.* the dried berries of *Piper nigrum* or an allied species, either used whole (PEPPERCORNS) or ground into powder.

c **1000** ÆLFRIC *Gram.* ix. (Z.) 44 *Piper*, piper [*v. r.* pipor]. *c* **1000** *Sax. Leechd.* II. 24 Meng p por wiþ hwit cwudu. *a* **1300** *Siriz* 279 in Mätzner *Altengl. Sprachpr.* 111/1 Pepir nou shalt thou eten, This mustart shal ben thi mete. **1362** LANGL. *P. Pl.* A. v. 155, I haue peper [C. vii. 359 piper] and piane, and a pound of garlek. **1488** *Nottingham Rec.* III. 269 For d. a quarter of pepur. **1543–4** *Act* 35 *Hen. VIII*, c. 10 They..shal for euer yelde beare and pay yerely..one pounde of pepper, in and for the acknowledgyng hym. **1562** TURNER *Herbal* II. 90 b, The vertue of all peppers in commun is to heat. *a* **1687** PETTY *Pol. Arith.* (1690) 46 Sugar, Tobacco, and Pepper..custom hath now made necessary to all sorts of people. **1781** GIBBON *Decl. & F.* xxxi. III. 223 *note*, Pepper was a favourite ingredient of the most expensive Roman cookery. **1856** EMERSON *Eng. Traits, Wealth*, Finding that milk will not nourish, nor sugar sweeten,..nor pepper bite the tongue.

(a)

PEPPER-AND-SALT.

Pe·pper, *v.* [f. prec. sb. (OE. had *piporian*, *piprian*, *gepiperian*, in same sense (so ON. *pipra*, OHG. *phefferôn*, MHG. and Ger. *pfeffer(e)n*, Du. *peperen*); but the current verb seems to have been formed anew in 16th c.]

1. *trans.* To sprinkle with pepper; to flavour or season with pepper; to treat with pepper. Also *absol.*

[*c* **1000** *Sax. Leechd.* II. 182 Sele þonne ʒepiporodne wyrtdrenc. *Ibid.*, ʒepipera mid xx corna. *Ibid.* III. 76 Pipra hit syþþan swa swa man wille.] **1581** and **1620** [see PEPPERED]. **1738** SWIFT *Pol. Conversat.* 142 This Venison is plaguily pepper'd. **1796** MRS. GLASSE *Cookery* x. 161 Dried salmon ..when laid on the gridiron should be moderately peppered. **1865** J. MACGREGOR *Rob Roy Baltic* (1867) 205 There is the blind that won't pull down or stop up, and the pepper-box that won't pepper.

b. *Falconry.* To wash (a hawk) with water and pepper, in order to cleanse her from vermin, etc. [So F. *poivrer*]

1618 LATHAM *Falconry* II. 34 Hauing on euening your water with pepper prouided, and when you haue, according to the order and accustomed manner, well washed and peppered her, take off her rufterhood. *Ibid.* 81 Vpon the receit of such a Hawke from the Cage, suddenly to make her gentle, by peppering, watching, and other such like accustomed vses.

2. To sprinkle (a surface) as with pepper; to cover, or fill with numerous small objects, spots, or dots, likened to grains of pepper; to besprinkle, dot, stud. Also *fig.* (Mostly in *pa. pple.*)

1612 J. DAVIES *Wit's Pilgr.* (1878) 46/1 Note the Lyning of the roialst Robe; Its powdred Ermyne, pepperd too with Stings. **1705** LADY WENTWORTH *Let.* 9 Mar. in *W. Papers* (1883) 40 Betty..affects to be afraid of the small pox, and thearfor I fear would be pepered with them should she get them. **1835** M. SCOTT *Cruise Midge* xxi, The neighbouring thickets were peppered with..small white-washed buildings. **1882** B. HARTE *Flip* ii, Her flushed face ..peppered with minute..freckles. **1896** *Moxon's Mech. Exerc., Printing* 422 Every page was peppered with italic.

3. To sprinkle like pepper; to scatter in small particles. Also *fig.*

1821 CLARE *Vill. Minstr.* I. 197 As grinning north-winds.. pepper'd round my head their hail and snow. **1899** MISS E. TH. FOWLER *Double Thread* xii, People go peppering them [words] all over the place, utterly unconscious of the awful responsibility.

4. To pelt with shot or missiles. Also *fig.*

c **1644** J. SOMERVILLE *Mem. Somervilles* (1815) II. 347 First peppering them soundly with ther shott. **1689** SHADWELL *Bury F.* I. i, There i'faith I pepper'd the Court with libels and lampoons. **1742** FIELDING *J. Andrews* I. xvi, I'll pepper you better than ever you was pepper'd by Jenny Bouncer. **1773** *Life N. Frowde* 135 She soon got into order and peppered us with her small Shot. **1866** GEO. ELIOT *F. Holt* ii, You may pepper the bishops a little. **1884** SALA *Journ. due South* I. xxiv. (1887) 327 Peppering the guide occasionally with Greek and Latin lore. **1885** *Century Mag.* XXX. 386/1 Galloping after us, and peppering us with shot-guns.

b. *intr.* To discharge shot or other small missiles (*at* something).

In quot. 1767 said of rain, to pour heavily; in quot. 1894 (*colloq.*) to 'go at it' vigorously: cf. *pelt*.

1767 GRAY *Let. to Mason* 11 Sept., We came peppering and raining back through Keswick to Penrith. Next day,—raining still. **1890** W. A. WALLACE *Only a Sister* 37 He could not possibly be peppering away at the pheasants in Sir James's covers. **1894** MORRIS in Mackail *Life* II. 300 The nightingales..O my wig, they were peppering into it.

(b)

Figure 2-15 *Sample Entries from* The Oxford English Dictionary. *(Oxford English* Dictionary, *copyright 1971. Reprinted by permission of Oxford University Press.)*

Handbooks and Manuals Handbooks and manuals are found primarily in specialized fields. They provide how-to and factual information, such as formulas and statistics, for their fields. If you are looking for career information, the *Careers Encyclopedia* and *Occupational Outlook Handbook* would provide information on what people do in various occupations and what the job prospects in a field are. Other examples are *Better Business Bureau Guide to Wise Buying, Book of the States, Reader's Digest Family Legal Guide, Engineering Mathematics Handbook,* and *Handbook of Chemistry and Physics*. See also *Reference Guides**.

Indexes Indexes are your guides to articles in *periodicals**. Using an index, you can locate an article on a specific page in a specific periodical. Indexes are published at regular intervals, perhaps as often as biweekly, and cumulate yearly. Thus, you can look in bound indexes for past years. Near the bound yearly volumes, you will find the latest biweekly, monthly, or quarterly unbound issues for the current year. You probably already know one major periodical index well—the *Readers' Guide to Periodical Literature*. The *Readers' Guide* references over 150 commercial magazines such as *Art News, Business Week, Motor Trend, Newsweek, Scientific American,* and *Sports Illustrated*. You can follow the *Readers' Guide* by looking up author and subject. The sample entries from *Readers' Guide* reproduced and explained in Figure 2-16 show how this index and most other indexes work. In the opening pages of every index you will find a list of the periodicals covered and explanations on how to use the index.

Beyond *Readers' Guide,* there are specialized indexes: *Humanities Index, Social Sciences Index, General Science Index, Applied Science and Technology Index, Business Periodicals Index, Index to Government Periodicals,* and many more. *The New York Times Index* will guide you to all the material published in the *New York Times* from 1851. The *National Newspaper Index* available only in *microform**, indexes the *New York Times,* the *Christian Science Monitor,* and the *Wall Street Journal,* our major national and international newspapers. There are so many indexes, in fact, that finding the appropriate one can seem like a

Sample subject entry: Diet

Rating the diets. D. M. Hegsted. il *Health* 15:21-2+ Ja '83

An illustrated article on the subject **Diet** entitled "Rating the diets" by D. M. Hegsted will be found in volume 15 of *Health*, pages 21-22 (continued on later pages of the same issue) in the January 1983 number.

Sample name entry: Lange, Jessica

Jessica Lange on Frances. por *Psychol Today* 17:22 Ja '83

about

One from the heartland. D. Ansen. il pors *Newsweek* 101:46-8 Ja 31 '83

An article by Jessica Lange will be found in volume 17 of *Psychology Today*, page 22, the January 1983 number.

An article *about* Jessica Lange will be found in volume 101 of *Newsweek*, pages 46-48, the January 31, 1983 number.

Figure 2-16 *Sample Entries from the* Readers' Guide to Periodical Literature.

BOTANICAL GAZETTE; a journal embracing all departments of botanical science. 1875. q. $37.50 to individuals; institutions $70. University of Chicago Press, 5801 S. Ellis Ave., Chicago, IL 60637 TEL 312-962-7600 (Orders to: Box 37005, Chicago, IL 60637) Eds. Edward Garber, Manfred Ruddat. adv. bibl. charts. illus. index. circ. 1,500. (also avail. in microform from MIM,UMI; reprint service avail. from UMI,ISI) Indexed: Biol.Abstr. Biol.& Agr.Ind. Chem.Abstr. Curr.Cont. Excerp.Med. Sci.Cit.Ind. Abstr.Bull.Inst.Pap.Chem. Field Crop Abstr. Forest.Abstr. Forest Prod.Abstr. Geo.Abstr. GeoRef. Herb.Abstr. Hort.Abstr. Gen.Sci.Ind. Plant Breed.Abstr. Rev.Plant Path. Soils & Fert. Weed Abstr.

Figure 2-17 *Sample Ulrich's Entry.*

problem. Actually, it's fairly easy to do. One good guide to an appropriate index in your field is Eugene Sheehy's *Guide to Reference Books,* which we discuss in *Reference Guides**.

Even more useful, perhaps, is *Ulrich's International Periodical Directory. Ulrich's* (pronounced *Ol-ricks*) lists and describes over 65,000 periodicals. The listed periodicals are organized by over 300 subject headings, such as agriculture, business and economics, ethnic interests, medical sciences, motion pictures, and political science. Figure 2-17 shows a typical *Ulrich's* entry. Notice that a good deal of information is provided about the listed periodical, including cost, editor, features, and circulation. Also provided are the names of the indexes and *abstracting journals** that cover the periodical, including, in our example, *Biological Abstracts* and *Biology and Agriculture Index*. With this information, you know exactly which indexes and abstracting journals will guide you to the articles you seek in that periodical.

Librarians' Glossary and Reference Book See *Catalog**.

Library of Congress Classification System See *Collection**.

Library of Congress Subject Headings See *Catalog**.

Manuals See *Handbooks and Manuals**.

Microfiche See *Microform**.

Microfilm See *Microform**.

Microform *Microform* is the librarian's term for materials greatly reduced in size through photographic techniques. Microform may be either *microfilm* or *microfiche*. Microfilm comes on a reel similar to that in a camera. Microfiche is a single sheet that may hold up to a hundred standard pages. Microform is increasingly used for storing *periodicals** and even some of the library's *catalog**. To read microform requires the use of a microform reader supplied by the library. Get acquainted with how microform is used in your library, how it is cataloged, and where it is stored. Learn also how to use the microform readers in your library.

Online Catalog See *Catalog**.

Open Stacks See *Collection**.

Periodicals Things that are published periodically are, not surprisingly, referred to as periodicals. They include the following: (1) Popular magazines, such as *Newsweek, Scientific American,* and *Sports Illustrated.* (2) Scholarly journals aimed at specialized audiences. For example, agronomists read *Crop Science;* English teachers read *College English.* The latest information in any scholarly field is usually found in its journals. As you progress in your field, you will need to get acquainted with its journals. (3) Business and professional magazines that report the latest news for business in general or for some trade or profession. *Forbes* and *Business Week* are examples of magazines of general business interest. *Computer Age* is an example of a specialized magazine for the computer industry. (4) Newspapers, both national and local. The *New York Times, Christian Science Monitor,* and *Wall Street Journal* carry a wide spectrum of national and international news. Most libraries also carry a selection of local newspapers.

Periodicals, except for newspapers, are bound yearly into book form. Some are becoming available in *microform**. Periodicals are shelved in special sections in alphabetical order. Current issues are found either on racks near the periodical section or in boxes next to the bound volumes.

Current copies of newspapers are found on racks in the library. Check with your librarian to learn their location. Because of their bulk, newspapers are usually not bound. If they are saved at all, it is in *microform**. Most college libraries will have, at least, the *New York Times* in microform. Most, too, subscribe to *Facts on File,* a weekly service that provides condensed, objective reports on current affairs. It is classified by subject, cumulates yearly, and is available back to 1940.

For information on how to find your way around in periodicals, see also *Abstracting Journals*, Indexes*, and Reference Guides**.

Reader's Guide to Periodical Literature See *Indexes**.

Reference Guides If you have glanced through this glossary, you have become aware that there are many reference books available to you—*abstracting journals*, dictionaries*, indexes*,* and so forth. Our description of them has been aimed primarily at alerting you to the existence of all the reference help you have available to you and providing you with explanations and examples of key items. To find exactly what you need, you must go to the reference guides themselves—books that classify, list, and describe the major reference sources you'll need, regardless of your interests.

The premier reference guide is Eugene P. Sheehy's *Guide to Reference Books,* familiarly called *Sheehy's.* This book and its supplements divide over 14,000 reference works into the following subject matter areas: general reference works, the humanities, history and area studies, and pure and applied sciences. Each of these is further subdivided. For example, astronomy is a subdivision under pure and applied science. Astronomy is further subdivided into general works, stars, navigation, and chronology. Figures 2-18 and 2-19 show typical pages from *Sheehy's* and give a good notion of what is available throughout the book. Get familiar with *Sheehy's*. It is an essential part of your education. We also recommend that you begin by reading the introduction to Sheehy's; it offers excellent advice on how to use a reference book once you have it in your hand.

Beyond *Sheehy's,* you can also find help in *American Reference Books Annual* and in *Guide to Reference Books for School Media Centers*.

Reference Section The reference section is the most used part of any library. Here the library gathers together all the reference works—*indexes**, *handbooks**, *yearbooks**, and so forth—discussed in this glossary. Some will be shelved where you can get to them freely. Others, more widely used, may be kept behind a counter; for these you'll have to ask the librarian. In most cases, you cannot check out reference works from the library but must use them in the reference section.

Every reference section will have a reference librarian or two on duty to keep an eye on things and to help you find information you need. Reference librarians are a hard working group of people, who will go to great lengths to help you. But the more you know about what you want when you ask a question, and the more specific the question, the more quickly they can help you (see pages 23–26). Spend some time in your library's reference section. Get acquainted with the librarians. Time so spent will save you a good deal of time later on.

Reserve Desk Most libraries have a reserve desk or even a reserve room. Here are kept books designated by professors for use in specific courses. Because everyone in the course needs access to the books, the reserve checkout time may be limited to a few days or even a few hours.

Sheehy's Guide to Reference Books See *Reference Guides**.

Ulrich's International Periodical Directory See *Indexes**.

Yearbooks Yearbooks are sort of a cross between *almanacs** and *handbooks**. Some supplement existing general encyclopedias, but most cover specialized subjects and areas. Issued yearly, they contain masses of valuable information. Science students, for example, would be particularly interested in the *McGraw-Hill Yearbook of Science and Technology*. Anyone interested in the United States should look into the *Statistical Abstract of the United States,* a source for almost any statistic about the United States one would care to know. A few of its subject matter areas suggest the spread of information available: *Population, Education, Elections, Social Insurance and Human Services, Science, Agriculture,* and *Construction and Housing*. See Figure 2-20 for a typical page of information from the *Statistical Abstract*.

Other useful yearbooks are *International Yearbook of Education, Commodity Yearbook, United Nations Statistical Yearbook, Europa Yearbook,* and *Yearbook of Astronomy*. See also *Reference Guides**.

Also published in Serbo-Croatian, Russian, German, and French. Aims to present in concise form "the essential and general statistical information on Yugoslavia, socialist republics and socialist autonomous provinces."—[*p.3*]. HA1631.S8

Zambia

Zambia. Central Statistical Office. Statistical year-book, 1967– . Lusaka, [1968?]– . Annual. (5th ed., 1971, publ. 1973) **CG244**

Includes tables on population and housing, health, education, labor, agriculture, transport, commerce and industry, trade, finance, etc.

C H

Economics

❖This area is a large one under which many related subjects are grouped: business and business management, commerce, finance and banking, insurance, labor and industrial relations, and various others. Many large libraries, both public and academic, will have special departments devoted to one or several of these subject fields, and in most large cities there will be pertinent special libraries, usually connected with large business or banking concerns. These libraries will have many more specialized sources than can be listed here.

In this section are included some of the bibliographies, indexes, dictionaries, and handbooks from which, or about which, information may be sought in a large general library.

Documents issued by the federal government are particularly useful in the field of economics. Only a few of the many valuable publications of the various departments and bureaus can be listed here. The U.S. Bureau of Labor Statistics, the Bureau of the Census, the Department of Commerce and its various bureaus, including the now defunct Bureau of Foreign and Domestic Commerce, and many others are prolific publishers. For further information consult the *Monthly catalog of United States government publications* (AG25).

GENERAL WORKS

Guides

Fletcher, John, ed. The use of economics literature. London, Butterworths; [Hamden, Conn.], Archon Books, [1971]. 309p. **CH1**

Librarians and economists have collaborated on this guide for the student and research worker. Includes chapters on the use of libraries, bibliographical tools, periodicals, unpublished materials, British and U.S. government publications, and on various subject areas within the field of economics. Indexed. Z7164.E2U8

Melnyk, Peter. Economics; bibliographic guide to reference books and information sources. Littleton, Colo., Libraries Unlimited, 1971. 263p. **CH2**

Includes sections on economic theory, economic conditions in various countries, private and public finance, commerce and marketing, international economics, economic geography, industry and transportation, labor economics, population and statistics, and a selected list of periodicals. Many annotations. Index. Z7164.E2M45

Bibliography

American University of Beirut. Economic Research Institute. A selected and annotated bibliography of economic literature on the Arabic speaking countries of the Middle East, 1938/52– . Beirut, 1954– . **CH3**

Title varies slightly.

A basic volume covering 1938/52 was published 1954 (199p.), with annual supplements beginning 1953; a second cumulation covering 1953/65 appeared in 1967 (458p.). A cumulation for the period 1938/60 was published by G. K. Hall, Boston, 1967 (358p.); in addition to cumulating the entries from the basic work and the annual supplements, some 800 new entries were added in that volume.

Classified arrangement with author index. Includes works in Arabic, English, and French. Z164.E15A6

Baranson, Jack. Technology for underdeveloped areas; an annotated bibliography. N.Y., Pergamon, 1967. 81p. (International ser. of monographs in library and information science, v.6) **CH4**

Lists 319 items (books and articles) in classified arrangement, with author, title, and subject indexes. Z7164.U5B3

Batson, Harold Edward. A select bibliography of modern economic theory, 1870–1929. London, Routledge, 1930. 224p. (Repr.: N.Y., Kelley, 1968) **CH5**

An annotated bibliography of books and periodical articles; listing is by subject and by author. Z7164.E2B3

Black, Robert Dionysius Collison. A catalogue of pamphlets on economic subjects published between 1750 and 1900 and now housed in Irish libraries. N.Y., Kelley, 1969. 632p. **CH6**

Comprises a union catalog of "pamphlets of economic interest published anywhere between the 1st January, 1750 and the 31st December, 1900" (*Introd.*) and now housed in one or more of the 17 cooperating libraries. Chronological arrangement with author and title indexes. Z7164.E2B6

Braeuer, Walter. Handbuch zur Geschichte der Volkswirtschaftslehre; ein bibliographisches Nachschlagewerk. Frankfurt am Main, Klostermann, [1952]. 224p. **CH7**

An international bio-bibliography of the history of political economy from ancient and medieval times to the modern day, with biographical sketches of important economists. Includes books, dissertations, and periodical articles.

Geiger, H. Kent. National development, 1776–1966; a selective and annotated guide to the most important articles in English. Metuchen, N.J., Scarecrow, 1969. 247p. **CH8**

A chronological, annotated listing of 350 books and articles on the cultural, economic, political, and social aspects of development. Author-title-subject index. Z7164.U5G43

Hamilton, F. E. Ian. Regional economic analysis in Britain and the Commonwealth; a bibliographic guide. N.Y., Schocken, [1970]. 410p. **CH9**

In seven main geographical sections with appropriate topical subdivisions: (1) The British Isles; (2) The British Commonwealth in general; (3) Africa; (4) Australia and New Zealand; (5) Canada; (6) South and South-east Asia; (7) The small territories. Z7165.G8H33

Hanson, Laurence William. Contemporary printed sources for British and Irish economic history, 1701–1750. Cambridge, Univ. Pr., 1963. 978p. **CH10**

497

Figure 2-18 *A Page from Sheehy's* Guide to Reference books. *(From Eugene P. Sheehy, ed.,* Guide to Reference Books, *9th ed. Copyright © 1976 by the American Library Association. Reprinted by permission of ALA.)*

CH40 Social Sciences | Economics | General Works

Dissertations

Wood, W. Donald, Kelly, L. A. and **Kumar, P.** Canadian graduate theses, 1919–1969; an annotated bibliography (covering economics, business and industrial relations). Kingston, Ont., Queen's Univ., Industrial Relations Centre, 1970. 483p. **CH40**

A classed listing of both doctoral and master's theses, including theses written by Canadians at non-Canadian universities. Nearly 2,500 items. Author index. Z5055.C2W6

Indexes and abstract journals

Documentation économique; revue bibliographique de synthèse. v.1– , 1934– . Paris, Presses Universitaires de France, 1934– . Quarterly. **CH41**

Subtitle and publisher vary. Suspended 1939–46; resumed with v.6, 1947.

At head of title: Institut National de la Statistique et des Études Économiques, Association de Documentation Économique et Social.

Offers abstracts of articles from American, Dutch, English, French, German, Greek, Italian, Portuguese, Spanish, Swedish, and Russian economic periodicals. Classified by subject with author index. Abstracts are in French. Author index in each issue, but no cumulation thereof since the abstracts are printed on perforated sheets in 3x5 card format which are meant to be detached and filed according to classification. Z7163.D6

Economic abstracts; . . . review of abstracts on economics, finance, trade and industry, management and labour. v.1–4,no.2, 1953–56. The Hague, Nijhoff, 1953–56. Semimonthly. **CH42**

Prepared by the Library of the Economic Information Service with the collaboration of the Library of the Netherlands School of Economics and the Library of the Ministry of Social Affairs.

Publisher varies.

Ceased with v.4, no.2 (whole no.22), May 1956.

Excellent abstracts of books and periodical articles in Dutch (with English summaries), English, French, and German. Detailed subject index in each issue, and cumulative author index for each volume. HB1.A1E2

Index of economic articles in journals and collective volumes. v.1– , 1886/1924– . Homewood, Ill., R. D. Irwin, 1961– . Annual. (v.10 covering 1968 publ. 1971) **CH43**

Title varies: v.1–7 called *Index of economic journals.*

Frequency varies.

Contents: v.1, 1886–1924; v.2, 1925–1939; v.3, 1940–1949; v.4, 1950–1954; v.5, 1954–1959; v.6, 1960–1963; v.6A, 1960–1963, Collective volumes; v.7, 1964–1965; v.7A, 1964–1965, Collective volumes; v.8– , 1966– , annual.

Now lists articles in English from the principal economics journals of various countries (about 140 titles in v.10). Arranged by a detailed classification scheme, with author index in each volume. Citations are full and precise.

Beginning with v.6A (covering 1960–63), indexes collective volumes such as *Festschriften,* conference reports and papers, collected essays, Congressional Committee hearings and special committee reports for United States and Canada, collections of English-language translations of foreign articles and essays. Z7164.E2I4812

Journal of economic abstracts. v.1–6, 1963–68. Cambridge, Harvard Univ., 1963–68. Quarterly. **CH44**

"An international journal published cooperatively by the contributing journals under the auspices of the American Economic Association."—*title page.*

Offers rather lengthy abstracts selected from some 35 contributing journals. Arranged by journal, with subject index in each issue and author index appearing annually.

Title changed with v.7, 1969, to *Journal of economic literature,* which continues to carry selected abstracts, reviews of recent literature, book reviews, etc., but is no longer strictly an abstract journal. HB1.J6

Dictionaries and encyclopedias

Bedrijfseconomische encyclopedie onder algemeene leiding van J. G. Stridiron. Utrecht, W. de Haan, 1947–52. 5v. and index. il. **CH45**

Signed articles with bibliographies. Each volume, A–Z. v.1 treats general economic problems; v.2, business economy and its general aspects; v.3, business economy in its special aspects; v.4, management; v.5, statistics and accounting.

Dictionnaire des sciences économiques, publié sous la direction de Jean Romeuf, avec la collaboration de Gilles Pasqualaggi. Paris, Presses Universitaires de France, 1956–58. 2v. **CH46**

A dictionary of terms used in the study of economics; international in scope. Includes biographical sketches of significant figures, excluding living persons. Many articles are signed; some have bibliographies. HB61.D5

Elster, Ludwig, ed. Wörterbuch der Volkswirtschaft. 4. völlig umgearb. Aufl. Jena, Fischer, 1931–33. 3v. il. **CH47**

1st ed. 1898 in 2v.

A standard German encyclopedia of economics, supplementary to the *Handwörterbuch der Staatswissenschaften* (CJ40n) which covered political science. Signed articles, bibliographies, and biographies of deceased persons. HB61.E5

Gilpin, Alan. Dictionary of economic terms. 2d ed. London, Butterworths, 1970. 276p. **CH48**

1st ed. 1966.

"The terms in this dictionary are those used largely in the United Kingdom, but a number in use in the United States of America and other countries have also been included."—*Pref.*

Hanson, John Lloyd. A dictionary of economics and commerce. 3d ed. London, Macdonald & Evans, 1969. 473p. **CH49**

1st ed. 1965.

Brief explanations of some 4,650 terms relating mainly to economic theory and applied economics. Emphasis is on recent developments. HB61.H35

McGraw-Hill dictionary of modern economics; a handbook of terms and organizations. Douglas Greenwald, ed. 2d ed. N.Y., McGraw-Hill, [1973]. 792p. **CH50**

1st ed. 1965.

Pt.1 lists and defines approximately 1,400 modern economic and related terms. Definitions were written for the non-specialist and are sometimes supplemented by charts, tables, or diagrams. Pt.2 alphabetically lists and describes 225 private and public organizations concerned with economics and marketing. HB61.M16

Palgrave, *Sir* **Robert Harry Inglis.** Palgrave's Dictionary of political economy, ed. by Henry Higgs. London, N.Y., Macmillan, 1923–26. 3v. (Repr.: N.Y., Augustus M. Kelley, 1963) **CH51**

1st ed. 1894–96; reprinted 1910 without change in the text, but with a supplement of new articles in v.3, p.693–803; a reprint of the 1910 edition, issued 1915–18, contains the same supplement but with cross references to the supplement incorporated in the main alphabet. The 1923–26 edition is printed from the stereotyped plates of the 1st ed., with some changes in the plates, and with a supplement which uses some of the material from the earlier supplement and adds some new articles.

A standard English work, including some general and foreign aspects of the subject, but largely limited to developments of economic study in the English-speaking world. Signed articles by specialists, and bibliographies. Useful and authoritative, but unfortunately not up-to-date. HB61.P17

Sloan, Harold Stephenson and **Zurcher, Arnold J.** Dictionary of economics. 5th ed. N.Y., Barnes & Noble, [1971]. 520p. **CH52**

1st ed. 1949.

500

Figure 2-19 *Page from Sheehy's* Guide to Reference Books. *(From Eugene P. Sheehy, ed.,* Guide to Reference Books, *9th ed. Copyright © 1976 by the American Library Association. Reprinted by permission of ALA.)*

No. **217.** Years of School Completed, by Region, Division and State: 1980

[**As of April 1.** Based on the 1980 Census of Population; see Appendix III]

Region, division, and state	Population, 25 years old and over (1,000)	Percent of population completing at least—			
		High school		College	
		1-3 years	4 years	1-3 years	4 or more years
U.S	**132,836**	**81.7**	**66.5**	**31.9**	**16.2**
Northeast	**29,903**	**82.4**	**67.1**	**30.8**	**17.2**
New England	7,438	84.3	70.5	34.6	19.2
Maine	662	83.4	68.7	29.4	14.4
New Hampshire	542	85.3	72.3	35.1	18.2
Vermont	295	83.3	71.0	34.7	19.0
Massachusetts	3,463	85.6	72.2	35.8	20.0
Rhode Island	575	79.3	61.1	28.3	15.4
Connecticut	1,900	83.7	70.3	35.9	20.7
Middle Atlantic	22,466	81.8	66.0	29.5	16.6
New York	10,721	81.7	66.3	32.2	17.9
New Jersey	4,504	82.3	67.4	31.5	18.3
Pennsylvania	7,240	81.6	64.7	24.3	13.6
Midwest	**34,085**	**82.9**	**68.0**	**29.4**	**14.7**
E. No. Central	24,066	83.4	67.3	28.7	14.5
Ohio	6,292	84.6	67.0	26.5	13.7
Indiana	3,136	83.4	66.4	24.6	12.5
Illinois	6,679	81.5	66.5	31.4	16.2
Michigan	5,254	84.9	68.0	30.0	14.3
Wisconsin	2,705	82.0	69.6	29.2	14.8
W. No. Central	10,019	81.8	69.6	31.1	15.3
Minnesota	2,346	83.3	73.1	34.5	17.4
Iowa	1,700	83.3	71.5	28.6	13.9
Missouri	2,919	78.3	63.5	27.2	13.9
North Dakota	365	75.2	66.4	35.1	14.8
South Dakota	390	78.0	67.9	31.7	14.0
Nebraska	912	84.9	73.4	32.8	15.5
Kansas	1,388	85.4	73.3	34.2	17.0
South	**43,691**	**77.4**	**60.2**	**29.4**	**15.0**
South Atlantic	21,994	78.9	61.3	30.3	15.7
Delaware	345	85.2	68.6	32.4	17.5
Maryland	2,499	83.5	67.4	34.9	20.4
South—Con.					
South Atlantic—Con.					
District of Columbia	399	83.0	67.1	41.5	27.5
Virginia	3,133	78.4	62.4	34.0	19.1
West Virginia	1,147	72.0	56.0	20.4	10.4
North Carolina	3,403	75.4	54.8	27.0	13.2
South Carolina	1,733	74.3	53.7	26.7	13.4
Georgia	3,086	76.3	56.4	27.9	14.6
Florida	6,250	82.4	66.7	31.6	14.9
E. So. Central	8,364	72.2	55.3	24.1	12.1
Kentucky	2,087	68.7	53.1	21.8	11.1
Tennessee	2,692	72.3	56.2	24.5	12.6
Alabama	2,217	75.0	56.5	24.7	12.2
Mississippi	1,368	73.0	54.8	25.6	12.3
W. So. Central	13,333	78.3	61.5	31.1	15.5
Arkansas	1,337	73.2	55.5	22.3	10.8
Louisiana	2,281	75.1	57.7	26.7	13.9
Oklahoma	1,770	81.6	66.0	31.2	15.1
Texas	7,944	79.3	62.6	33.8	16.9
West	**25,157**	**86.8**	**74.5**	**40.9**	**19.3**
Mountain	6,335	87.6	75.2	39.5	18.8
Montana	451	85.7	74.4	36.5	17.5
Idaho	514	87.4	73.7	37.2	15.8
Wyoming	255	90.0	77.9	37.9	17.2
Colorado	1,664	89.4	78.6	44.1	23.0
New Mexico	707	82.3	68.9	34.7	17.6
Arizona	1,559	85.0	72.4	38.0	17.4
Utah	705	93.0	80.0	44.1	19.9
Nevada	480	90.4	75.5	35.1	14.4
Pacific	18,822	86.5	74.3	41.4	19.4
Washington	2,439	89.7	77.6	40.2	19.0
Oregon	1,580	88.5	75.6	38.5	17.9
California	14,044	85.8	73.5	42.0	19.6
Alaska	211	91.0	82.5	43.7	21.1
Hawaii	548	83.8	73.8	38.8	20.3

Source: U.S. Bureau of the Census, *1980 Census of Population*, vol. 1, chapter C (PC80-1-C).

Figure 2-20 *Page from* Statistical Abstract of the United States. *(From U.S. Bureau of the Census, Statistical Abstract of the United States, 104th ed. Washington, DC: US Government Printing Office, 1984, 145.)*

Exercises

1. On pages 20–21, we describe for you a leisurely exploration of your library as a means for you to get to know the resources available to you. The following exercise closely follows the course of the described exploration. The material requested enables you to examine the right sources and to take the right books into your hands. To complete this exercise, you will need a dozen four-by-six-inch note cards and notebook paper. When asked to record material, do so in the manner prescribed by your instructor.

A. Stop by your library's *circulation desk**. Obtain any material available there about the use of the library. Find and record the answers to the following questions:

1) What are the library's hours?

2) Does the library have *open* or *closed stacks**?

3) Which of the following *catalog** tools are available: *Card catalog**? *COM catalog**? *Book catalog**? *Online catalog**? Other?

B. Find the two-volume *Library of Congress Subject Headings** (LCSH). Using the LCSH as your source, find and record several headings and subheadings for a discipline that interests you. (In subsequent activities in this exercise, we refer to this discipline as "your discipline.")

C. Using the headings obtained from the LCSH as an aid and your library's *catalog** as a source, prepare bibliographic cards for three books in your discipline. Obtain one of the three books. Using it as a source, complete three note cards by writing as follows: a verbatim quote, a paraphrase, and a summary.

D. Record the answer to this question: Does your library use the *Dewey Decimal Classification System** or the *Library of Congress Classification System**?

E. Using ready reference sources such as *almanacs**, *dictionaries**, *encyclopedias**, and *atlases**, find and record the requested information. Briefly indicate the source for each item (for example, *American Heritage Dictionary* or *Stat Ab, USA*):

1) Choose a country whose name begins with the same letter as your last name (for example: Jones, Jamaica). If you have to, go forward or backward in the alphabet until you find a country that begins with the closest letter. Obtain and record the following information for the country:

a. name
b. population
c. form of government
d. colors in flag
e. principal exports

2) Obtain and record the following information about someone famous in your discipline:

a. name
b. month, day, and year of birth
c. town or city of birth
d. principal contributions to the discipline

3) For an occupation typical of one that might be followed by someone who graduates from college in your discipline, obtain and record the following information:

a. name of occupation
b. job prospects
c. typical salary range
d. typical work performed

F. For your discipline, record the name of at least one source in each of the following categories. (If your discipline lacks a source in any of the listed categories, say so, but explain how you know this.):

1) *Indexes**
2) *Abstracting journals**

3) *Dictionaries**
4) *Encyclopedias**
5) *Periodicals**
6) *Handbooks and manuals**

Prepare one bibliographic card and one note card from each of three of the items you have listed (six cards in all).

G. If your library has the *New York Times* on *microform**, find and record several headlines from its front page for the date you were born.

2. You may at this point in the course have to consider gathering library information for a paper due later in the term. Perhaps, as a result of thinking about that paper, you already have a topic, an audience, and a purpose. Now is a good time to conduct an analysis of your library problem, using the techniques we describe on pages 23–26. Consider the following questions:

A. How familiar are you with the subject?

B. How much material will you need?

C. In what disciplines will you conduct your research?

D. What kinds of reference sources will help you?

E. How much time will your library project take? Prepare your analysis for presentation in a manner precribed by your instructor.

3. Using the analysis you prepared for Exercise 2 as a guide, prepare a working bibliography for your paper. If your library does not have enough resources available of the kind you need to complete your paper successfully, rethink your topic and consult with your instructor. If there are enough resources available, use the bibliographic card and note-card techniques described on pages 29–32 to gather information for your paper. From time to time, review your material in the manner described on pages 32–33. Be prepared to show your bibliographic cards and note cards to your instructor and to review your material with him or her.

3

Composing: Using Logic and Rhetoric

Figure 3-1 *The information-knowledge-wisdom hierarchy. The caveman (left) has lots of information (facts and ideas); he selects and organizes useful information into knowledge (center), but he does not achieve wisdom until he has integrated his knowledge into a whole that is more useful than the sum of its parts. (Tom Chalkey. Reprinted with permission from* The Futurist, *published by the World Future Society, 4916 St. Elmo Ave., Bethesda, Maryland, 20814.)*

In the discovery stage of the writing process, you generate a good deal of information. In the composing stage, you organize, write, and revise that information into a coherent composition. The use of logic and rhetoric is an essential part of that process.

Simply stated, logic is the thinking process that underlies writing. Rhetoric is the process of displaying that thinking for others to examine. In classical times, logic and rhetoric were thought of as being separate. Today, we don't see the separation as being nearly as clear-cut. If, for example, you follow our advice in the discovery part of the process, and begin by linking occasion, purpose, and audience with your subject matter, you have begun to use logic and rhetoric in a unified way. However, the ancients were not altogether mistaken. It is one thing to think logically about a subject and another to present thoughts so that others can understand and accept them. For example, in thinking about a subject she knows well, an expert might skip over steps in the logical process and still arrive at correct conclusions. But, in the presentation of her conclusions to an audience, she would be persuasive only if she displayed her logic step by step. We have all had teachers who obviously knew their subject matter, and who had thought about it deeply, but who, sadly, could not present that subject matter to their students in an understandable or persuasive fashion. Their logic may have been without fault, but they failed at rhetoric.

Rhetoric involves the consideration of such things as purpose, audience, and occasion. Purpose, audience, and occasion may help decide what language and style we choose to present our concepts. They may be factors behind the order in which we present the points of an argument. They may determine whether in the argument we appeal to emotion or rationality.

Have you ever thought your way through an argument to support your request for money from someone? Then you have engaged in logic. Have you then thought about how to present that argument? For example, have you had to decide which points would best support your case and maybe even the best time of day to present the argument? Then you have engaged in rhetoric.

The cartoon used at the head of this chapter is our starting point.[1] Look for a moment at the mythical caveman and what he is doing in the cartoon. In the first frame, the caveman is subjected to numerous sense impressions—from the grass, rabbits, sunshine, water flowing, and so forth. He is absorbing information but doing nothing with it. In frames two and three, he is doing something with the information that makes it useful to him. In the terms of the cartoon, he is turning information into knowledge and wisdom.

What he is doing, of course, is selecting and ordering bits of knowledge into integrated systems of knowledge. He is realizing that rabbits eat grass, that he can eat rabbits but not grass. In the last frame he gains the wisdom of realizing the interdependency of all the systems and knowing the ecological consequences of creating an imbalance of nature. *The key to the growth of knowledge, and the beginning of wisdom, is the way in which we select and order the information we have.* It is what we refer to as logic.

In selecting and ordering your available information, you are following a process of integration that is common to every thinking person. You are trying to bring order out of chaos. We all face this problem constantly and most often deal with it, as did our cavemen, by creating a series of systems and subsystems that we can organize into different levels of importance. To use a term we will employ again, we organize the systems and subsystems into a hierarchy.[2] Hierarchies exist everywhere in human endeavor. For instance, the United States has a federal system, fifty state subsystems, and numerous county, city, and other local sub-subsystems. In the same way, the army breaks itself into divisions, regiments, companies, and squads. By so ordering our governing systems, we break them into small enough units, with few enough lines of communication, so that they become humanly manageable.

In thinking about our information, we follow a process that is essentially identical. We organize our information into systems and subsystems and thus create a hierarchy to impose order. We can illustrate the method of creating hierarchies in thinking and writing with two strategies commonly used, classification and generalization.

Classification

In classification, we create knowledge by integrating our facts into categories based upon similar characteristics. We can show you how classification works very simply with an example that may be right in the room where you are reading this book.

By this time in your academic career, you may have gathered several shelves full of books. In fact, you may have enough books by now that you are having trouble finding the ones you want. Staring at your books, you receive sensory information—mass, colors, words, designs, and so forth. You are much like the caveman in the first frame of our cartoon. But now a purpose forms in your mind. You wish to order your books so that you may find them more easily. You think about the kinds of books you have: fiction, poetry, history, reference, mathematics, and science seem to be the main categories. Armed with these categories, you look at the books again so that you don't merely see a green book labeled *The World Almanac* and *Book of Facts*; you now also see a reference book. Next to the almanac is a thin paperback called *The Double Helix*. "A-ha," you say, "a science book." You are creating a system.

Armed with your system, you divide your books among the shelves in an organized way—science here, fiction there, and so on. When you survey the results, you decide to go a step further to create subsystems. You organize the fiction books by authors' last names. The science books seem to break down best by disciplines—biology, chemistry, physics, and others. You systematize your history books by continent: American history, Asian history, European history. You have created a hierarchy that has brought order out of chaos. But hold on. Might there be some other way to order your books?

Perhaps you have some books that you seldom read, but you want to display them as a form of scholarly decoration. Now your purpose shifts. Your aim is not to provide easy access to your books, but rather to find a way to make them pleasing to the eye. You look at your books with this different purpose. Ignoring titles and subjects, you notice color and size. You notice that some books have better bindings than others and some are thick enough to stand alone, perhaps with a vase or small sculpture next to them. Using your aesthetic categories of size, color, quality, and mass, you create a display that pleases your eye and, you hope, the eyes of others.

Notice what has happened in both examples. You have used your purpose to plan a hierarchy. Use of your hierarchy allows you to select what you consider to be the right material and ignore the rest. As you have classified your books, you can classify all kinds of information. Consider for a moment all the roads in your state. Can you think of some system to classify all of them? You'll do best if you have some purpose in mind. Perhaps your interest is in how roads are funded. With that in mind, the information that states are organized into different political units—for example, the state itself, plus counties and cities—may seem pertinent. With those political categories behind your classification strategy, your organization and thinking may go more smoothly. Alternatively, you may have an engineering interest in road construction. If so, classification by road surface—gravel, asphalt, concrete—may be the most useful approach.

Classification, a logical hierarchy, becomes a rhetorical hierarchy when the writer uses it to organize a written presentation. In the following paragraph, the writer sets up a classification hierarchy. He is discussing how the planet Mars evolved. In order to do so, he classifies the major forces of change:

> The major challenge in understanding how the planets evolved is to decipher the fragmentary records left by major physical and chemical processes. We know that meteoric impact was the dominant process on Mars during the first half billion years of its history. After that time, impact rates rapidly declined, and volcanism, water, and interaction with the atmosphere became dominant forces of change.[3]

Once the classification hierarchy is laid out in this introductory paragraph, the writer can then proceed to use the hierarchy as the basis for a clear and well-organized discussion.

All information is classifiable and thus can be systematized into useful knowledge. In creating a hierarchy based upon classification, be sure to use only one classification for each rank of classification. For example, the classification of *gravel, asphalt and concrete* is allowable, but *gravel, asphalt, country road* is unworkable. If you follow this one simple rule, you will avoid the pitfalls that lead to faulty classification.

Generalization

Perhaps the thought process we use most in dealing with information is generalizing from the particular bits of information we have to reach a conclusion. This generalizing from particulars is called *induction*. Because induction is so central to our thought processes, we cover it in some length.

Induction

In the early part of the 19th century, Charles Darwin took an extended scientific voyage around South America aboard an English ship named the *Beagle*.

In the course of the voyage, Darwin made many observations and gathered numerous specimens of plant and animal life. The observations and specimens were interesting in and of themselves, but for a period they remained, by the definition of our cartoon, information and not knowledge. However, in 1838, something occurred in Darwin's mind. He relates the incident himself:

> In October 1838 I happened to read for amusement Malthus on Population, and being well prepared to appreciate the struggle for existence which everywhere goes on from long continued observation of the habits of animals and plants, it at once struck me that under these circumstances favorable variations would tend to be preserved, and unfavorable ones to be destroyed. The result of this would be the formation of new species. Here then I had a theory by which to work.[4]

"Here then I had a theory by which to work." There is no better introduction to induction. In induction, we don't simply look at facts and manipulate them to reach conclusions. In induction, we form a theory, a hypothesis of some sort, and then take it to our facts. The hypothesis becomes our measuring rod. If the facts fit the hypothesis, we know we are on the right track. If the facts don't fit, either they or the hypothesis is wrong. If the facts check out, we must discard the hypothesis. If the facts seem suspect, we may stay with the hypothesis a while longer.

Darwin spent 20 years checking his facts and observations against his hypothesis before he was willing to state that he believed his hypothesis to be accurate.

We all constantly use induction as Darwin used it, albeit on a lower level. Recently one of us had dinner out with his wife and some friends. Shortly after dinner, one of the friends became sick. The rest of us hypothesized that this occurred because of something he had eaten at dinner. We applied rules of both sameness and difference to check out our hypothesis. The sick friend had had a veal cutlet. But so had one other person who did not get sick. Everyone, including the sick man, had had coffee, so coffee was ruled out. We went through the list in this way until we found a significant difference. Everyone except the sick man had had a salad before the main course. He had had soup. "There," we said, "the soup caused the sickness."

Were we absolutely sure of the confirmation of our hypothesis? No, not completely. You must face a disagreeable fact. All conclusions reached by induction are opinions. Even when all the facts check out and the accuracy of the hypothesis seems overwhelming, it remains an opinion. For example, our sick friend may have been suffering from a flu virus. Therefore, even though we operate on such conclusions all the time, it pays to be cautious about them, and like good scientists we should be alert to new hypotheses that may fit the facts better. Until we have such a new hypothesis, or a new set of facts, we operate with the hypothesis that best fits the existing facts.

In Chapter 2, we called your attention to *The Statistical Abstract of The United States*. This reference work, published annually by the Bureau of the

Census, contains a huge collection of information about the United States. In it you can find information about population, birth and death rates, education, health and nutrition, and much more. It is not, however, a book of knowledge. You must create your own knowledge by forming hypotheses and inductively checking them out against the information the book contains.

Let's try such a hypothesis: *In the United States, women are more accepted in the trades and professions in the 1980's than they were 10 to 20 years ago.* Armed with this hypothesis, we can seek facts to deny or substantiate it. Looking in the *Statistical Abstract*, we find the following facts.

Percentage of Women Enrolled in Professional Schools[5]

	1966	1982
Agriculture, forestry	2.7	56
Business	23	49
Engineering	1.9	21

Percentage of Women in Selected Trades[6]

	1972	1982
Carpenters	3.6	7
Brickmasons	0.5	1.7
Electricians	0	.7
Plumbers	0	.8
Auto mechanics	0.5	1
Telephone installers and repairers	1.9	10.9

In all categories checked, more women were training for a profession or engaged in a trade in 1982 than was so in the 1960's and 1970's. In some cases the growth was considerably more significant than others, but the hypothesis is supported. For a full study, of course, we would need to gather much more information than we have provided here to substantiate our hypothesis.

Two things are necessary for the successful use of induction. First, you must be able to get facts to work with. Second, you must have a hypothesis of some sort to apply to the facts. Facts by themselves are not enough. Induction consists of checking out your hypothesis against the facts. In such checking, you must be rigorous and honest and ready always to let go of a hypothesis that doesn't square with the facts.

Be wary when you are working with induction. Don't make the mistake of generalizing from too few particulars. For example, you may read in your newspaper of several basketball players found guilty of accepting bribes to change the outcomes of games they have played. "A-ha," someone may say, "basketball players take bribes. You can't trust any of them." Wrong. Several basketball players were convicted of taking bribes. There is insufficient evidence to go any further than that statement. To do so would unjustly brand many innocent people as criminals. Induction is not perfect even when we have ample evidence. Its use when we act hastily on insufficient evidence can lead to very faulty conclusions.

Another error in inductive reasoning—a *fallacy*, as such errors are called—is concluding that because some event followed another event, the event that occurred first must have caused the second. Logicians have given this fallacy a Latin name: *post hoc, ergo propter hoc*. (That is, *after this, therefore, because of this*.)

For example, suppose you were a detective investigating the basketball bribery case. You might in your investigation note that the players began to accept bribes *after* a new coach had been appointed for the team. Noting that, you might well be suspicious of the new coach, but it would be an example of the *post hoc* fallacy to leap to the conclusion that the coach was guilty. You would have to push your investigation much further. In doing so, you might find the coach is entirely innocent—that, in fact, the real cause was that several of the players fell so deeply into debt that the temptation to take bribes became too much for them.

It is to avoid such fallacies that scientists control their experiments so carefully. Horticulturists, for example, experiment with the effects of different length light periods on Easter lilies. In doing so, they carefully control all the other variables, such as temperature, fertilizer, and moisture. They want to be able to conclude with a high degree of certainty that the different light periods cause the results observed. Outside the laboratory, we lack such rigid controls and must, therefore, apply induction with even greater care.

Deduction

Closely related to induction is deduction. In induction, we examine many particulars to confirm or deny a generalization. In deduction, we apply a generalization already accepted to some particular to draw a conclusion about that particular.

In its classic form, deduction is used in a syllogism in which the first statement is the general principle. The second statement relates some particular to the general principle. The third statement draws a conclusion about the particular based upon the relationship. In this fashion, note this example:

All jockeys are short.
John is a jockey.
John is short.

In a syllogism, if the first and second statements are true, the third, if properly stated, has also to be true.

Do not make the error of reversing the second and third statements of the syllogism:

> All jockeys are short.
> John is short.
> John is a jockey.

Obviously, a great many short people find occupations other than being jockeys.

Like classification, generalization is used rhetorically as well as logically. When using a syllogism rhetorically, we usually present it in an abbreviated way, particularly if the general principle of the first statement is widely known and accepted. We might write, for example, "Knowing John was a jockey, I expected him to be short." Although thoroughly disguised, the syllogism is present in this statement.

Typically in a well-organized presentation, we move back and forth between induction and deduction. Earlier, we presented data about women in the professions and the trades. Using that data rhetorically, we might first use induction to establish a general principle and then use the general principle deductively:

> By 1982 women represented 56 percent of the enrollment in schools of agriculture and forestry, 49 percent in business schools, and 21 percent in engineering schools. However, in the trades, such as carpentry, plumbing, and auto mechanics, the percentages of women actually engaged in the trade ran much lower, on the order of 1 to 7 percent. In general, then, if you are a woman, you might be more accepted in the professions than in the trades.

Because we are aware we are dealing with many human variables, we have, in a common-sense way, qualified our syllogistic use of our general principle with the words, "in general" and "might." Obviously, some women might be more accepted in the trades than in the professions. Nonetheless, the classical syllogism underlies what we have written:

> Women are more accepted in the professions than in the trades.
> You are a woman.
> You would be more accepted in the professions than in the trades.

We have used classification and generalization to illustrate the way in which we use logic and rhetoric to create and present knowledge. There are other strategies besides these two major ones. We turn to them now to treat them in an abbreviated fashion.

Basic Strategies

As we have seen, writing is a thinking process in which we select and integrate pieces of information into a hierarchy. The experienced writer can do this much more quickly than can the inexperienced writer. Experienced writers already recognize when their purpose and audience call for classification, generalization, or one or more of the other strategies available. Through experience, they know how to select and order the details they need. Because this is so, a good preparation for writing is reading. In reading, you experience the solutions that skilled writers have found for their writing problems. Often, then, when you need such solutions, you'll be able to recall them, consciously or perhaps even unconsciously.

Although we cannot reproduce for you the experience of reading and absorbing the solutions that writers before you have found, we can offer some help. We can explain and demonstrate some of the basic writing strategies, namely, *topical order, comparison, causal analysis, description, narration, definition*, and *argument*. All involve the selection of material and the construction of a hierarchy to integrate the material selected. Each can be used in the design of an entire essay or for a piece of an essay. In this chapter, we discuss how to use them in the composing process.

Topical Order

A topical plan involves perhaps the most basic use of systems and subsystems that we have in writing. Suppose you have a large, general topic, say, investing in the stock market. A writer who had that topic broke it down into the following subtopics:

What Investment Means to You
What You Should Know about Common Stocks
How and Why Stock Is Sold
What You Should Know About Preferred Stocks[7]

In a topical hierarchy, you break your topic into subtopics, which, in turn, you can break up into sub-subtopics, and so on.

Here is how a topical approach can be used on a small scale:

> There are four reassuringly simple components of Casa Zeus's solar consciousness: siting, landscaping, tightening, and the blocking of energy loss at night. "The first thing you do," Woods points out, "is position the house so most of the windows face south, and can be passive solar collectors. You don't *increase* the number of windows; you simply *move* them.

"Then you change the microclimate to produce the macroclimate you want. Landscaping techniques alone can save 10 to 20 percent of your energy costs." Woods "bermed" the northwest corner of the house for example—banked an earthen rise against it, both as insulation and to divert the prevailing wind up and over the roof.

Casa Zeus is, of course, well insulated, but its prime weather barrier is compulsive attention to tightness.[8]

And so on, as the writer works through each of his four subtopics.

Comparison

In comparison, which includes contrast as well, the writer puts together several things—objects, processes, people, whatever—and compares and contrasts them by similar characteristics. It is a technique that can be used simply to inform and explain, as in this example, in which Uranus and Neptune are compared and contrasted by several of their characteristics to each other and to other planets:

Their births in the cold and dark domain of the outer solar system gave Uranus and Neptune, the seventh and eighth planets from the Sun, characteristics that differ from those of Jupiter and Saturn, the other giant gas planets.

Both Uranus and Neptune have only about one-fifth the mass of Jupiter and are almost the same size: Uranus is approximately 32,200 miles in diameter, and Neptune, 31,000 miles. Uranus, like Saturn, has dense rings, whereas Neptune does not—although, like Jupiter, Neptune may possess a tenuous ring.

All the gaseous planets have rocky cores of about the same size, but the amount of hydrogen and helium enveloping the cores differs vastly. Jupiter and Saturn are made up mostly of hydrogen and helium—the components of their atmospheres. Uranus and Neptune are mostly carbon, nitrogen, and oxygen—the main components of their cores.

Despite their similarities, however, Uranus and Neptune each possess distinguishing characteristics. For example, although Neptune is slightly smaller in diameter, it is more massive, being equal to about 17 Earth masses. Uranus is equal to about 14.

The most obvious difference between Uranus and Neptune is in the direction their axes tilt. Uranus is tipped over on its axis and, in its current orbital position, points its southern pole at the Sun. With its moons traveling in the planet's equatorial plane, the Uranian system resembles a bullseye facing the Sun. But Neptune's axis, like Earth's, has only a slight tilt of 28 degrees.[9]

Comparison in the form of analogy is a powerful tool in writers' hands, enabling them to relate something unknown to the readers to something they already know. Through the relationship, the reader comes to understand the new thing or, perhaps, to see it in a new way. Here is an example of analogy being used skillfully and amusingly:

> It is always difficult to grasp and convey the significance of a technological trend which is progressing at an exponential rate and which shows no sign of letting up. An analogy with a more familiar technological development might help. If the internal combustion engine had developed as rapidly as the central processing unit of the modern computer since 1945, a Rolls Royce would now have 45,000 horsepower, cost $4, and do 3 million miles to the gallon!
>
> In aviation, if jet technology had developed at the same rate as the computer has in the past 25 years, we would be traveling to Europe in 7 minutes at a cost of 2¢, and the airplane would be the size of a shoe box.[10]

Comparison can also be used on a larger scale as a form of argument (see pages 71–74) in which you justify the choice of one thing over another, based upon how well it meets a set of criteria. You might argue, for example, that car X is better than car Y because it has lower maintenance expenses, better handling characteristics, and better gas mileage. You would, of course, provide evidence to support these three statements.

Causal Analysis

In causal analysis, we link effects together with their causes, attempting to demonstrate that the effects did, indeed, result from the causes. We generalize from the evidence we possess, using both induction and deduction (see pages 58–62). Be careful in a causal analysis to avoid the *post hoc* fallacy and the fallacy of generalizing from insufficient evidence (see pages 60–61).

In this example, we give you the opening sentences in a causal analysis, followed by a sample of the evidence presented:

> The chief requirements for success in world markets remains to make world-class products, products that satisfy customer needs, no matter *who* those customers are, no matter *where* they are. But a major problem remains for American Industry. That is the strength of the dollar. A strong dollar benefits American importers and American tourists, but its increasing strength hurts American producers trying to sell their goods abroad. . . .
>
> Example one: At a recent public bid for road compactors in Indonesia the U.S. bid price for each unit was 44 percent higher

than the low bid from Italy and 23 percent higher than the second highest bid from Sweden. We didn't have a chance. In another typical public bid situation, this time for portable air compressors for Korea, U.S. bid prices surpassed all the others. Our bid, based on estimates from our North Carolina plant, was 36 percent higher than the successful Belgian price. We did not have a chance.[11]

Description

One purpose of description is to make your reader see. For the moment, let's think about description in visual terms. Suppose someone asked you to draw a face.[12] You would likely proceed in something like the following manner. First, you would draw an oval:

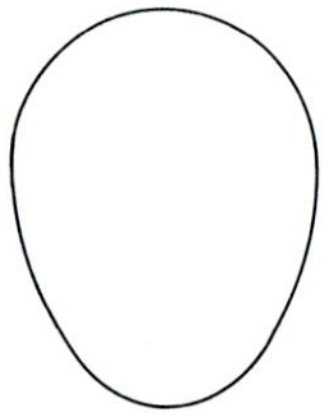

The oval is your basic system. Next, you would add the major features as subsystems:

Next, you would add details, such as eyelashes and teeth, which are sub-subsystems:

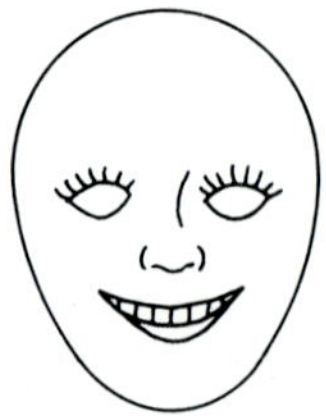

Even if you have a low level of artistic ability, by thinking and acting systematically, you could create a recognizable face.

In planning a written description, you would proceed in a similar fashion. Here is a description of a body scanner, a complex x-ray machine used for exploring the human body:

> The resulting machine looks like something out of science fiction. It is, in essence, a huge horizontal cylinder that rotates, with a smaller stationary cylinder inside.[13]

The "huge horizontal cylinder" equals the system. The "smaller stationary cylinder" equals a subsystem.

The writer goes on to select and add details about the "huge horizontal cylinder," in the same way that we added eyelashes to the eyes in our drawing:

> This outer cylinder is a complex marvel. Twenty feet long and weighing more than 15 tons, it is cantilevered out into space, held up only by a triangular-shaped bracket at the end opposite the patient. Fourteen X-ray tubes are lined up around half the cylinder.[14]

The writer of this example and you in your writing are in control of the hierarchy. You can make it as simple or as complex as your purpose and audience make necessary. You can have the equivalent of a stick figure or a fully drawn human being:

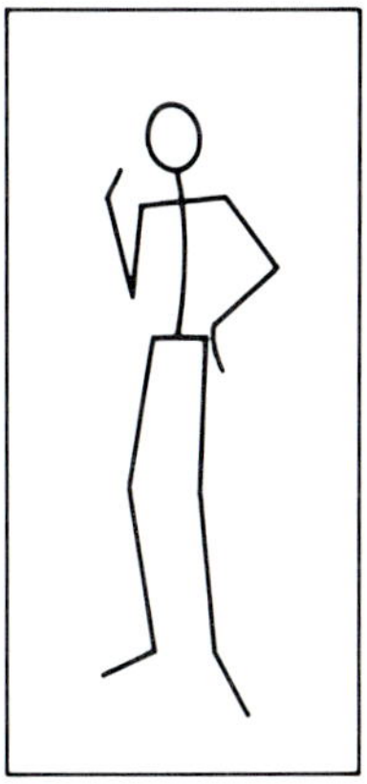

Description can be scientific and technical, as is our body-scanner example, or it can be used to evoke an emotional response. The next, highly selective, passage is meant to make you feel the sturdiness and warmth of the object described:

> The *Catherine J* is a brand new boat. She draws six feet below the water line, which makes her extraordinarily stable for her 38-foot length. There's a snugly heated cabin, and an entire arsenal of electronic equipment.[15]

Our last example is a description of an African landscape. It is meant to be both informational and somewhat evocative. Notice in it how the point of view of the observer—in this case, quite literally where he is standing—can influence the description. The observer is atop a tower:

> I had walked with Dau and the others . . . to small camps near ephemeral water holes, but on the ground it was too confusing, the change in altitude and vegetation too subtle, the sun too nearly overhead to provide any sense of where I was or from where I had come.
>
> For the first time from the tower, I could see an order to the landscape. From up there on the tower, I could see the long thin border scar, could trace it off to the horizon to both the north and the south. But beyond that, no evidence, not the slightest sign of a human hand. The Bushmen camps were too few in number, too small and well-hidden in the grass and bush to be visible from here.[16]

Narration

Narration is probably the simplest method of creating organizational hierarchies. It involves putting events in chronological order. Most often, the order is start to finish, but as we all know from books and movies, flashbacks in time are also common in narration. Narration is often used to put action into description. See how it works in this description of the body scanner in action:

> In a basement research room at Mayo Clinic in Rochester, Minnesota, a black and white television screen displays the rib cage, lungs, and beating heart of a nine-year-old child. The image, recorded during an examination months earlier, looks for a moment like a conventional x-ray. Then the figure rotates, and we are suddenly seeing through the rib cage from the side, then the back, the front again, all in full three-dimensional detail.
>
> The picture moves in on the pulmonary arteries, which are not getting enough blood to the child's lungs. First the rib cage dissolves from the screen, then the backbone, then the tissues of heart and lungs, leaving only the arterial tree. A dye has been injected into the child, and the blood vessels right down into the capillary beds, stand out like a nova suspended in space.[17]

We now see the scanner, and we see it in time. Notice also that the writer is working with two systems of time. The present: "The black and white television screen displays the rib cage. . . ."; and the past: "A dye has been injected into the child. . . ."

A major use of narration is relating past events. As in all writing, you select the details that help you achieve your purpose. In this example, the writer's purpose is to exemplify the confusion about nuclear power in the United States:

> Two decades ago this month, in March 1964, the Jersey Central Power and Light Company applied for a construction permit to build the Oyster Creek nuclear power plant, and the age of commercial nuclear power was born. Oyster Creek was the first nuclear plant planned by a utility strictly on the merit of competitive economics. Largely because of the potential for cost savings, U.S. utilities ordered 222 more nuclear power plants over the next 10 years, making it one of the world's fastest growing industries, which has brought us billions of dollars in savings.
>
> Alternatively, 10 years ago, Public Service Indiana ordered two nuclear units that it called Marble Hill. For several years, while many other nuclear plants ordered around that time were being canceled, Marble Hill was the last order for a nuclear plant in the United States that was still under construction. Earlier this year, over a decade after the plant was originally announced, the utility had to cancel Marble Hill because of the financial drain caused by its construction. One unit was little more than half completed, and the other only one-third, but the utility had already spent $2.5 billion on the project, which now has little chance of ever generating a single kilowatt-hour. To many observers, this cancellation—along with other problems that were being faced by several nuclear plants under construction—symbolized a closing curtain on the age of nuclear power in the United States. So from that perspective, 1984 is not an anniversary of the beginning of the nuclear age, but the beginning of the end.
>
> How can government officials and the public, who will ultimately determine the fate of nuclear power, make sense of these conflicting views?[18]

Definition

Misunderstanding the meaning of a term can result in confusion, misinterpretation, and error. If you were discussing salary with a potential employer, you would want to be sure whether $20,000 a year meant *gross* salary or *net* salary. If you assumed *net* salary (take-home pay), you might be disappointed when you received your first paycheck.

How well a piece of writing communicates depends largely on how clearly the reader understands the words used by the writer. As a writer, you will use definition to define terms that you think will be unfamiliar to your readers or that might be interpreted in a way you didn't intend.

Short, concise definitions abound in writing. In the passage quoted earlier about Casa Zeus' landscaping, the writer states that the builder, Woods, "'bermed' the northwest corner of the house for example—banked an earthen rise against it, both as insulation and to divert the prevailing wind up and over the roof." The phrase after the dash provides the details that define the term *bermed*. In the passage about the effects of a strong American dollar, the writer defines "world-class products" as "products that satisfy customer needs, no matter *who* those customers are, no matter *where* they are." Such definitions may sometimes be placed in a glossary at the end of a paper, but more likely, as in the passages cited, they will be placed in the text near the term defined.

At the heart of such definitions is the familiar hierarchical arrangement. The writer organizes the definition into three parts: the term to be defined, the class to which the term belongs, and the characteristics that set it off from other members of the class.

Term	Class	Characteristics
world-class products	products that satisfy consumer needs	no matter *who* those customers are, no matter *where* they are

Sometimes a short, concise definition is not adequate to explain a complicated concept. At such times, the writer needs to extend the definition by using one or more of the strategies already discussed. For example, *radiation* can be defined by causal analysis, explaining its sources and its effects. Terms that are commonly confused, such as *velocity* and *acceleration*, can be defined by comparing their similarities and contrasting their differences. As illustrated in the passage on the body scanner, terms that refer to unfamiliar things and processes can be defined in part by description and narration. In the following definition of *urbanization*, the writer begins by connecting the concept to changes in distribution of population, providing a concise meaning ("migration by the rural population into big cities") and providing statistics to show the growth of big cities since 1700.

> The enormous growth in world population has been accompanied by considerable changes in its distribution. One of the most marked features of the population growth has been urbanization—migration by the rural people into big cities. These grow in consequence much more rapidly than world population as a whole. Statistics regarding the growth of big cities in recent centuries illustrate the development.

In the year 1700, no more than 40 cities in the world had populations of over 100,000, whereas the lists first published in 1870 of all cities (over 100,000) in the world put them at 164. By 1900 the number had risen to about 300, and by 1950 to 670. . . . By 1970 the number of cities with over a million inhabitants had [reached] 152, most of the increase occurring in Asia. China has at least 17 of these giant cities, Japan and India 8 each, and Central and South America 15. In North America there are 8, in western Europe 13, in the Soviet Union 10, and in Africa 5.

The writer concludes his definition by using causal analysis and comparison to explain the effects of urbanization:

Owing to heavy concentrations of people, industry, and traffic, the physical and mental strains and stresses are generally greater in big cities than in small towns. As studies made in Great Britain and the United States show, in a big city there are on the average 15% less sunshine, 30% less ultraviolet radiation in winter, and 10% more rain, hail, or snow. There are 10% more cloudy days, 30% more mist in the summer, and 100% more fog in winter. . . . In consequence of the high level of air pollution in big cities, many diseases occur on a large scale far more often. In cities of over 1 million inhabitants, lung cancer is twice as rife as in the country. Bronchitis and other lung ailments are also much more frequent. Apart from these physical effects, excessive urbanization also produces widespread suffering in the psychological and social spheres. . . .[19]

Argument

In argument, your purpose is to demonstrate the probable truth of your position. We say *probable* because argument is almost always a combination of induction and deduction, and, as we have already seen, induction can only give probability, not certainty (see pages 58–61).

Generally we do not argue in areas in which we can have objective certainty. If we were to argue over which was taller, the Washington Monument or the Eiffel Tower, we could settle the argument quickly by going to a reference work, in this case our dictionary. There we would learn that the Eiffel Tower at 984 feet is taller than the Washington Monument at 555 feet, 5-1/8 inches. There is no further argument.

Also, we should avoid argument in those areas where opinions are purely subjective and cannot be supported by fact. For example, whether someone likes or dislikes Brussels sprouts, football, or hard rock is purely subjective. To argue such things is usually both pointless and painful.

We do and should argue in those areas where we deal with opinions that can be supported by evidence of some sort. Most often we argue by stating a thesis—a major opinion—and then supporting that thesis with facts and perhaps other opinions. Argumentation uses either induction or deduction, usually both.

In our example,[20] a government official argues that Americans are ill-prepared to live in an interdependent world. First he states his thesis:

> There is ample evidence that the United States today faces a "knowledge gap," just as we faced a "missile gap" in the 1960s. I refer not to our knowledge of technology or science or economics. The Nobel prizes awarded each year to Americans indicate that we are doing well in those areas. Rather I am talking about our knowledge of the now shrunken world and our competence to deal with it.

Next, he establishes our involvement in the world with facts like these:

> Like it or not, America is involved with the world. Nationally, one out of every eight manufacturing jobs depends on exports. One out of every three dollars of U.S. corporate profits is derived from international activities. Exports of American goods and services contribute nearly $200 billion to our gross national product.

He states again and supports his thesis that we lack needed skills to deal with an interdependent world:

> By temperament and training, we Americans are not well equipped to deal with our new situation. We are thrown into contact and conflict with peoples whose histories and motivations we scarcely understand.
>
> Can we, for example, comprehend the new forms of political change, quite distinct from Western models, that are evolving before our eyes? Or, how many educated Americans—aside from a few scholars—appreciate in even the vaguest way, the dynamism and values of Islamic cultures? Worse still, few of us speak anyone else's language. The 1979 report of the President's Commission on Foreign Language and International Studies—known as the Perkins Commission after its chairman James Perkins—indicated that only 8 percent of U.S. colleges and universities had a foreign language entrance requirement, as against 34 percent in 1966 and an astounding 85 percent in 1915. . . . The Perkins Commission raised the important question: How well equipped are we to make an effective response to our new situation?
>
> The fact of the matter is that we seem woefully unprepared to respond effectively. Consider:

> —only one in twenty undergraduates enrolls in courses dealing with foreign peoples and cultures.
>
> —only about one percent of college and university faculty members go abroad each year.
>
> —and fewer than two percent of high school graduates have any foreign language competence.

The writer calls upon other authorities to support his thesis:

> Former State Department official Harlan Cleveland stated the problem well: "It has been hard enough to try to prepare the nation's youth for responsive and responsible positions in local and national affairs. Now the system is asked to help young Americans become responsive and responsible citizens of an interdependent world. The new assignment," he said, "would be ridiculous if it were not also imperative."

The writer details some of the efforts that have been made to increase international knowledge and awareness in the United States. He closes with a summation and a call for action:

> Let me close by suggesting that we are at a pivotal point in our history. We are late in realizing it. Building appropriate educational systems is a long-range task, but I believe it prudent to consider the following possibilities:
>
> —that "interdependence" could prove to be a brutal phenomenon for our civilization;
>
> —that we are not now, as a society, prepared to cope with the implications of that possibility. . . .
>
> However real the impediments to an effective response, and they exist, we cannot afford to turn away from involvement.
>
> Education that teaches us to celebrate rather than condemn cultural diversity, to understand rather than undermine differing traditions and beliefs, to respect rather than revile mankind's infinite variations—such education may not be enough to preserve our precarious perch on the favorable side of history, but surely the effort must be made.

Argument is one of our major uses of language. We argue to convince others that our convictions are justified, to sell goods and services, to change the opinions of others, to get others to take actions we desire, and so forth. To live successfully in the world, we should learn to argue well.

Bits of information and data are worth little until they are integrated into a system of knowledge. In this chapter, we have shown you some of the logical and rhetorical strategies for such integration. In the next chapter, we discuss and demonstrate a process through which you can use these strategies in creating and presenting knowledge.

Exercises

1. Two of the key terms used in this chapter are *logic* and *rhetoric*. In your own words explain these two terms. Show in what ways logic and rhetoric are similar and in what ways they are different. Use examples to illustrate your points.

2. On pages 57–58, we define and describe classification. To illustrate the process, we use the classification of books and of roads. We quote a passage about the planet Mars to show classification in action. Write an essay modeled after pages 120–127 in which you define and describe classification. You must provide your own examples of classification. Also be prepared to use your essay as a basis for a class discussion of classification.

3. On page 60, we show you how induction and deduction can be used with information gathered from the *Statistical Abstract of the United States*. We form a hypothesis about women in the trades and the professions, and then, using information from the *Statistical Abstract*, we determine if the facts support or refute the hypothesis. Browse through a collection of facts, such as the *Statistical Abstract, The World Almanac and Book of Facts*, or *The United Nations Demographic Yearbook*. See what sorts of information the collection contains. Form a hypothesis that can be tested by information from your source. Write an essay in which you state the hypothesis, and then, by applying induction and deduction to your information, support or refute the hypothesis.

4. One of the best ways to learn something is to teach it to someone else. For this exercise, the class is divided into seven groups. Each group takes as its responsibility one of the basic writing strategies described on pages 63–74: topical order, comparison, causal analysis, description, narration, definition, and argument. Members of each group will teach the rest of the class how this particular strategy works. In order to do so, each group will have to gather samples of the strategy to use in class. The group should consider for each sample the following questions:

- What is the evidence that the sample follows the designated strategy?
- How has the writer used the strategy to integrate data into knowledge?
- What was the author's purpose?
- Who was the audience for the sample?
- Does the strategy chosen fit the material, purpose, and audience? What is the evidence for the conclusions the group reaches in this matter?
- Could the author have used some other strategy? If so, would the other strategy have been superior or inferior to the one chosen? Why?

4

Composing: Planning, Writing, and Revising

The composing process is a cycle of planning, writing, and revising, as portrayed in Figure 4-1. You probably best begin it by reviewing what you have done in the discovery process. Serious writers are constantly reviewing. They think about their material, and almost absorb their material. They are constantly checking material against purpose and the needs of their audience. As they write, they stop from time to time to read over a few previous paragraphs or pages. It's a way of keeping the brain on track, to keep it off thoughts of lunch, friends, tennis games, and so on. It's a way of stocking the mind so that in periods when you are not consciously working, the unconscious mind can keep busy for you—solving problems and making connections that the conscious mind has missed. As necessary as reviewing is as a beginning, don't overdo it. It can become procrastination, a way of putting off the tough work that lies ahead. After you review, get down to the work of composing.

We present composing as a three-stage process: planning, writing, and

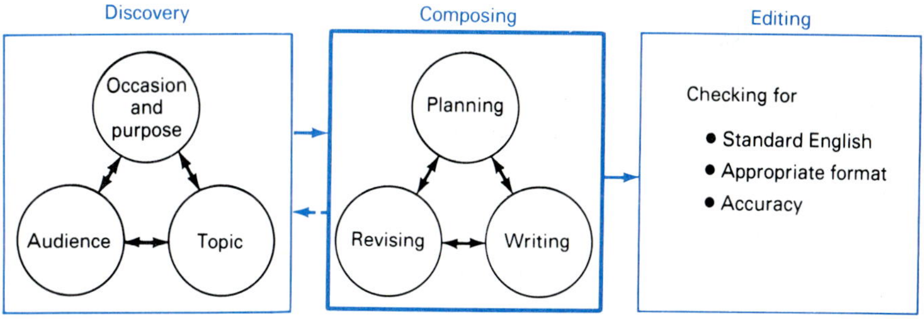

Figure 4-1 *The Composing Process.*

revising. It may seem somewhat linear in our presentation. We caution you that it is not, at least not necessarily.

Composing is not linear because writing can occur at any one of the three stages. You may be composing a small outline to get your ideas lined up and suddenly find yourself developing one of the ideas in a paragraph. If that happens, don't fight the process. In writing, take what you can get when you can get it. Some writers go directly from the discovery stage to the writing stage with little or no planning. The rough draft becomes in effect their planning stage.

Composing is not linear because revising goes on at all three stages. You tinker with your plan even as you make it. As you write, you may stop abruptly when you have the notion that a sentence won't do. You scratch it out or wipe it off the screen and start over again. If your draft refuses to go well, you may need to go back to the planning stage.

Nevertheless, there is a flow from planning to revising that does occur. Most writers do take time to jot down a simple word-phrase outline, as much to clarify their thinking as to serve as a guide to writing. A few even take time for rather elaborate outlines, complete with topic and subtopic headings. There is a time set aside mainly for the hard work of writing the first draft. There is a time when the draft is completed and the main order of business is revising. Therefore, we will discuss planning, writing, and revising in that order. But remember that composing is a dynamic business and that all three stages can be occurring simultaneously.

Planning

Be sure of your purpose before moving into planning. To a large extent, purpose determines the hierarchy you will use to present your material. In Chapter 1 (pages 7–8), we discuss the four major purposes for writing. In Chapter 3, we discuss the major logical and rhetorical hierarchies used in writing. In planning, you bring purpose and hierarchies together. Here are some of the possibilities:

- *To present or explain knowledge you possess or to define terms.* In most cases, this first of the four purposes will be less complex than the other three. The hierarchies you are most likely to choose are *topical order, classification, description, narration,* and *definition,* either alone or in combination.
- *To explain and defend a thesis.* Remember that each advanced purpose will probably include the earlier purpose. In this purpose, notice that you are called upon to *explain* your thesis. Also, consideration of your audience may cause you to include background information and definitions. So you may well begin your planning by considering such hierarchies as *topical order, classification, description, narration,* and *definition*. But to defend your thesis calls for an *argument* in which you clearly state your thesis and attempt to demonstrate its plausibility. In doing so, you will certainly use *induction* and *deduction*.

• *To present an evaluation of something.* What are you evaluating? You will need to explain. By what criteria are you evaluating it? You will need to define such criteria and perhaps explain how you arrived at them. If you are evaluating something by comparing it to something else, then *comparison* is likely to be the hierarchy you use. Again, you are likely to have to present background information and your evaluation is likely to be an *argument.* Remember that in an evaluation you are expected to reach a conclusion: "This movie is excellent." "This process is too dangerous and costly." "This administrative policy discriminates unfairly." And so forth.

• *To present and support a recommendation.* To be acceptable, a recommendation must be preceded by an evaluation. People may not accept your recommendation to see a certain movie unless you convince them by your evaluation of it that it is worth seeing. Your evaluation may have to include a brief *narration* of the plot. If you are trying to convince readers to accept Plan A, you will have to evaluate the plan and perhaps show through *comparison* its superiority to Plan B. Recommending as a purpose can include any and all of the previous three purposes and any and all of the hierarchies.

Working with these purposes and your knowledge of your readers and the occasion, you are able to look at ways to plan your paper. To illustrate, return for a moment to the paper about the Three Mile Island nuclear accident that we used in Chapter 2 (see pages 26–33). As you may remember, in that example we proposed that you were gathering material for a term paper in a class on public policy. You had gathered considerable material and had formed a hypothesis to focus your work:

> The TMI accident created enough public anxiety and controversy to affect seriously the public nuclear policy of the United States Government.

As you now think about that hypothesis, you see clearly that your purpose will be to explain and defend a thesis. You remember that your public policy professor has only a layperson's knowledge of nuclear power and will therefore need some background information. You begin to see your paper as having a two-part organization. The first part will deal with the TMI accident itself. You will probably narrate the events, explain some of the technical points involved, and discuss the seriousness of the accident. The second and larger part of your paper will be an argument in defense of your hypothesis. You begin to see some of the points you will be working with. There was a large, well-documented public reaction to TMI. Since TMI, governmental regulatory policies have been tightened. Since TMI, the atomic power industry has been in serious trouble. You have correlations; you will need to establish causality.

Working for even a short time in this manner, you may produce a plan more complex than you can hold in your head. When this happens, you need to freeze your plan temporarily so you can review it. A simple outline works well for this purpose. It brings together for you your principal ideas, selected details from your notes, and possible hierarchies. Constructing a simple outline is a step toward writing a fully organized and developed paper. But think of the freeze as only temporary. Your outline is a working document. Expect it to change.

Even though your outline may change, the time spent on it is more than repaid by these three advantages:

- It lays out your organization in highly condensed form so that you can see the overall picture of what goes into the paper. The outline form makes it easy for you to verify that all points and supporting material have been included. It also helps you cope with interruptions that break your train of thought. To resume writing, you may have to reorient yourself to your overall plan.
- It is produced by dividing topics into subtopics and, if necessary, by dividing subtopics into lower-level segments. This logical division aids greatly in developing a hierarchical structure.
- It uses short phrases or sentences to identify topics and subtopics. Because it is easier to tinker with outline entries than to move paragraphs and sentences, it is easier to rearrange material.

Most of the time, you can and should work with an informal outline, a list of words or phrases that represent the topics and subtopics you wish to cover in a particular order. Since it is for your own guidance, it can be quick and sloppy, as is the following outline on bulimia, an eating disorder that predominantly affects young women who have an overwhelming desire to be thin.[1]

Profile of a bulimic
- Definition of bulimia
- Becoming trapped in the binge-purge cycle
- Deceiving characteristics
- Emotional characteristics
- Physical characteristics

Relationships of a bulimic to her mother
- In infancy
- In adolescence
- In adulthood

Overwhelming emphasis from society to be thin
- Changing emphasis on women to be thin
- Mass media's message of thinness

Changing roles of women in America
- Participating in male roles
- Pressures to work and be a homemaker

Treatment of bulimics
  Hospitalization
  Outpatient therapy

Notice how the writer's outline clearly indicates that her purpose is to present and explain knowledge. To do so, she has chosen a topical order, a hierarchy often picked for this purpose. Notice, however, that she has chosen to present the relationships of a bulimic to her mother in chronological order, the typical order of narration. The simple outline has helped the writer to shape her paper. At this stage of development, many writers will choose to begin their draft. Others may want to complete more items on the outline, such as organizing the details for the many subsections of the paper, checking to see if there are deficiencies of information, and making sure the coverage and sequence is appropriate for the purpose and audience.

If you have created notes as part of the discovery process, it is a good idea at this point to arrange them in the order of the outline. When you do so, you will appreciate having taken your notes on easily shuffled cards (see pages 28–32). Some people, in fact, go directly to card arrangement as a form of outlining and skip the written outline altogether.

Sometimes you may be required to write a formal outline. Your teacher may have you submit such an outline so that he or she may check the purpose, scope, and organization of a paper you are developing. When you are part of a team of writers working on the same document, an editor or team supervisor may require a formal outline for the same reason and also for these:

- to designate who is responsible for each part of the paper;
- to provide a blueprint of the overall structure of the document, especially its completeness, coherency, and unity;
- to keep track of and evaluate the progress of the team writing project.

When you have completed your outline, you will have (1) listed the major points of your paper, (2) placed under each major point the subordinate points by which it is to be expanded, and (3) arranged the order in which your ideas are to be presented. The outline is only a skeleton of your paper, but writing it will clarify your thinking, organize your material, and give you much of the momentum you need to start actually writing.

But you should not regard the paper as fully and completely organized. Seldom will you have everything laid out in an organized manner. As you actually write—especially at the most specific level of your paper—you will continue to organize and perhaps even reorganize as better connections and more specific ideas occur. Most of your paragraphs and sentences will be organized ad hoc, because you won't know for sure if a particular writing strategy works until you try it out.

Writing the Rough Draft

Much of the work has been done by the time you are ready to write the rough draft. All the collecting, analyzing, planning, and organizing—the activities we discuss in Chapters 1, 2, and 3, and so far in this chapter—have primed your mind. You know who your readers are and why you are writing to them. You have organized your material, have a plan that represents your governing organization, and have arranged your notes to match your plan. You may even have a tentative title, lead, and perhaps several topic sentences.

Now you are ready to put all your work to this point on the line—literally. When you complete the rough draft, you will know how inadequate your efforts have been and about how much more work you have to do.

How do you write a rough draft? There is no simple way to do it; there are several approaches, including no doubt some which no one has tried yet. You will find some writers who say they begin by writing and rewriting their introduction until they get their thesis, purpose, and plan stated clearly and their relationship with their readers established. They believe that once they get the opening in reasonably good shape they can write the rest of the paper relatively easily. You will find other writers who state that they try to write the end of their paper first in the belief that it is easier to write the rest once they know the final idea they want to lead up to. You will find still others who say that they begin anywhere they can in the hope that once they start writing they can more easily pull their best ideas from the unconscious. They are all right—up to a point. Writers write rough drafts just about any way they can.

Regardless of where you start, set aside a fairly large chunk of time—perhaps as much as three or four hours, with only a short break or two. You will need that much time to draft a passage that you can return to. After that initial long session, you can work in smaller installments if necessary.

A convenient way to begin is to think of your paper in very general terms. On the most abstract level, all essays consist of three parts: (1) the beginning or introduction, (2) the middle or body, and (3) the ending. This abstract framework can be visualized like this:

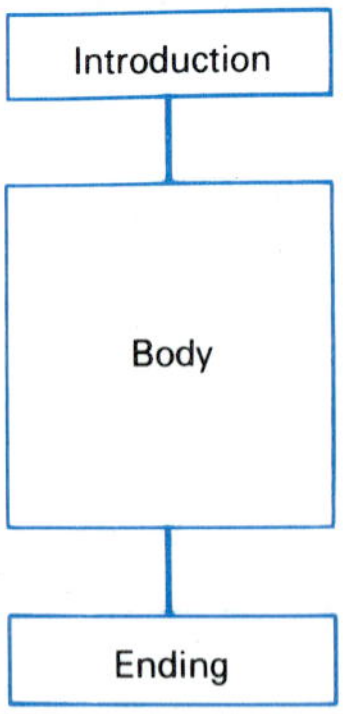

Try to imagine this three-part structure underlying all your writing. It may seem fairly rigid, and it is. The parts of almost all writing appear in this order and in this proportion. But this does not mean that the writing is mechanical. As we have already seen in our discussion of basic writing strategies in Chapter 3, "Composing: Using Logic and Rhetoric," the body of the paper can be organized many different ways to fit the purpose, audience, and subject matter. As you write, you will continue thinking things through, sorting and combining information as new ideas occur and new relationships are found. But the three-part structure will remain.

It probably makes little difference what part of your paper you tackle first. Just because the introduction is read first doesn't mean that it has to be written first. If you have an idea of how to begin your paper, try writing the introduction. If not, don't worry too much about it and get on to the body of your paper. You can get back to the introduction later. As you write, concern yourself not only with organization but also with displaying organization to your readers.

Writing the Body

Writing the body of the paper first makes a lot of sense, because in organizing your material you have been organizing the body of the paper. It is also easier to tell what kind of introduction is required once you have written the body.

Because most of your writing will move from general to specific, we suggest that you try concentrating first on the major points in your outline. Choose one of your major points and write about it, for it is certain to end up as part of your paper. Look for ways to develop an important idea.

Concentrate on one major idea at a time and follow your notes as you have arranged them. For each major entry in your outline, ask yourself these questions: What do I need in order to develop this point? Do I have enough examples and details to support my contention? Do I need to define a key term? Would an analogy help? Have I provided the readers with answers to who? what? when? where? how? why? How does this idea relate to the previous one? To the next one?

As you write, more ideas will probably occur. You will start to remember all kinds of things—stray bits of data, part of what somebody wrote or said about a point you plan to cover, an idea that you thought you had forgotten. Jot them down and try to develop them, but don't be too worried at this point about completeness. If a detail doesn't come, leave a blank, flag it for later work, and continue. Write everything you know about the point, then move on to the next point and write everything you know about it.

It is important that you continue getting your ideas on paper or into the word processor. There will be times when you will do some quick revising, anything from changing your mind about a word or detail to restructuring part of a paragraph. But don't start extensive revising prematurely. Don't get bogged down at this point worrying about grammar, spelling, punctuation, word choice, or even paragraph breaks. You may feel that some of your sentences are choppy and that some of your ideas are not expressed as clearly as you would like. Of course, the more focused an idea, the more precise and clear your words will be and vice versa. But unless a better connection or word occurs immediately, keep pushing. Don't stop to polish a sentence or paragraph into final form. Remember that what you are creating can always be changed.

If you find yourself losing your forward momentum, try to get your bearings by reading your last few paragraphs or checking your outline to pick up the track. Don't write for more than several hours at a time. Try to stop at a point where you're sure of what's coming next. It will make beginning again less of a chore. When you are not writing, get away from it completely. Watch TV, read, play tennis, go for a walk, take a nap. Let your unconscious mind work on your writing problems. You will be amazed how effective this technique can be. When you return to your writing, take the time to read over a previous page or two to refresh your mind before you get to work.

Writing the Introduction

The introduction, whether short or long, informs readers what the piece of writing is about and interests them in the subject. In some forms of writing, for example magazine articles of a light nature, the writing may not get read if the opening doesn't immediately interest the reader. In other forms of writing, for example, business reports, readers may be more tolerant of a dull opening, and, in fact be suspicious of an opening that tries too hard to gain their interest. In introductions, like everything else, readers and occasions have to be considered.

Here are the openings to two light magazine pieces that get their readers into the article quickly and provide a hook to catch their interest.

> Here's a cheerful thought. Some knowledgeable people believe that black widow spiders, like locusts and jack rabbits, come in plagues.[2]

> In the fifth chapter of Matthew's Gospel, Christ is quoted as saying that the meek shall inherit the earth, but another opinion lately suggests that, no, more likely it will go to the cockroaches.[3]

It is no accident that these openings hook most readers. The writer gets quickly to the thesis and sets the mood at once.

More formal pieces of writing usually require a more discursive introduction that answers questions like these: What is the purpose of the paper? What are its major ideas? What is its plan of organization? A good introduction of this type answers these questions explicitly, as in these two examples, the first about educational technology, the second about computers in college:

Relationships between instructors and students in higher education take different forms, particularly as higher education adapts its structure to new audiences. I argue that this remains true even as "instructor" comes to include instructional technologies, that one's view of student-instructor relationships will and—should—color one's view of instructional technology, and these views connote very different roles for technology in collegiate learning.

I begin with two vignettes from my own undergraduate education, followed by four technological counterpoints.[4]

Between Fall 1982 and 1984, the proportion of entering college freshmen reporting that they "frequently" or "occasionally" wrote a computer program increased 85 percent, from 27.3 percent to 50.6 percent. This past fall, three of every five entering freshmen reported completing at least half a year of computer science in high school. And almost a fourth of them report they used a personal computer "frequently" during the year prior to entering college.

Are changes in college computing comparable? Are campuses and faculty prepared to build on the familiarity of these students with computers?[5]

The introduction is where you win or lose your readers. To win them, you must interest them. Keep in mind who your readers are and how much orientation and background information you have to provide to bring your subject and purpose into focus for them.

Writing the Ending

No matter how brief or long the paper, writing the ending challenges your abilities as much as does writing an introduction. This is because you must end your paper by (1) giving a sense of completeness or closure, (2) focusing the thought of the reader on the thesis, and (3) leaving the reader in the appropriate mood. To do these things requires you to wrap up things by pointing the reader back to the beginning of your paper.

The ending of a brief paper is often an echo of the lead. The two endings that follow are from the columns about black widow spiders and cockroaches that opened with the leads quoted on page 82. Each deftly achieves the three functions of an ending.

Plenty has been written about red hourglasses and poisonous bites; precious little about the biology and population dynamics of the black widow. Who *does* know what graceful intricacies lurk in the brain of *Latrodectus*?[6]

> With luck maybe it won't happen—that ultimately ugly event foreseen so vividly by Jonathan Schell [The Nuclear Holocaust]. With luck, and with also a gale of informed and persistent outrage by citizenries more sensible than their leaders. But with less luck, less persistence, what I can't help but envision for our poor raw festering planet, in those days and years after the After, is, like once before, an Age of Cockroaches.[7]

Longer and more argumentative papers require endings that finish more strongly than merely by echoing the lead. Good endings summarize the major points made in the body, restate the thesis, or if appropriate state one or more recommendations. These attributes are clearly visible in the following ending that completes the paper about educational technology whose introduction you saw on page 83.

> For educational technology to improve higher education, two things must happen. First, faculty must learn to consider educational technology in terms of their own teaching style, consciously adapting one to the other where they perceive benefits. Second, and far more difficult, organizational traditions must come to accommodate educational technologies, and vice versa. Both require careful collaborative assessment of traditional pedagogy, including its structure, and of new educational technologies.
>
> There is risk here; some ideas, even well-considered ideas, just won't work. This requires a commitment to evaluation. An emphasis on collaborative thought and experimentation, combined with an organizational commitment to accommodation and evaluation, will permit the best of outcomes; educational technology can support, extend, and complement what works in higher education, rather than simply replace it, and thereby bring productive and lasting change.[8]

Just as these writers vary their endings according to their purposes, you should make your endings serve your purpose. When your purpose is primarily to inform, you should summarize the major points you have made and leave the reader with a clear restatement of your thesis. When your purpose is to argue a point, try recapping your argument to demonstrate the flow of your logic. When you are attempting to persuade the reader to take a particular course of action, end with your recommendations. Sometimes, you need to do all of these.

Completing the Rough Draft

The ultimate goal of writing the rough draft is to produce enough material so that you can start revising. Don't be dismayed if your rough draft seems choppy and if it looks messy, as long as you can read it. Nobody but you will see this rough draft. In fact, your rough draft may be so rough that you might want to consider it what Peter F. Drucker calls a "zero draft—the one before the first draft."[9] Even if you have to discard much of what you have written, you are loosening up and getting a clearer notion of what you are trying to say.

After you have completed the rough draft, make a clean typed copy. You will probably be able to make a few small improvements as you type; you will get a good idea of what you have produced; the draft will look neater; and you will feel good.

But even with nice-looking copy, you will probably be disappointed in some ways with your first draft. Just remember that you have written a *rough* draft. With concentration and hard work you can take that imperfect draft and make significant improvements to it. As you revise, you can do this over and over again, coming up with better results each time.

Revising Your Paper

After you have created the rough draft, you need to *concentrate* on revising it. Concentrated revision involves reflecting on what you have written to see what needs to be done to make your paper as organized, developed, accurate, and clear as possible. To revise successfully, you must slow things down and look for problems.

It is crucial that you distance yourself from your rough draft. If possible, lay the draft aside for a day or two. Return to your draft by reading through it. Try to see your draft as your reader will see it. This is difficult but necessary. As the writer, you can see the connections between ideas even if you haven't made these connections clear. The reader will not. As the writer, you know, or should know, the meanings of all the words you use. The reader may not. As you read, make notes to yourself in the margins of your draft. Notes should be similar to these: *Connection here is unclear. Tone is too emotional here. Style is too stuffy and formal for content.* Or they should reflect the reverse: *Tone is too light for the seriousness of the ideas. Need more detail to be convincing here.* And so forth. Our Chapter 11, "Principles of Style," will be helpful to you in revision. Its purpose is to aid you to achieve a style that is clear and appropriate to your situation and audience. Useful for you, too, are the tool chapters, particularly Chapter 6, "Words," Chapter 8, "Sentences," and Chapter 9, "Paragraphs."

As you revise, pay close attention to developing your ideas adequately, to displaying your organization for your readers, and to achieving good prose style.

Developing Ideas Adequately

Your paper develops a thesis. Most of your paragraphs are built around particular ideas. Beware of undeveloped points. Check to see that the thesis is stated clearly and that details are adequate and accurate. Readers want facts and explanations of facts, so look for places that need more details and explanation. If you are writing a paper about patients' fears of invasive medical tests, make sure that you have defined and given examples of such tests. Is the definition clear? Are the examples familiar? If you state that there can be risks involved in some complicated tests, verify that you have provided ample evidence to back up your assertion. Have you pointed out that such tests require the informed consent of the patient? Have you explained what is meant by "informed consent"? Answering these questions is not always a simple matter. Several times you may have to go full circle from your draft to the occasion, purpose, and audience, and through your notes back to the draft.

Check the accuracy of your facts. Go back to your notes to see if you have transcribed them accurately. If the facts aren't complete in your notes, don't guess at them. Are your sources reliable? Will your readers regard them as authoritative? Relying on information from sales and promotional literature and little-known publications to substantiate your points is unwise. Continue your research until you have found the elusive data and have looked at the best sources of information. Avoid the appearance of not having done your homework or not having enough material for your paper.

Displaying Organization

Review the organization of your material. Does your paper plunge immediately into the details or does it present the big picture first? Do your introduction and the topic sentences state your principal ideas clearly? Can you see the relationships between the parts and between the parts and the whole? Do the section- and paragraph-breaks hold up? Are there smooth transitions from section to section? From paragraph to paragraph? From sentence to sentence? Are there any gaps? Does your paper work smoothly from the abstract to the detailed, from the general to the specific, or vice versa?

After you are confident that your organization is logical, make sure that your readers can follow it easily. A hard lesson for many beginning writers to learn is that no matter how careful their research or how painstaking their attention to the details of their ideas or how hard their work on the introduction, body, and conclusion of their paper, the success of their writing depends upon the active and willing participation of their readers. Readers have to be aware of how a piece of writing is organized; they must be aware of the progress of thought. Making them aware of these things is the responsibility of the writer.

Unfortunately, most inexperienced writers do not display their organizational pattern in explicit ways to readers. Because their governing organization and the relationships of their ideas are very clear to them, they believe that they are equally clear to readers as well. Even when it occurs to them to take a stab at an introductory overview, they feel vaguely uncomfortable about being *grossly* clear. What inexperienced writers don't realize is that one reason why readers have limited capacity to recall what has been read is that they have difficulty understanding how a piece of writing is organized. They depend upon the writer to provide clear signals on how content is organized.

Good writers know that plunging immediately into the details of their presentation places an enormous burden on their readers and that presenting the big picture first enables their readers to move smoothly into and through the details. Thus, good writers are sticklers about providing forecasting statements that anticipate what is to come, topic statements for paragraphs that introduce the subject of the paragraph, and connective devices that signal relationships. They know that readers do not regard these as grossly clear signposts, only as clear signposts.

Work on providing those signposts.

A statement of how you have organized a particular passage in a paper is particularly valuable to your readers. In addition to enabling them to anticipate your organization, it helps focus their thoughts on your theme and purpose and sets the context for your discussion. Here are three passages that contain such statements. The statement of how the material is organized is italicized.

The first is from a student essay titled "Terminal Wait in the Computer Center." It describes a problem all too familiar on many college campuses, and it proposes changes to correct the situation:

> As you stand in the corner of the computer center, your watch flashes four minutes after three in silver, digital numbers. You wait because your computer project is due tomorrow and forty-eight bodies occupy the forty-eight terminals in the room. After waiting an hour, your mouth begins to feel dry, so you go over to the water fountain to get a drink, and taking your last sip, notice someone getting out of his seat. Excited, you rush over, pick up your backpack, turn around to make a beeline for that empty terminal, only to find it again occupied. Somebody who just walked in the door now sits at the terminal you have waited to get for an hour. Frustration, anger, and feelings of injustice boil over from within you. Have you ever experienced this situation? Many students have. Currently our university operates student use of its computer terminals on a first-come, first-serve basis, with no limit on the amount of time an individual uses a terminal. This method causes problems as students have to wait to use a terminal, do not have enough time on the terminal to run a program, and therefore become utterly frustrated and discouraged. The time has come to change the current method of computer terminal usage by students. *Students should sign up for specific blocks of time to use a terminal, professors should consider the amount of computer time used for an assignment for grading, and students should have to pay for any time used beyond that allotted for the assignment.*[10]

The second example is from a speech by a well-known authority on nuclear power that analyzes the outlook for the development of nuclear power in the United States:

> Much of the problem of sorting out the reality of nuclear power is a matter of perspective. As a nation we tend to focus on short-term crises and solutions, not the long-term strategies that are necessary to take us beyond the age of inexpensive fossil fuel. *Today I would like to discuss one long-term perspective: to examine the status of nuclear power today, to describe the obstacle that it must overcome to make any additional contribution to U.S. energy supply beyond the plants already "in the pipeline," and to make some specific recommendations that should help bring nuclear power back into a realistic long-term perspective.*[11]

The third is from a chapter of Stephen Jay Gould's book of essays, *The Flamingo's Smile: Reflections in Natural History:*

> *In this essay, I shall discuss two taxonomic systems (theories for the classification of organisms) popular in the decades just before Darwin published the Origin of Species.* Both assumed reasons other than evolution for the ordering of organisms; both proposed a scheme based on the number five for placing organisms into a hierarchy of groups and subgroups. Both argued that such a simple numerical regularity must record an intrinsic pattern in nature, not a false order imposed by human hope upon a more complex reality. *I shall describe these systems and then discuss how evolutionary theory undermined their rationale and permanently changed the science of taxonomy by making such simple numerical schemes inconsistent with a new view of nature.*[12]

Previewing statements like these (in addition to a table of contents and headings in longer, more formal papers) get main points in focus quickly and forecast the organization of supporting ideas. When topic statements of paragraphs relate directly to preview statements in the introduction and to summary statements in the conclusion, readers are able to follow the writer's line of thought easily. Read the rest of "Terminal Wait in the Computer Center" to see how its author threaded his three proposals throughout the essay. We will repeat the preview statement from the introduction and italicize the topic statements and summary statement in the conclusion.

> *. . . Students should sign up for specific blocks of time to use a terminal, professors shouid consider the amount of computer time used for an assignment for grading, and students should havve to pay for any used beyond that allotted for the assignment.*
>
> *Having students sign up for specific blocks of time includes*

setting up and coordinating the procedure by the school, and tightening participation by students. A schedule coordinator needs to direct the flow of computer usage. The coordinator would need a logbook in which to record the name of the person reserving the terminal, and the specific terminal and hour reserved. Students would be required to telephone or visit the schedule coordinator's office to make a reservation no earlier than the day before the reserved time. The Student Recreational Center incorporates the same method in the use of racquetball courts, eliminating the problem of waiting for a court. Surely the same method for computer terminals will stop the problem of waiting for a terminal.

Having the amount of computer time used for an assignment as part of the student's grade requires programs set up for this and extra work by the professor. Programs would need to collect the user time for each student. The professor would then collect from the computer the total computer hours each student used for an assignment, and then devise a plan to incorporate the time into the grading system. A possible grading system may mean giving ten extra points for zero to two hours of computer use, five points for two to four hours, zero points for four to six hours, minus ten points for six to eight hours, and minus twenty points for more than eight hours. Hours used and points given or taken away change depending on the difficulty of the assignment and the ability of the class. This method will cause students to prepare their program beforehand rather than tying up a terminal for hours.

Giving students a set amount of computer time, and making them pay for any overtime would involve setting rules, writing programs, and coordinating the procedure. First, one would need to figure out the number of computer hours sufficient for each student per assignment or semester, and how much to charge per hour of overtime. *Second*, the computer must know how many hours of computer use each student has and when to disallow a user entry into the system because of overtime. *Third,* a coordinator needs to collect money from the students, and allow them back into the system once they have paid for extra time. Making students pay for overtime will keep their time on the computer to a minimum—especially when time turns into loss of money.

Using a sign-up schedule, considering time usage in grading, and charging students for overtime may not perfectly solve the problem, but they do offer some forms of relief from the current method of computer usage at our university. Having a sign-up schedule definitely takes care of the waiting problem, and the other two options give students extra incentive to spend less time on a terminal, giving more people an opportunity to use it. Think about it next time you experience "terminal wait" in the computer center.

We won't attempt to discuss everything that is effective about this short essay, but we do believe that you would agree that the author uses at least four techniques to keep the parts of his essay together and help readers predict both organization and content:

- a clearly stated thesis statement ("The time has come to change the current method of computer terminal usage by students.");
- a direct partitioning of his proposal for corrective action into three parts ("Students should sign up for specific blocks of time to use a terminal, professors should consider the amount of computer time used for an assignment for grading, and students should have to pay for any time used beyond that alloted for the assignment.");
- a topic statement at the beginning of each paragraph that directly relates that paragraph to the thesis and overview statements;
- an ending that restates the main points of the argument to create a sense of closure and to reinforce the main idea that readers will carry away from the essay.

The italicized passages are placed where the writer's skill and the reader's need converge. If we removed any of the italicized information, readers would find it difficult to anticipate the discussion and to exclude unlikely directions the paper might take. In fact, the italicized passages are so important that we would find it very difficult, if not impossible, to come up with another satisfying way to make the paper easy to read.

In longer, more formal papers, consider displaying your overall organization through the use of a table of contents and matching headings within the paper. See pages 169–175 for guidance. In paragraphs and sentences, cohesive devices help readers follow a writer's train of thought. Among such devices are pronoun references, repetition of key terms or phrases, transitions, and parallel structure. (See pages 153–158 and 204 for a discussion of these devices.) As you revise to display organization—highlighting principal points and making it easy for readers to follow your presentation—check overview statements and summaries to see that they reflect the ideas of your discussion. Check every numbered list to see that there is no inconsistency. If you see items 1, 2, 3, and 5, find out why item 4 does not appear. You may have simply misnumbered or accidentally omitted a point, or you may have intentionally deleted the passage and forgot to renumber. Be sure which.

Achieving a Good Prose Style

Once you are satisfied with your changes in content and organization, concentrate on style. Look for words that can be deleted without changing the meaning of the passage. Rewrite unnecessary passives and make certain that most of your sentences conform to the basic subject-verb-object or complement pattern and that sentence cores are easy to spot. (See Chapter 8, "Sentences.") Be sure that words, allusions, analogies, and tone are appropriate to the occasion and audience. (See Chapter 11, "Principles of Style.") Check every pronoun to see that it has a clear antecedent. Try to express every idea so clearly that every reader of your intended audience will understand—the first time through—precisely what you mean.

Continuing to Revise

As you revise for completeness and accuracy of details, for organization, and for style, you may see a misspelled word or an ungrammatical expression that you can correct easily. Go ahead and correct it, but don't worry too much about such things now. Probably the least productive thing you could do now is to focus on spelling, grammar, and punctuation. Instead, work on making those changes that affect meaning and make your writing easy to read. Save the tidying up for later. When you become more experienced and adept at revising, you will be able to work simultaneously on content, style, and mechanics. For now it is best to work on major, substantive changes.

If you have made several big changes in a passage, you may want to recopy it so that it is neat and ready to go through another revision. You may spot areas to change as you recopy; this is normal. Make them before you forget them. Half-born ideas and unexecuted changes are here one minute and gone the next.

Our suggestions on revising the rough draft also apply to further revisions. Don't be too quickly satisfied with your revisions of the first draft. Be prepared to go over your revised draft much the same way you worked on your rough draft. Most accomplished writers count on revising several times. Here's what John Kenneth Galbraith, a leading economist and an accomplished writer with more than twenty books to his credit, has to say about his writing and revising:

> There are days when the result [of my writing] is so bad that no fewer than five revisions are required. In contrast, when I'm really inspired, only four revisions are needed. . . .[13]

By the time you produce a final draft of your paper, you should be able to point to several improved drafts.

When you are through revising, you are ready for the final edit, the subject of our next chapter.

1. Write an essay for your school's paper on some campus organization, facility, or situation (good or bad). Decide whether your main purpose is to define and explain, to defend a thesis, to present an evaluation, to present and support a recommendation, or a combination of these purposes.

Consider the occasion and audience for the essay and review the major rhetorical hierarchies to see which ones seem appropriate for your purpose. Because your essay is intended for the school's paper, it will have to be fairly short, but it can be much longer than a letter for the editorial or opinion page. What kind of introduction and ending will your paper have? What techniques will you use to reveal the organization of the content of your essay?

Use the process presented in Chapter 4 to write the essay, and submit the essay to your writing teacher for comments. When your essay has been returned, revise it, if necessary, and submit it to the editor of your school's paper for possible publication.

2. To learn more about what writers think and do when they compose, interview somebody who has recently had an article published in a local newspaper or magazine. The person might be a faculty member or student at your school, a relative or acquaintance, or a complete stranger. Focus the interview to get that person's views on her or his composing process. How conscious was the author about methods of planning, composing, and revising? Did the author work from an outline—either informal or formal? Why, or why not? What parts of the manuscript were written first? last? How often did the author pause to read what she or he had written before continuing to write? How consciously did the author consider the occasion and purpose for writing? How aware was the author of her or his relationship to the audience? What did the author find easiest about composing? the most difficult? How extensive and essential was revising? Was the author surprised by any unexpected responses from readers?

If the author has had several pieces of writing published, how typical was the process of composing this most recent article compared to the others? Does the author's writing process change in some situations or with some writing tasks? Are there similarities between the author's composing process and the process discussed in Chapter 4?

Organize your interview notes into some order—such as (1) planning, (2) writing, (3) revising, and (4) similarities and differences between the author's composing process and that discussed in Chapter 4. Write an essay for your writing teacher and classmates that reports the results of your interview.

3. Use the question in Exercise 2 to analyze your own composing process. Describe your composing process in an essay for your writing teacher and classmates.

4. Analyze an earlier paper that you would like to revise. What would you do differently? What needs to be redone? Write a paper for your writing instructor, proposing the rewrite and explaining what changes you would make in the rewrite. If the instructor approves your proposal, rewrite the paper and submit both the original and the rewrite to your instructor.

5. Direct an essay toward students in your former high school or for incoming freshmen. Explain the writing process described in Chapters 1 through 5 of this book and detail what you have learned from it.

5

Editing

Editing is the last stage in the writing process. It includes, when appropriate, the final preparation of your manuscript for typing or word processing, and also the final proofreading before you turn the typed or printed paper over to its readers. You normally will not enter the editing stage until you are satisfied that you have drafted as well as possible in the composing stage or until you have run out of time for composing. As illustrated in Figure 5-1, in editing you should see that your work meets the standards of acceptable standard English, that your format is appropriate and helpful to the reader, and that your facts, calculations, and graphics are accurate.

Some writers find editing anticlimactic and give it insufficient time and effort. Such an attitude can be a dreadful mistake. Some readers, both in college and the workplace, measure writers' abilities as much by the writers' grammatical correctness as by their sense of organization and style. Papers, otherwise well written, can be rejected or failed because of incorrect grammar and usage or poor or inappropriate format. You may consider such rejection or failure as unfair, but we're afraid you can't wish it out of existence. Also, some errors can be more troublesome than are careless lapses in conventional usage. A decimal point in the wrong place could ruin your presentation. A misplaced comma could change the meaning of a sentence. A factual error could lead your reader to mistrust

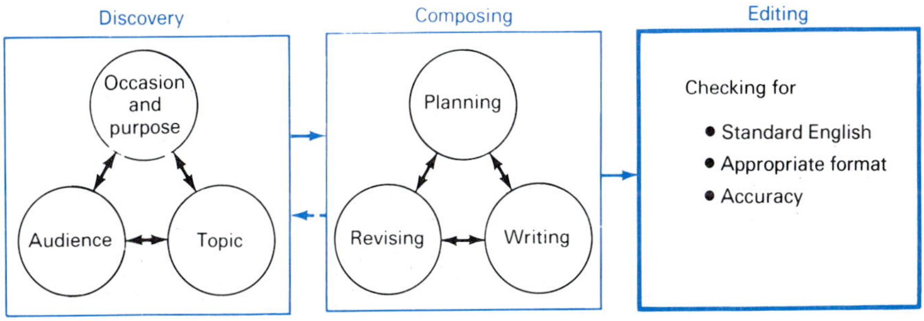

Figure 5-1 *The Editing Process.*

your entire argument. In editing, your job is to make sure that everything is as it should be. It is an important task.

You will find some of our tool and handbook chapters helpful in editing. Chapter 7, "Grammar," lays a groundwork for understanding exactly what grammar and usage are and why correct grammar and usage are important. Chapter 10, "Format," will guide you through some of the intricacies of page layout, documentation, and graphics. Pages 218–226 in Chapter 11, "Principles of Style," describe and tell how to correct twelve major usage errors that writers make. Chapter 12, "Conventions," describes and tells how to use correctly such conventions as abbreviation, punctuation, and capitalization. Chapter 13, "Glossary of Grammatical Terms," defines the terms that writers must know to discuss grammar, usage, and conventions. Use the list of marking symbols printed inside the back cover as a guide to specific problems and conventions.

Exactly how you correct the errors you find depends to an extent on how you are working and on the demands of your audience. If you are preparing your final draft on a word processor, you have the luxury of being able to change, delete, and move material electronically. Word processing removes much of the drudgery of editing. But you will frequently still be working with your manuscript on paper rather than on screen. For example, you may be preparing a draft manuscript to be retyped or word processed by a professional or by yourself. Or you may be working with what you hope is the ultimate draft of your paper. It exists on paper, out of the typewriter or printer. Furthermore, you may know that your reader will allow two or three pen-and-ink corrections per page. In the second case, you'll need to be particularly neat and legible with your corrections. In the first case, you can be somewhat less neat, but you still must be careful and legible. In either case, it is a good idea to learn to use professional proofreader's marks. Most professors will understand them; all professional typists should know them. We print a complete list for you inside the back cover. In the accompanying illustration, we show how to use the major marks when correcting a paper.

- To insert an omitted letter, punctuation mark, or word, place a caret (^) just below the line where the letter or word should go and write the letter or word directly above it:

```
    e
Nuclar waste can be stored and aged several years before
   ^
burial which significantly reduces heat generated by the

waste.
```

If you have omitted one or more lines of text or a couple of sentences, it is best to retype the page.

- To insert an ommitted space, place a # just above the line where the space should go:

```
   #
Thechoice of waste form may be glass, ceramic, or synthetic

rock.
```

By the way, the name for the symbol # is octothorp.

- To add punctuation marks, use the following:
  —to add quotation marks or an apostrophe, use the inverted caret (∨):

  Goethe said: "The Daemonic is that which cannot be explained by Reason or Understanding."

  Hamlet's reason for not killing Polonius when he first had his chance is clear.

  —to add a comma, insert it where you want it and make a caret (∧) over it:

  From a practical point of view, the protein sources of greatest interest are presscake from oil seeds, e.g. cottonseed flour, soybean products, and peanut flour.

  —to add a period, insert it where you want it and make a circle around it:

  Varsity teams compete during the year with other teams in the Ohio River Valley. Intramural teams are organized in nearly every physical activity in which students are interested.

  —to add a colon, semicolon, question mark, or exclamation mark, insert it where you want it without any additional markings.

- To delete a single letter in the middle of a word, draw a vertical line through it and make close-up marks (⁀‿) to delete the space:

  One of the most important duties of the assistant trainer is tapping ankles and wrists.

- To delete a single letter at the beginning or end of a word, make a delete mark (ℓ) through it:

  If Ernest Hemingway was the American kexpatriate, T.S. Eliott was the transplanted American in Europe.

- To delete a single blank space, make close-up marks (⁀‿):

  Construction costs are estimated at $ 160 per Kilowatt hour.

- To replace a wrong word or a badly misspelled word, draw a line through it and write the correction immediately above it.

  Opponents might ~~agree~~ argue that distance apparently provides adequate protection.

Don't cross out or erase original words so that they can no longer be read. You may have second thoughts about your substitution and wish to undo it.

- Transpose letters or words this way:

```
Whether additionla processing plants should be built by
private and business industry or the government is far from
clear.
```

- To change a capital to a small letter, draw a diagonal line through the capital letter:

```
As early as 1975 Utility Companies began deferring and even
cancelling orders for nuclear power plants.
```

- To change a small letter to a capital, draw three horizontal lines directly below the letter you wish to capitalize:

```
Technical experts from Oak Ridge National laboratories have
proposed several methods of disposal.
```

There are no particular tricks to editing other than attending scrupulously to the task. Because you have revised your paper several times, you will have the problem of being overly familiar with it. Therefore, if time allows, let your paper sit for a day or two before you edit it. The time away from your paper allows you to gain some distance from your work and to refresh your mind. By now you have probably worked long and hard enough on your paper that your mind is a bit dull. To edit in this condition would be unwise, for this is when errors can be overlooked easily and some real boners be made.

When you are ready to begin, clear off your desk so that you have plenty of room to work. You may have to spread out pages so that you can check to see that changes made are consistent. Make sure there is no coffee, soda pop, or food nearby that could spill on your manuscript.

We suggest that you slow things down as you edit, reading slowly—line by line, word by word, and with long words letter by letter. There are several ways to do this. One way is to read your paper aloud, because you will not be able to speak as rapidly as you can read silently. Another way is to use a ruler or other straight edge or pencil to guide your eyes along each line. If you are editing on a word processor, scroll the text up one line at a time, reading that line carefully before you bring the next line into view. You might even want to change the line spacing temporarily to triple or quadruple space to isolate each line even more.

Yet another way to slow things down is to do several editing passes, focusing on a specific type of potential problem each time. Use the following checklist as a guide.

• Find and correct typographical and mechanical errors in your text. There are predictible errors in this category. Listed here are ten errors, totaling 69.9 percent of this type error found by professional proofreaders:[1]

Errors	Percent
Letters omitted	14.5
Substitutions	14.1
Space omitted	10.7
Punctuation mark omitted	10.5
Letters or words transposed	6.6
Words omitted	5.9
Small letter for capital	2.9
Full line omitted	1.7
Spelling error	1.6
Capital for small letter	1.1

• Check the mechanics of your punctuation. Check to see that you have used a hyphen in the correct place to divide words at the end of lines. Be certain of your placement of punctuation with other marks of punctuation, especially with brackets, parentheses, and quotation marks. Look up in Chapter 12 any point of punctuation that you have doubts about.

• Correct grammar and usage, such as subject-verb disagreements, noun-pronoun disagreements, incorrect pronoun case, and dangling modifiers, all covered on pages 221–225. Watch out that you don't confuse words that sound or look alike, such as *effect* and *affect, compliment* and *complement, council* and *counsel, through* and *though*.

• Proofread your graphics. Doublecheck all tables and figures for accuracy. Use a calculator to check percentages and totals in tables and charts. Make sure that all formal graphics are labeled and numbered correctly and that they are referred to in your text.

• Check for consistency. Be alert to inconsistencies in facts, dates, spellings, people's names, and so on. Doublecheck anything that appears odd, such as dates that are off by a century (*1985* instead of *1895*, etc.) or totals that seem to be way off (*22 nuclear reactors* instead of *222 nuclear reactors*, etc.).

• Look for errors in format. Watch especially for incorrect spacing, indentation, and margins. Avoid leaving a heading or subheading standing alone at the bottom of a page or a short line at the top or bottom of a page. Check the sequence of page numbers and their position.

• Doublecheck the sources of quoted material. Make sure that every source cited is included in the list of works cited at the end of your paper. Our Chapter 10 provides guidance in these matters of documentation. However, in college, documentation is sometimes governed by a style book, perhaps published by a professional association or by the English department at the school. If in doubt, check with the professor making the assignment. Just be sure to use an accepted, consistent documentation style.

Figure 5-2. *Editing Style Sheet*

AB	CD	EF	GH
IJ	KL	MN	OP
QR	ST	UVWXYZ	Abbreviations
Numbers	Punctuation	Citation Form	Miscellaneous

As you can see, you have lots to look for. To help you keep track of the details and to maintain consistency throughout your paper, especially if it is a long one, we suggest that you use a style sheet similar to the one in Figure 5-2. It consists of a series of boxes arranged alphabetically, followed by boxes for other stylistic matters. If, for instance, you decide to spell the word *gauge g-a-u-g-e* instead of its variant *g-a-g-e,* you would enter the word *gauge* in the "G-H" box for easy reference. If you decide to spell out numbers below 10 and use figures for numbers 10 and above, you would put a brief note to that effect in the "Numbers" box. Use the boxes to record your decisions on capitalizing certain words, hyphenating particular compounds, and so forth.

How well and thoroughly you edit depends to some extent on the time available for the task. Obviously a term paper can and should be edited more carefully than an impromptu essay or the answer to an examination question. How well and thoroughly you edit also depends somewhat on your personality. Some writers are hasty and sloppy with their editing. Others are obsessive about editing, almost to the point where they can't submit a paper for fear that an error lurks somewhere within. We suggest that a middle ground is the best approach. Do allow yourself enough time to edit a paper at the appropriate level. But get on with your work. Do the best job that time and patience allow and get your paper in when it is due.

Exercise

Try your editing skills on the following passage and check your corrections and proofreading marks with the copy on page 100. (For a complete list of proofreader's marks, see the inside back cover.)

During his own lifetime Macaulays writtings were extremely controversial, but by the time of his death his defenders were in the majority and the pb=lic had accepted him as the greatest writer of their generation But beginning with a series of a ttacks by Mathew A rnold during the 1860s and well extending into the middle of the Twentieth Century, Macaulay's posthumous rreputation has been controlled by Arnold and arnoldians. During this period, however an increasing credible defense of Macauly has been made by the Maculay family protectors -- the Trevelyans and their freinds. While the opinions of twentieth-century literary critics and academicians have been pretty much repititions of the nineteenth centuiry Arnoldian view, the major development has been the acceptance of Macaulay by historians. Literary critics and scholars, however,continuing to regard Macaulay's writing as spawned by extreme wrathe and his integrity compromised by political allegiance, prefer to treat him as a literary pariah. Many historians, on thelother hand, now regard his History as consumate historical writing.

During his own lifetime Macaulays writtings were extremely controversial, but by the time of his death his defenders were in the majority and the ~~pb-lie~~ public had accepted him as the greatest writer of their generation. But beginning with a series of a ttacks by Mathew A WD rnold during the 1860s and well extending into the middle of the Twentieth Century, Macaulay's posthumous rreputation has been controlled by Arnold and arnoldians. During this period, however an increasing credible defense of Macauly has been made by the Maculay family protectors -- the Trevelyans and their freinds. While the opinions of twentieth-century literary critics and academicians have been pretty much repititions of the nineteenth centurry Arnoldian view, the major development has been the acceptance of Macaulay by historians. Literary critics and scholars, however, continuing to regard Macaulay's writing as spawned by extreme wrathe and his integrity compromised by political allegiance, prefer to treat him as a literary pariah. Many historians, on the lother hand, now regard his History as consumate historical writing.

II

The Writer's Tools

6

Words

Helen Keller, blind and deaf from the age of two, thus had two of the major routes of learning denied to her. At the age of seven she was given into the care of a young teacher of the blind, Anne Sullivan. Helen Keller was later to describe as magic that moment when she recognized that a certain sequence of taps in her hand by Anne Sullivan stood for a substance she was simultaneously feeling, water. With that experience, she learned what it meant to symbolize, to create an abstraction for the thing itself. Once the concept of symbolizing and abstracting was clear to her, the road to learning language, to communicating with others, to sharing and transmitting knowledge, was open to her.

Primitive human beings, perhaps a million or more years ago, made the same discovery, that symbols could be created, perhaps with sound, perhaps with hand signals, perhaps with some combination of the two. Using these symbols, people could communicate about the world they knew, even when the objects of the world were not physically present. They could talk and think about a stream, an animal, or a person far away in either space or time. With these symbols, with these *words,* human beings could accumulate knowledge and pass it on: This is how you gather a certain berry, make a certain tool, catch a certain fish.

Progress was now possible because each generation could add to and pass on the accumulated knowledge store. The development of language was humankind's greatest achievement. The mental effort it took minimizes by comparison the effort that went into such modern achievements as atomic power, space flight, or computer technology. When finally, only some ten thousand years ago, human beings devised ways for writing words, the ability to accumulate and transmit knowledge increased many-fold, and civilization and science as we know them began. Because of words and the other symbols developed in music, mathematics, science, and art, we all inherited the potential to gain knowledge of the world the day we were born. It is there for the taking if we learn to understand and manipulate symbols.

In this chapter we talk about words. (In Chapter 7 we talk about grammar. The two together give us language.) First, we deal with words as abstractions.

Second, we discuss the origins of English. Finally, we discuss how we create words when we need them.

Abstraction

Thinking of words as abstractions, semanticists (students of words) have developed the abstraction ladder, a way of thinking about the level of abstraction of a word. At the bottom of the ladder is the thing itself, an IBM Displaywriter, for instance. The Displaywriter consists of numerous bits and pieces, made of copper, steel, plastic, and other materials. These, in turn, are composed of molecules and atoms and whirling electrons. This is the thing itself. To talk about this thing, we have to name it, so we do. We call it an *IBM Displaywriter*. In so doing, we have abstracted from the thing itself. Moving up the ladder, we can refer to the Displaywriter as a *word processor*. We are now more abstract; that is, we are slightly further away from the thing itself. We have lost some of the advantages of exactness but have gained the advantage of putting the Displaywriter into a larger class. We can now think about what the Displaywriter has in common with the word processors of other manufacturers. But we lose sight of certain particulars that belong to the Displaywriter alone. Moving up the ladder still further, we can think of the Displaywriter as an *office machine*. Again we move further away from the real thing and join a larger class that includes typewriters, duplicating machines, and so forth. We might choose to end our ladder at *machine,* where yet more individual characteristics are lost and a yet larger class is joined. Or we could go higher on the ladder with words like *asset, wealth,* and *thing*.

Abstraction is indispensible in human communication. The higher abstractions, concepts like *democracy, wealth, loyalty, truth,* would be almost impossible to discuss without words for them. Words are the tools with which we think. They are a shorthand way of dealing with the world around us. But remember that the higher on the ladder you go, the further you get from reality. Often in communication you must come down the ladder, closer to reality, to make your point. It is why in an argument we may say, "Wait a minute. We have to define our terms. We're throwing about the word *freedom* here. What do we mean by it anyway? Freedom from what? to do what?"

Going to the dictionary at this point might help, but probably would not resolve the problem. In the dictionary, we would find such definitions as "the condition of being free of restraint," "liberty of the person from slavery, oppression, or incarceration," "political independence," "possession of civil rights," and "exemption from unpleasant or onerous conditions." We will probably only begin to define *freedom* by coming down the abstraction ladder and using examples of our own that relate to the argument. We will need, perhaps, to use homely examples, such as the philosopher John Stuart Mill's reminder that a man's freedom to swing him arm ends short of another man's nose. When *freedom* is defined satisfactorily by such forays into reality, then the argument will be able to proceed. But it is also possible for the argument to break down if one of the participants has never really experienced freedom. In some cases, even the best and most skillfully constructed definitions may not work. Language can fail when the people using it have never experienced the reality from which the words are abstracted.

Words as tools are enormously powerful, so powerful, in fact, that they can, if we're not careful, control our thoughts and emotions. Think of the difference in value judgments implied if we use the word *shrewd* to describe someone rather than *smart,* or the difference between *clever* and *intelligent.* Words have connotations; that is, they have levels of association and emotional meaning, beyond their literal meaning, their denotations. A *Negro,* according to the dictionary, is simply and objectively a member of the black race. A *black* fits precisely the same definition. The denotations of the two words are the same. Yet, we know that during the 1960's *black* almost totally replaced *Negro*; *Negro's* connotation became too much of a burden for the word to carry.

Poets, novelists, politicians, and advertisement writers know they can influence, even control, our emotions by choosing words with the right connotations. The ad writer who, in a description of a robe says, "Surround yourself with the luxurious warmth of pure cashmere" knows well the connotations of words like *luxurious, warmth, pure,* and *cashmere.* (See also pages 216–217.)

With abstractions, we often run the risk of pigeonholing, of stereotyping, people. We use words like *priest, teacher, doctor,* and *politician.* Such words are high on the abstraction ladder. Each represents a large class of people. Perhaps we have had pleasant or unpleasant associations with some members of one of the classes. If we allow such associations to control our thinking about the whole class, we will not look clearly at the things in themselves, the real people at the bottom of the abstraction ladder.

Abstraction makes language possible and is utterly and completely necessary if we are to live as human beings, but like many of the other things that make us human, we must use it with great care.

The Origins of English

English is a member of a language family known to us today as Indo-European. The people we call Indo-Europeans lived some five thousand years ago in Central Europe, somewhere east of what is now Germany and west of the Ural Mountains. We know little about the people but a great deal about their language. Linguists, by tracing backwards from modern languages such as English and French through such ancient languages as Old German and Latin, have been able to reconstruct the original sparse Indo-European wordstore from which most of our modern words have come. For example, one such Indo-European root word is *bhreg,* meaning *to break.* From this one root, by various changes and combinations, have come thousands of words in the modern European languages, including such

English words as *break, bray, breach, brash,* and, with a slight shift in pronunciation, *fracas, fraction, fragile, fragment, frail, infringe, and refract.*

We do know that through migration and conquest the Indo-European language eventually was spoken all over Europe, through parts of the Middle East, and into India—hence the term, *Indo-European*. The modern descendents of the Indo-European language include many major languages spread over several branches: Albanian, Armenian, Balto-Slavonic, Celtic, Germanic, Hellenic, Indian, Iranian, and Italic. (See Figure 6-1.) There are, of course, many other language families in the world, approximately a hundred. Some of the prominent ones are the Semitic (Arabic and Hebrew), Afro-Asiatic, Central Saharan, Niger-Congo (the last three all African families), Sino-Tibetan (which includes the Chinese languages), Athapaskan Indian (including several Amerindian languages), and Malay-Polynesian (the language of many Pacific peoples). Scholars have found no evidence for any common ancestor for all these language families.

Among the Indo-European languages, English is a comparative newcomer, only some 1,400 years old. In the middle of the 5th century A.D., several tribes from Northern Germany—the Angles, Saxons, and Jutes—invaded and colonized what is now known as England. They drove out the existing population, Celts, many of whom settled in Wales and Scotland. In this colonization was the beginning of English. The invaders spoke a Germanic language, which we refer to today as Anglo-Saxon or Old English. Old English had a German word store and a complicated German grammar (see pages 125–126). Today Old English is as difficult to read as a foreign language, but many of our everyday words are descended from this period, words such as *man, woman, house, drink, sleep, foot,* and *fire*.

In the eighth through the tenth centuries, another Germanic people, the Danes, invaded England, establishing settlements in the Northeast. As a result,

BRANCH	LANGUAGE
Albanian	Albanian
Armenian	Armenian
Balto-Slavonic	Lettish, Lithuanian, Great Russian, White Russian, Ukranian, Polish, Czech, Slovak, Bulgarian, Serbo-Croation, Slovenian
Celtic	Gaelic, Irish, Welsh
Germanic	Dutch, Plattdeutsch, English, German, Yiddish, Icelandic, Norweigian, Danish, Swedish
Hellenic	Greek
Indian	Hindi, Urdu, Bengali, Punjabi, Marathi, Nepali
Iranian	Kurdish, Persian, Afghan
Italic (Latin)	French, Spanish, Portuguese, Italian, Rumanian

Figure 6-1 *Modern Indo-European Languages.*

many Scandinavian words made their way into English, such as *law, dregs, egg, loan, flat, ill, flit, cow,* and *thrive*. Perhaps a thousand such words were borrowed, most of them dealing with common, everyday concepts.

In 1066 an event occurred that had a profound effect on English—the Norman Conquest. Under William the Conquerer, the Normans defeated the English at the Battle of Hastings and took control of England. The Normans, as their name implies, were *North-men*, Scandinavians who had settled in France during the ninth and tenth centuries. The land of their settlement came to be known as Normandy. The Normans, though remaining free of French domination, took on many of the trappings of French civilization, including replacing their Scandinavian language with French. In essence, then, in 1066, England was conquered by a group of French-speaking Scandinavians.

The Normans took firm control of England, driving out the English upper classes and exploiting the English peasantry. The courts, the church, the army, and the government were all in the hands of the Normans. As a result of the Conquest, England became a land of two languages—English for the lower classes and French for the upper classes. This condition of two languages lasted for about two hundred years. In 1204, Normandy was subjugated by the King of France. With Normandy in French hands, the Norman nobles in England began to think of themselves as English. This political development hastened what had already begun, the speaking of English rather than French by the Norman upper classes. By the fourteenth century English was once more the dominant language in England for all classes. But the years of Norman domination and the use of French had had their effect.

During the years when the two languages existed side by side, thousands of French words passed over into English. As might be expected, the importations were the kinds of words that would be used by a ruling class: words used in governing, such as *crown, duke, empire, royal,* and *statue;* church words like *clergy, baptism, communion, pray,* and *sacrament;* military words like *army, navy, combat, sergeant, lieutenant,* and *captain*.

Much of our legal language is French: *crime, justice, bar, bill, slander,* and *legacy*. Many of the triplet expressions that lawyers are so fond of using come to us from this period. Lawyers of the time expressed concepts in both English and French, and sometimes Latin, in an attempt to be understood by all. As a result we still live with such cumbersome expressions as "to sell, transfer, and convey the property," where *sell* is English, *transfer* is Latin, and *convey* is French. In wills we find not only an estate being left to the heirs but also the "rest, residue, and remainder" of that estate. *Rest* is English, and *residue* and *remainder* are French.

Our familial relationships are expressed in both English and French. Close family relationships are expressed in English: *father, mother, brother, sister*. The relationships of the extended family are expressed in French: *aunt, uncle, niece, nephew, cousin,* and the *grand* in *grandfather* and *grandmother*. For many reasons, the ruling class kept better records of the extended family than did the peasants, and they did it in French.

Many of our words for dress and food are French, words adopted during the Norman rule: *gown, robe, lace, satin, sable, diamond, dinner, supper, feast, appetite, roast, stew,* and *fry*. It was Sir Walter Scott in *Ivanhoe* who pointed out that frequently the word for the animal on the hoof is English and the word for the meat on the table is French, as in *cow/beef, pig/pork, calf/veal* and *deer/venison*. The social comment seems inevitable: The English speaking peasants took care of the animals; the French speaking Norman aristocrats ate the meat.

Indeed, it would be surprising if something as intimate to our relationships as language would not be affected by social distinctions. We can see many reminders of the English-Norman social hierarchy in modern English. Ordinary folks live in *houses* (Eng.), rich people in *mansions* (Fr.). Railroad workers join a union called a *brotherhood* (Eng.); college men join *fraternities* (Fr.). Sculptors practice an *art* (Fr.), stonemasons a *craft* (Eng.). We can see reminders of the hierarchy in writers trying to impress their audiences with French (or Latin) words for the simpler English words: *utilize* for *use, initiate* for *begin, terminate* for *stop, prior to* for *before, subsequent to* for *after,* and so forth.

We all know the vulgar connotations of certain Anglo-Saxon four-letter words, for example, those referring to the bodily wastes. We also know that it is not vulgar to refer to the same wastes using French or Latin words, for example, *excrement* and *urine*. It would seem, therefore, that the vulgarity lies not so much in the thing described as in using peasant language to describe it—another hangover of the social structure of Norman times. (Indeed, the very word, *vulgar,* comes from a Latin word meaning *common people*.)

The wholesale importation of French, a Latin-derived language, into English made easier the later importation of Latin words into English during the sixteenth and seventeenth centuries. From medieval times Latin had been the language of scholars. Many scholars also knew some classical Greek and considered it, like Latin, to be superior to English. During the sixteenth and seventeenth centuries, scholars felt that English was inadequate to the demands of the cultural and technological changes sweeping Europe as a result of what we think of as the Renaissance. To enrich English, it seemed natural to them to reach into Latin and Greek. They brought thousands of Latin words, often without alteration, into English—words such as *education, scientific, appendix, delirium, create,* and *consolidate*. Greek importations were also numerous—for example, *anonymous, catastrophe,* and *thermometer*. This willingness to go outside the English word store for needed new words has had a lasting effect on English. As we'll see when we look next at the creation of new words, we are still borrowing words whenever it is convenient.

Word Creation

No one really knows how many words we have in English, but a conservative estimate would be from 600,000 to a million. How many words does a native

English speaker know? Again there is no definite answer, but the range is probably somewhere between 10,000 to 20,000 words. Educated people who read a good deal undoubtedly exceed 20,000, though they may not write or speak all the words they can understand. As we have seen, thousands of words from many sources have been in English for hundreds of years and in Indo-European for thousands of years. And as users of our language, we have many ways of creating new words when we need them. Association is perhaps the most potent principle in the making of new words. It is through association, for example, that we coin new words from people's names and other proper nouns. The term *boycott* comes from a Charles Boycott, a nineteenth-century land agent in Ireland whose tenants refused to deal with him because of what they considered his unfair practices. Thus we *boycott* an industry or country that we consider to have acted unfairly in some way. Through such similar associations we have *sandwich, morocco leather, tabasco sauce, wisteria, lynch,* and *schrapnel,* all from names and proper nouns.

Association with the concept of *break* is at work in all the words we list as descending from the Indo-European word *bhreg* (see pages 105–106). To *bray* is to utter an earsplitting sound, a *fracas* is a fight in which things may get broken, something *fragile* is easily broken, and so forth.

Sometimes, unfortunately for our easily grasping the meaning of a word, the associations are buried in a language such as Latin or Greek, languages that may not be familiar to us. For example, most of our common Anglo-Saxon words such as *mouth* and *eye* have Latin adjectives, in this case, *oral* for *mouth* and *ocular* for *eye*. *Oral* and *ocular* are probably widely enough used to be familiar to most people, but how about *avian, stellar, lupine, ovine, vulpine,* and *olfactory?* Do you know the common nouns connected with each of these Latin adjectives? (In order: *bird, star, wolf, sheep, fox,* and *smell*.)

Such is also the case with *sychophant*. If you look up *sychophant,* you'll find not only its definition but the fact that its root is a Greek word meaning *fig-shower;* that is, one who shows figs. How in the world did *fig-shower* come to be applied to a self-serving flatterer? As some of the better dictionaries will explain, there is a Mediterranean gesture of the fig, a waving of the hand, fingers up, with the ball of the thumb pressing against the balls of the first and second fingers. Today, it is largely a gesture of contempt for someone. In ancient Greece, the gesture was used in court to denounce a criminal. Thus, a *fig-shower* was one who curried favor with the authorities by denouncing people to them. Through similar associations we have created *apple-polisher* and other words less elegant to express the same concept as found in *sychophant*.

Frequently, when we need a new word, we simply take an old word and give it a new meaning. The new meaning always has some association with the old meaning, and the word, normally, keeps its original meaning as well as adding its new one.

The common word *head* typifies this kind of language change. *Head,* a Germanic word, in its original sense stands for that knob that sits on top of the neck. Think of some of the associations we can have with this knob. It is globular in shape. On a human being it is on top; on a four-footed animal it is in front. It is the seat of our reasoning powers; it is in command of the rest of the body. Now think of some of the ways in which we use the word *head*. We speak, for example, of the *head* of a company. A *head* of cabbage. The *head* of a nail. The *head* on a beer. The *head* of a coin. Twenty *head* of cattle. The *head* of an engine. We use it in phrases such as, "Keep your *head,*" "Don't lose your *head,*" "*Head* him off," "Bring the issue to a *head,*" and "Go to the *head* of the class." Indeed, there are so many uses for *head* that in the *Oxford English Dictionary* (OED), that complete dictionary of the English language, the entry for *head* takes up six pages.

Notice that the new meanings always have some association with the original meaning. A *head* of cabbage is globular in shape. The *head* of a company is at the top and in command. When we *head* people off, we get in front of them. If we bring an issue to a *head*, we bring it to the top or the forefront so we can examine it. And so on.

Many of the common words in our word store have been used in this manner. Parts of the body, particularly, are used this way. In the OED, the definitions for *foot* fill five pages (Go to the *foot* of the class.). *Hand,* like *head,* fills six pages (The big day is at *hand*. Give him a *hand*.). *Finger* and *nose* each have two pages in the OED (I can't put my *finger* on the right answer. *Nose* out the trouble if you can.).

Obviously, words like *head* and *foot* cannot be understood if we see them alone. We have to see them in context to know the writer's intended meaning.

Frequently in this word change, we widen the meaning of a word, usually because the concept behind the word is useful. This widening process is sometimes called *generalization*. In baseball, the compound *raincheck* was coined for the ticket given to patrons if a game is cancelled because of rain. The ticket can be used at a later game. Implicit in *raincheck* is the concept of postponement. We have extended the use of the word based upon that concept. We commonly say things like, "Sorry, I can't make your party. May I have a raincheck?" Are we asking for a ticket to a baseball game? No, we're saying, "We really would like to come to your house. Please ask us again at some later time."

Conversely, we can narrow the meanng of a word, a process often called *specialization*. For example, *disk* (or *disc*) in general use can refer to any flat, circular object. But its meaning can also be narrowed to mean specifically a phonograph record or a disk used to store computer information. In this case, the generalized and specialized meaning of *disk* exist side by side. In other cases, the specialized meaning may supplant the general one. For instance, *deer* was once synonymous with *animal*. Today, it refers to a specific kind of animal.

Another way to use existing words is to form them into compounds. To look at *head* again for a moment, going back to the OED we find that words using *head* as the front part of a compound fill nearly five pages. We have *headache, headband, headline, headman,* and many others.

Words such as *headache* are sometimes called self-explaining compounds. That is, if we know English reasonably well, we can probably puzzle out the

Word	*Prefix*	*Common meaning*
precept	pre-	before
detain	de-	away, from
intermittent	inter-	between
offer	ob-	against
insist	in-	into
monograph	mono-	alone, one
epilogue	epi-	upon
aspect	ad-	to, towards
uncomplicated	un-	not
	com-	together with
nonextended	non-	not
	ex-	out of
reproduction	re-	back, again
	pro-	forward
indisposed	in-	not
	dis-	apart from
oversufficient	over-	above
	sub-	under
mistranscribe	mis-	wrong
	trans-	across, beyond

Figure 6-2 *Masterwords. (From* Efficient Reading, *Sixth Edition, by James I. Brown. Copyright 1984 by D.C. Heath and Company. Reprinted by permission of the publisher.)*

meaning of *headache* and *headman* without too much trouble. But many compounds are not nearly as easily understood. Think of the layers of association that a foreigner would have to work through to understand compounds like *soap opera, carhop,* and *rat race.*

Sometimes in compounding we shorten one or both words in the compound and form a blend. Thus we make *brunch* from *breakfast* and *lunch, smog* from *smoke* and *fog, motel* from *motor* and *hotel,* and *medicare* from *medical* and *care.*

We also feel quite at home in clipping single words, forming shorter versions of them. This is particularly true when the words are common words. We speak and write *plane* rather than *airplane* (or *aeroplane*). *Baby sitters* become *sitters. Telephones* become *phones.* The *soap operas* become simply the *soaps. Mathematics* becomes *math. Cab* and *taxi* are clips of *taxicab* which, in turn, is a blend of *taximeter cabriolet.*

In a method similar to compounding and blending, we coin many new words by joining prefixes to existing words. Most of the common prefixes are used over and over again. Professor James I. Brown listed fourteen common prefixes with their meanings and sample words, calling them *masterwords.* We show Professor Brown's word list in Figure 6-2.

In Figure 6-2, *Ob-* in *offer* and *ad-* in *aspect* illustrate a process called assimilation. It is difficult to say *obfer* or *adspect,* so we change the pronunciation to the easier-to-say *offer* and *aspect*. The spelling follows the pronunciation. Knowing the meanings of prefixes can help you when you meet a strange word. Knowing that *trans-* means *across* or *beyond* is a help in figuring out such words as *transaction, transalpine, transcribe,* and *transfusion*.

As we do with prefixes, we coin words by using suffixes. We take *-ette*, meaning *small* or *feminine*, attach it to *cigar*, and create *cigarette*. With *-ette* we coin *drum majorette, dinette, suffragette, bathinette*, and so forth. With *-ize, we create Americanize, colonize, hospitalize, dramatize, moralize*, and *itemize*. With *-ism*, we create *fascism, communism, alcholism, terrorism, patriotism*, and *witticism*. With *-logy* we produce *phraseology, physiology*, and *psychology*.

Most suffixes have been a regular part of the language for centuries, such as *ic (Gaelic, analytic), -ster (gangster, trickster)*, and *-er (zipper, runner)*. Others have been formed more recently by a process called *analogy*. In analogy, the wordmaker may reason something like this, "Hmm, we're having this long walk for charity. It's long, almost like a marathon. Hey, that's it. We'll call it a *walkathon*." We have, in essence, created a new suffix, *-athon*. With a slight accommodation in spelling, we have used it to create *telethon* for long television fund drives. Conceivably, we could form words such as *jogathon, readathon*, and *teachathon*. Taking off from *alcoholic* in the same analogous way, we get *foodaholic* and *saltaholic*. From *hamburger*, we take *-burger* and create *tacoburger, pizzaburger, cheeseburger* and *chickenburger*. We are forever ingenious with our language.

We can tell a great deal about ourselves by looking at the words we use and create. We can trace historical associations and technological growth and discover what we find distasteful or frightening.

Historically, most of the immigrants to the United States have left their mark in American English, as did the Amerindians they found here. From the Amerindians we have words for foods and animals, such as *hickory, pecan, persimmon, pone, squash, succotash, chipmunk, moose, muskrat*, and *skunk*. They also gave us the political words *caucus, powwow*, and *Tammany*.

From the French voyageurs and trappers, who lived closely with the Amerindians, we have words for animals and natural features, such as *butte, chute, coulee, prairie*, and *rapids*. They also gave us *chowder*. From the Louisiana French we have *bayou, cajun, creole, levee*, and *Mardi Gras*.

From the Blacks have come African words, most incorporated during early times, and, of late, terms from what has come to be called Black English. African terms include *banana, banjo, chigger, goober, juke, tote, voodoo*, and *yam*. Many of us now know Black English words like *afro, blood* (fellow Black), *nitty-gritty, rap* (in the sense of *talk*), and *soul food*.

We should expect that a group as large and influential as our German immigrants would put many words into American English. The German love for good food and drink is shown in the presence of words like *delicatessen, frankfurter, hamburger, bock beer, dunk, lager, stein, schnapps, liverwurst, noodle, pretzel, pumpernickel, sauerbratan, sauerkraut*, and *wienerwurst*. The Germans were not afraid to speak directly, and from them we get *bum, fresh, loafer, nix, ouch, phooey, scram, shyster*, and *spiel*. They also gave us *pinochle, poker, seminar*, and *semester*.

The contributions that Italians have made to American eating habits show in the common *pizza* (and *pizzeria*), *spaghetti*, and *tutti-frutti*. For the true aficionado of Italian food, we have *antipasto, minestrone, pasta, cappelletti, lasagna, ravioli, tortelloni, dulce*, and *espresso*.

The first Jewish immigrants to America came primarily from Western Europe and spoke the language of the countries from which they emigrated: German, French, Italian, and so forth. Hebrew, when used, was reserved for religious ceremonies. Therefore, these immigrants contributed few peculiarly Jewish words to American English. In the late nineteenth century, however, a second, larger wave of Jewish immigrants came from Eastern Europe. Most of these had Yiddish as a common language. Yiddish is a language that was developed by Jews in medieval times and that mixes together German, Hebrew, and several Slavic languages. Many Yiddish words have made their way into American English. Common words for popular foods such as *bagels* and *lox* and *blintz* are widely known. To *nosh* means to *snack* and is much used in the Eastern United States. Perhaps the most interesting borrowings from Yiddish have been the vigorous words used to describe human characteristics and foibles. Most Americans would recognize *schnook*, *schlemiel* and *schmuck* as types they would not want to be. Depending on its context, *chutzpah* (daring, brashness) may be good or bad. Eastern Americans would likely recognize the meanings of *gonif* (thief), *meshuga* (crazy), nudnik (pest), *schlepper* (a lazy slob), and *schnorrer* (a constant borrower).

More loan words have come into American English from Spanish than from any other language, from early times in the Southwest to today when words are being introduced by thousands of Spanish speakers in New York, Miami, New Orleans, and the Southwest. Just a small sampling would include *aficionado, alfalfa, bodega, bracero, burro, bronco, cabana, cafeteria, chili con carne, corral, coyote, embarcadero, filibuster, incommunicado, lariat, lasso, loco, macho, machete, marina, poncho, ranch, rodeo, stevedore, tornado*, and *vigilante*.

Great events, such as wars, leave their mark on language. World Wars I and II gave American English many new words or popularized older words that had not been in general use. From World War I we have *blimp, chow, dog tag, dud, khaki, KP, pom-pom, red tape,* and *rookie*. World War II gave us *blockbuster*, *blitzkrieg* (later clipped to *blitz* and now a common word in football), *flak, GI, gobbledygook, gung ho, Jeep, radar, shack up*, and *snafu*. The Vietnam War and era contributed words such as *counterinsurgency, the domino theory, fire fight, hawks and doves, sit-in,* and *the silent majority*.

Perhaps the greatest event in this century has been the unprecedented growth of science and technology. Radio, movies, television, air travel, space travel, computers, automobiles—all have been developed in this century. We have had enormous leaps forward in medicine, agriculture, astronomy, and in all the basic sciences. Such rapid developments call for new words by the thousands, many of which are known to the masses of us and not just to the specialists.

The automobile has changed our lives like few other technological developments ever have. It is close to all of us, and we have developed a huge vocabulary for it. The word *automobile*, itself, was created in 1870 from the Greek *auto*, meaning *self*, and the Latin *mobile*, meaning *moving*. As we do with many familiar words, we clipped *automobile* to auto. The synonym, and perhaps even more common word, *car*, comes from a Latin word for cart or wagon. The two words, *automobile* and *car*, are survivors of many words coined for this new vehicle such as *autopher, autovic, autobat, diamote*, and *self motor*.

As the automobile was developed, its parts had to be named. The terms developed are familiar to most of us: *bumper, radiator, hood, carburetor, spark plug, windshield, windshield wiper, transmission, differential, power steering, accelerator, trunk*, and many more. We had to name things that were part of the automobile way of life, such as *license plate, garage, traffic cop, ticket, motel, jaywalker, hitchhiker, interstate, drive-in* and *drag race*.

Like the automobile, medicine is close to most of our lives, and most of us know a fair amount of medical terminology. However, there is a difference between medical terminology and automotive terminology. Though based upon an advanced technology, automobiles are widely owned and operated. Therefore, many automotive words tend to be common words used in a new way (*hood, trunk*) or self-explaining compounds (*windshield, windshield wiper*). Notice, however, that even in automobiles the more technical terms may be from Greek or Latin, as are the Latin-based *carburetor* and *transmission*. Most highly technical words are likely to be coined from Greek or Latin. Medical terms are no exception to this practice that still persists today among scholars and scientists, partly because Latin and Greek still do have universal application and partly because such words seem more prestigious than common words.

Would we take that symbol of the doctor, the *stethoscope*, as seriously if it were called *breastwatcher*, the translation of the term? Would we be more or less frightened by *cholesterol* if we knew it as *bile solids*, which would be a fair translation of the two Greek components of the word? Would we pay as much to a *toothstraightener* as we would to an *orthodontist*? Would it help our understanding to know that the *-itis* in all the following medical terms means *inflammation*: *appendicitis, pancreatitis, prostatitis*, and the frightening sounding *reflux esophagitis*, the medical term for what most of us know as *heartburn*? How about *gastritis* from the Greek *gaster* for belly and *-itis*: in other words, a *belly ache*? In any event, the scientific and scholarly habit of using Latin and Greek roots for new words is not likely to die out, and we will continue to live with words like *arteriosclerosis, homeopathic, bronchoscope, apperception,* and *deoxyribonucleic acid* (thankfully, shortened to DNA).

Our creation of some words reveals our fears and those things we find somehow distasteful or uncomfortable. Noah Webster, who in the nineteenth century gave us the *American Dictionary of the English Language*, also edited the Bible to remove or change words that referred to sex or to the elimination of body wastes. In Webster's Bible, *teat* was changed to *breast*; *stones* (the Bible word for testicles) became *peculiar members*; and *leg* was changed to limb. In the same century, a Thomas Bowdler did the same favor for Shakespeare, producing a cleaned-up version of his plays. From Mr. Bowdler, in fact, we derive the term *bowdlerize*, meaning to expurgate taboo words from a piece of writing.

Before we smile at these nineteenth-century gentlemen, we have to recognize we do the same thing when we substitute euphemisms for terms we consider too explicit. Death is a subject we find fearful. We speak of people *passing away*. One of us remembers while in the Air Force referring to fellow flyers who were killed as having *bought the farm*. Funeral parlors have *slumber rooms* and *viewing rooms* where the *dear departed* are kept. The United States State Department won the 1984 Doublespeak Award from The National Council of Teachers of English for replacing "killing" with "unlawful or arbitrary deprivation of life."

Old age is distasteful to many of us, so we ironically speak of *senior citizens* and *golden age* clubs. Crippled people make us sorrowful or embarrassed, as we consider our relative good fortune, and we coin euphemisms to refer to them. They become *handicapped* or *disadvantaged* or *disabled*. We speak of the blind as *vision-impaired* and the deaf as *hearing-impaired*. A wheelchair becomes a *mobility aid*.

One of the problems with euphemisms, beyond the fact that they are frequently inaccurate or vague, is that eventually they become as associated with the feared or distasteful things as the original words, and new euphemisms then have to be coined. For example, one of us teaches veterinarian students who used to write of *dispatching* animals killed for experimental reasons. As *dispatch* became too closely associated with the act of killing, the term *sacrifice* was substituted. In the nineteenth century, *toilet* was a quite respectable word in American English, but now it has lost ground. Few people have *toilets* at home. Rather we have *bathrooms* or *powder rooms*. In public places we have rest rooms, separated into *Men's* and *Women's*. In schools we have *lavatories* or *Boy's* and *Girl's*. The Army has *latrines*, and the Navy has *heads*. The English have *water closets*. On interstate highways, toilets have become *facilities*. Some waterfront restaurants have *Buoys's* and *Gull's*.

Closely related to euphemism is what is sometimes called the "genteel tradition"—the desire to replace simple, concrete words with high-sounding ones. In the genteel tradition *undertakers* become *morticians, funeral directors*, and even *grief counselors*. *Press agents* become *public relations consultants* and *sales clerks* become *sales representatives*. *Janitors* become *custodians* and *teachers* become *educators*. *Newspapers, radio, television*, and *magazines* become the *media*, and *libraries* become *instructional media centers*. *Center*, in fact, is becoming quite popular. *Hospitals* are becoming *medical centers, town hall* is now the *government center*, and *schools* are becoming *learning centers*. Even *bowling alleys* are becoming *bowling centers*.

Euphemisms are probably more comical or sad than harmful in most instances, and sometimes they may even be useful for softening hard reality. But too often they can be used to cover some nasty doings or disguise their true intent. The Vietnam War gave us *pacification*, which sometimes included destroying the enemy, *protective reaction* for air attacks, *escalation* for an enormous increase of American troops in Vietnam, *New Life Hamlet* for *refugee camp* and *incursion* for *invasion*. Bureaucratic language, of which these words are examples, often seems written with the desire to confuse, obscure, impress, or some combination of all three. We boggle at some of the words in this sample:

> Very briefly, the program will provide very intensive supervision to a relative small number of sophisticated recidivist delinquent youth who have been failures in all other dispositional alternatives, including institutionalization.

We wonder why the writer is not willing to come down the abstraction ladder a few rungs and breathe a bit of reality into this report. Does *institutionalization* mean *jail*? What are those mysterious *other dispositional alternatives*? *Sophisticated* is a word high on the abstraction ladder and has too many meanings to be useful in this context. The writer would be better advised to come down the ladder and say what is meant: *worldly, refined, corrupted, complex, champagne-drinking*, or whatever. In dealing with bureaucratic language, it frequently pays to seek out the intended meaning of the words used.

Abstracting, borrowing, compounding, blending, attaching prefixes and suffixes, creating euphemism—in all its forms (practical, sublime, and silly), the creation of language is an intense and peculiarly human activity. Can anyone create a word? Yes, of course, but no one has to use it. In the early days of the American space program, someone created the term *A.O.K.* The public relations people and broadcasters associated with the program would say, "The mission is going well. The astronauts report everything is A.O.K." The term had a slight vogue because of the high interest in the program, but it filled no need that was not already being filled by *O.K.* Therefore, its use has died out.

On the other hand, someone created the prefix *mini-* from either *minimum* or *miniature*. It is a prefix that identifies the thing symbolized by the word it is affixed to as being smaller than other members of its class. Thus, a *minicar* is smaller than other cars, and a *miniskirt* is shorter than other skirts. *Mini-* has been enormously successful. We hear about *minibuses, minicabs, minicourses, miniseminars, minisermons, minicruises, miniconferences*, and so forth. Obviously, *mini-* filled a need and has gained a place in the language.

Words mean whatever the people who use them want them to mean, but words are also social contracts in the same sense that not stealing is a social contract: that is, we won't steal from you if you won't steal from us. In the same way, we agree that the mammal over there with certain characteristics is a *dog*. Our choice of the word *dog* may be completely arbitrary, but once the contract is made, we should not be hasty in breaking it. If you were to persist in calling a *dog* a *weg*, other people would consider you strange and obstinate. It is unlikely that you would succeed in changing the rest of us. On the other hand, you may introduce a new breed of dog, perhaps a cross between a wire-haired terrier and a spaniel, and call it a *wirespan*. Should the breed succeed and achieve recognition by the American Kennel Club, you would have contributed a new word into English that would last as long as the breed (unless, of course, someone clipped it to *wire* or *span*).

What we are saying, then, is that the speakers of a language, English or any other, are the arbiters who decide whether a word changes, lives, or dies. The doctrine is called *usage*. Dictionary makers employ usage in determining which words go into their dictionaries and how these words are defined. Here is how the makers of the *American Heritage Dictionary (AHD)* describe their work:

> Only a trained human reader can spot and mark a shift in meaning. Thus the special citations used in *AHD* are collected by citation readers who underline each word being cited and mark off the passage in which it appears. Such citations are then typed on notecards and placed on file. Then when the time comes to update the dictionary, editors consult the citations to see how often a new word or meaning has been used and in how many publications it has appeared. If the word or sense seems to be well established in the language, an editor can use that information in the citations to help in defining the word. Citations also help a definer write a definition that is limited enough to be specific and broad enough to cover closely related applications of a word.
>
> A full-scale updating of the *AHD* comes once every two or three years; but every year, with each new printing, a number of editorial changes are made. The *AHD* has to keep up not only with new usages but also with new nations and leaders, new trends and inventions, new concepts and concerns. At each updating there are always some new entries to be added and some existing entries to be expanded or redefined. For example, the *AHD* now defines a *camper* as a vehicle as well as a vacationer, and *cosmetic* is now applied not only to make-up but also to anything that is merely decorative rather than functional, superficial rather than substantial.[1]

As the makers of the *AHD* make clear, dictionary makers are not lawgivers. Rather, they are historians who record what we are doing in language, so that we can check to see what the social contract calls for at the moment. In fulfilling their historical function, the editors of the fourth and latest supplement to the *Oxford English Dictionary* have added such words as *self-service, security blanket, sitcom, superpower, teenager, unisex, word processor, yo-yo, yuck, yuppie, zap, zilch*, and *zillionaire*.

A couple of maxims of the day come to mind as we conclude this chapter. The first is "Use it or lose it." Words are a gift to us all. Like our other gifts, they are meant to be used. By reading, speaking, and writing, we keep alive that in us which is uniquely human. The second maxim is "Use it, but don't abuse it." A language is meant to be used and changed and made to fit the needs of its users. But remember the social contract. Don't abuse the privilege.

Exercises

1. Most commonly used words have many different meanings that have evolved through the processes of association, generalization, and specialization.

Also, such words are often compounded with other words to form new words. *The Oxford English Dictionary* (OED) is a rich source of etymological and historical information that demonstrates such evolution. Words such as *head, foot, hand, peak, pick*, and *harvest* fill up many pages with their definitions. Choose such a word in the OED. Write an essay based upon the word's etymology that demonstrates how association, generalization, specialization, and compounding have been employed to give new meanings to the word. Be prepared to discuss your essay in class.

2. This chapter discusses the following ways of word creation: association, generalization, specialization, compounding, blending, and clipping. Also discussed are the use of prefixes and suffixes, foreign loan words, words from great events, words from science and technology, euphemisms, and words from the "genteel tradition." Divide the class into groups, each of which take several of these methods of word creation as their teaching responsibility. The group will find example words and, using the examples, demonstrate to the rest of the class how the methods work.

3. Choose a highly abstract word like *loyalty, bravery*, or *democracy*. As a group, the class should define the word. A good technique is to begin by brainstorming the concept (see pages 9–10). The brainstorming can be followed by a discussion in which ideas that truly relate to the concept are selected and strengthened through such strategies as exemplification, generalization, and comparison. The discussion can become the basis for individual essays on the word discussed. Or, alternatively, the discussion can be used as a model for individual essays on other words chosen by the writers.

4. Advertisements, poems, and political speeches all demonstrate that in many instances the connotations of words are more important than their denotations. Connotation is often important in fiction and even journalism. Divide the class into groups, each of which prepares and leads a class discussion on the use and effect of connotation in one of these mediums. Such discussions can serve as sources and models for individual essays. (A tip: the publication *Vital Speeches of the Day* is a good source for political speeches.)

5. Many users of English, even rather expert ones, sometimes mistakenly use one word for another. For various reasons, certain pairs of words are frequently confused in this way. Look up the following words in a dictionary. Be prepared in class to distinguish between the items in each pair. You should be able to use each listed word correctly in a sentence:

acute, chronic
affect, effect (noun and verb)
alternative, alternate
appraise, apprise
bait, bate
complacent, complaisant

comprise, compose
continual, continuous
deprecate, depreciate
discreet, discrete
disinterested, uninterested
fewer, less
flaunt, flout
fortuitous, fortunate
imply, infer
lay, lie (recline)
oral, verbal
principal, principle
raise, raze
sit, set
site, sight

6. This exercise can serve as a basis for a discussion, talk, or essay. With the help of a dictionary and a thesaurus, compile a list of synonyms and near synonyms—for example, *stout, corpulent, fat, obese, fleshy, beefy, plump, rotund, tubby, roly-poly, heavy-set, thickset, stocky, brawny, burly, portly*, and *stalwart*.

What are the differences in denotation and connotation among the words? Are any of the words exact synonyms and completely interchangable? Which words would leave you with a favorable impression of the concept or person to which it is applied? Which unfavorable? Are some of the words completely neutral? Would some of the words be more appropriate in one context than another, for example in a light, humorous essay, but not in a formal technical report? Trace the etymology of some of the words. Does the source (for example, Old English, French, or Latin) have an effect on the present connotation of the word?

7

Grammar

In Chapter 6, we discuss words, the semantic component of language. Words, however, by themselves do not a language make. The words have to be put together in a system that shows us the relationships among them. That system is what we know as *grammar*. We can illustrate the need for grammar easily enough by scrambling a Sentence (A) so that it loses its grammar, as in Sentence B:

> A. The term "family" refers to a group of two or more persons related by blood, marriage, or adoption and residing together in a household.
>
> B. Or term the refers of related more and a together residing adoption household to family group a blood two marriage or persons in by.

Clearly, the string of words in Sentence A is a recognizable sentence. The string in Sentence B is gibberish. Another, often amusing, way of producing gibberish is by keeping the grammatical system but replacing meaningful words with nonsense syllables, as in Sentence C:

> C. The fram "wampunction" sojers to a kump of ame or lex waconies wasatched by hax, ligamy, or morician or mabing upjeter in a gluhat.

In Sentence C, although it's nonsense, the reader has a sense that something is being said. This comedy trick is accomplished by so-called double-talkers. The trick is done by keeping relationship words like *of* and *by* and grammatical endings such as *ing* and *ed*.

What is it that a grammatical system must accomplish for its users? To answer that question completely would take many books. The complexity of grammar can be gauged by one linguist's statement that "Ten linguists working full time for 10 years to analyze the structure of the English language could not program a computer with the ability for language acquired by an average child in the first 10 or even five years of life."[1] But we can sketch a few of the things a grammar does for its users. It indicates who or what is acting in a situation and who or what is receiving the action *(Mary hit the ball. John stroked the cat.)* It shows time relationships. *(Anne is writing. Anne wrote. Anne will write. Anne had written her letter before I wrote mine.)* It indicates moral obligation. *(Anne should have written to me.)* Grammar distinguishes the singular from the plural *(book, books).* It indicates questions and negative replies. *(Do you want to go to the movies? No, I'd rather not.)* It tells us in what direction things can be found and where things are in relation to other things. *(Go to the corner and turn right. The cat is on the table.)* It shows possession. *(John's coat. The coat of John.)* To accomplish all these things and many more, the English grammatical system depends heavily on word order and relationship words such as prepositions and articles. These are called *syntax.* Supplementing syntax is a system in which we continually alter words to show their role or relationship in a sentence. Thus we show the past tense of *break* by changing it to *broke* or the possessive case of *woman* by adding an 's. This use of *inflections,* as these word alterations are called, is known as *morphology.* (Don't confuse this specialized grammatical use of the word *inflection* with the more common meaning of the word, which is to change the volume or tone of voice.)

Thus, language is broken into a semantic portion (words) and grammar (syntax plus morphology). Let's look at the system in action in a fairly simple sentence:

Paul kissed Mary.

In this sentence we depend largely, though not completely, on syntax for understanding. *Paul* precedes the active past tense verb *kissed,* so we know he is the actor in the sentence—the kisser. *Mary* comes after the verb, so we know she is receiving the action, and is the kissee. Morphology plays a role because the addition of *ed* to *kiss* makes the verb be in the past tense. You knew all that, even if you had never heard of the concepts of syntax or morphology before—or if you had never heard of a verb, for that matter. As we will show you shortly, if you are a native speaker of English, you knew most of your grammar before you ever stepped into a schoolroom.

English depends heavily upon syntax for showing grammatical relationships. This is so true that in the sentence, "Him and me climbed the tree," we understand that *him* and *me* did the climbing even though the morphology of the sentence is telling us that the tree and not the boys did the climbing. Syntax is so important in English that the mere moving of a word can alter the meaning of a sentence drastically. Recently, newspapers quoted a senator as referring to the President as "the most powerful *single* man in the free world." Unless something was going on that the country was unaware of, the senator most certainly meant "the *single* most powerful man in the free world."

This heavy dependence upon syntax is not universal to all languages. In classical Latin, morphology played a major role. For example, these two Latin sentences have identical meanings, "Paul kissed Mary":

Paulus Mariam basiavit.
Mariam Paulus basiavit.

The word endings identify Paul as the subject of the sentence and Mary as the object, regardless of the word order. If we wanted to indicate that Mary was kissing Paul, we would have to change the endings in this manner:

Maria Paulum basiavit.

By contrast, in English "Mary kissed Paul" is quite a different sentence from "Paul kissed Mary," though the results may be equally satisfying.

The following English sentence is somewhat more complicated:

The boys chased John and him toward Mary's house.

In this sentence, we recognize again that word order tells us *The boys* are the subject and *John and him* are the objects of the action. The prepositional phrase *toward Mary's house* tells us in what direction the boys chased John and him.

The is important in the sentence because it is a signal that we are talking about some specific boys. *Boys* without the use of *the* would mean "boys in general." Hence, we call *the* the definite article.

Morphology plays a more important role in this sentence than in the simpler *Paul kissed Mary*. In this sentence, there are four inflections: the plural *s* on *boys,* the past tense *ed* on *chased,* the use of the accusative pronoun *him,* and the possessive *'s* on Mary.

Just as classical Latin shows us that we can't take word order for granted as the major way to show the grammar of a sentence, Chinese shows us that we can't take inflections for granted either. Chinese is even more lightly inflected than English. It has, for example, no plural forms or past tense. Therefore, in Chinese a sentence might read (in the equivalent English), *Boy kiss Mary*. To indicate time, the Chinese speaker would have to add the Chinese equivalent of *today, tomorrow,* or *two hours ago*. If Mary were being kissed by more than one boy, the Chinese speaker would have to add a number, such as *Two boy kiss Mary yesterday*. This simpler grammatical system in Chinese should not be taken as a sign that Chinese is a primitive language. Chinese is one of the oldest languages on earth, and evidence supports the view that the older a language is the more its grammatical structures are simplified.

Non-native speakers of a language have to learn these grammatical rules in an artificial way. If you have ever studied a foreign language, you know what a difficult task it is. But what about native speakers? How do children in the first five to ten years of their lives master a system so complex that in the words of Professor Breyne Arlene Moskowitz quoted earlier, ten linguists working for ten years could not analyze it completely enough to program it into a computer. In an excellent article, Professor Moskowitz reviews what linguists know about the process of language acquisition in children.[2]

Children learn most of the grammatical structure of their language during the first five years of their lives, before they ever enter a schoolroom. They learn language from their family and their friends, and they learn it only if they interact with speakers of the language. This interaction is vital. A child exposed to a television set but who is not given the chance to interact with speakers would not learn the language.

Adults living with children seem, perhaps quite unconsciously, to structure their language to make it easier for the children to interact and comprehend. They use a simple vocabulary and they talk in shorter sentences, often with exaggerated intonation. For example, the slight rise in our voice at the end of a question such as, "Are we going now?" may be elevated beyond normal in speaking to a child. We may simplify the pronunciation of words to make them easier for children, so that *stomach* becomes *tum-tum*. This use of what is sometimes called "baby talk" is found in all languages and cultures and is apparently not only a sign of affection but a useful teaching device.

In this comfortable environment, children begin to talk in one-word sentences. *Wa-wa* spoken with a rising tone is a request for water, or, if the tone is sharp enough, even a command. *Doggie* spoken quietly may simply indicate the presence of the animal. *Doggie* with a rising intonation or in a scream indicates fear and even terror. Thus, while in one-word sentences children are mastering vocabulary, they are are also beginning to show a feeling for syntax as well.

Children pass rather quickly through the one-word stage to a two-word stage. Here syntax is clearly used to show relationships: possession *(Daddy coat)*, actor-action *(Dog running)*, action-object *(Drink milk)*, and location *(Cup here)*. Children can, by stringing together these two-word sentences, carry on fairly complex conversations, as in this one reported by Professor Moskowitz between a child named Brenda and a linguist:

BRENDA: "Tape corder. Use it. Use it."

LINGUIST: "Use it for what?"

BRENDA: "Talk. Corder talk. Brenda talk."[3]

Children pass from the two-word stage not into a three-word stage but into what Professor Moskowitz calls telegraphic speech. In this stage, they produce short sentences in which they gradually master proper word order, learn function words such as prepositions and articles, and inflections. Hence, they master syntax and morphology. During this learning process, children generalize from what they hear, form hypotheses about how language works, and try the hypotheses out. Weighing how their hypotheses seem to work or not to work, they construct for themselves a grammatical system. Quite sensibly, children master the simpler things first and leave more complex things for later. (For this reason, it seems to do little good for parents to correct children excessively in an attempt to speed the learning process. In fact, such parental behavior may interrupt the process in ways that are harmful to the child.)

In learning the past tense of verbs, children go through six stages in which they generalize language rules out of the language they hear.

In the first stage, children master the present tense (i.e., *I talk, I come, I go*). In the second stage, they may learn to use a few irregular verb past tense forms *(I came, I went)*. In the third stage, children recognize that people use a *d* or a *t* sound to indicate past action, so they generalize this knowledge to all verbs, including the irregular ones *(I talked, I comed, I goed)*. Parents may view this stage as a regression because the correct irregular forms of *I came* and *I went* are no longer used. Actually, at this stage, the children are demonstrating a mastery of generalizing the rules from what they hear.

In the fourth stage, children generalize from the fact that in some words the *d* or the *t* sound is actually pronounced as a separate syllable *(I need-ed)* and apply the added syllable to all past tense verbs, producing *talk-ed, go-ed,* and even *went-ed* as two syllables rather than one.

In the fifth stage, children sort out which past tense forms are simply a *d* or a *t* sound without adding a syllable *(I played, I walked)* and which require the extra syllable *(I need-ed, I weed-ed)*. In the sixth stage, children figure out that some verbs don't fit the generalized patterns and restore *I went* and *I came* to their speech.

In learning plurals, children go through stages quite similar to those involved in learning the past tense, working their way through pronunciations such as *boy, boys, boysez,* and *boys* and *man, men, mans, manez, menez, mans,* and *men*. In the same way, children learn the rules for forming questions, negatives, passive voice, all the tenses, and the myriad of other grammatical structures that allow them to carry on intelligible conversation with their fellow speakers of the language. At the same time, of course, children are learning vocabulary, about two thousand words by the age of five.

We hasten to add that children do all this without knowing a verb from a tow truck and certainly without any knowledge that they are learning something called "past tense" or "passive voice." They are simply generalizing from what they hear, forming hypotheses from their generalizations, and trying out their hypotheses in a trial-and-error way until they get the structures right.

Where do the grammatical structures of a language come from? In the most profound sense, we have no answer for that question. Just as we really don't know when exactly human beings first thought of using spoken words as symbols for reality, we also don't know when they thought of the grammatical ways of showing the relationships among the words. Presumably, in the development of language, the development of words and grammar must have kept pace with each other. What we do know is that any language we can examine—whether it be classical Greek, modern French, or the language of a primitive people such as the San of South Africa—has a fully developed grammatical system.

Though we can't document the beginning of any grammatical system, we can examine grammatical change in recorded languages. For example, now that you know what grammatical inflection is, we can talk about the decay of certain grammatical inflections in English. As you know from Chapter 6, the origins of English lay in the Germanic languages spoken by the Angles, Saxons, and Jutes who occupied England from the fifth century on. The language that these people spoke from approximately 450 to 1150 we know today as Old English.

Old English, like most European languages of the time, was heavily inflected. Unlike Modern English nouns, Old English nouns still showed what is known as *case,* mainly through the use of inflection. Case provides a way of showing the relationship of nouns or pronouns in a sentence. In our pronouns, we still show case by inflection. In the nominative case for pronouns used as subjects, we have, for example, *he* and *she*, and in the accusative case used for objects of verbs and prepositions, *him* and *her*. In both nouns and pronouns we still have genitive (possessive) case, as in *John's, Mary's, his* and *hers*. Modern English nouns, with the exception of the genitive, show case not by inflection but by placement in the sentence. Hence, *Paul kissed Mary* is a very different sentence from *Mary kissed Paul*.

Old English nouns had four cases: *nominative* (for subjects), *accusative* (for direct objects), *genitive* (for possessive), and *dative* (for indirect objects). Thus, in Old English, the word for *hound* shows this pattern:

	Singular	Plural
Nominative	hund	hundas
Accusative	hund	hundas
Genitive	hundes	hunda
Dative	hunde	hundum

By the time we reach Middle English (1150–1500), the English system of noun inflection has greatly decayed. If we examine *hound* again, we find something close to Modern English:

	Singular	Plural
Nominative	hound	houndes
Accusative	hound	houndes
Genitive	houndes	houndes

Except for a rarely used *hounde,* the inflections for the dative case are gone.

In Modern English, we have introduced the complication of the apostrophe in the genitive:

	Singular	Plural
Nominative	hound	hounds
Accusative	hound	hounds
Genitive	hound's	hounds'

In Old English, adjectives had to follow the case of the noun and in addition had to change depending upon whether the noun was considered masculine, feminine, or neuter. The adjective *good,* for example, came in all the forms shown in Figure 7-1.

In Modern English, we have left only the form *good,* that serves for all cases and genders, and for singular and plural. If you feel like breathing a sigh of relief for the complications you have been spared, it would be perfectly justified. Why did these changes come about? Likely, they were caused by the invasion of England by two other peoples. In the years between 787 and 1042, the Danes invaded England and occupied large areas along the northeast coast. The Danes were a Germanic people with a grammar and a vocabulary similar in many ways to Old English. However, many of their inflections were different from those of Old English. Thus, in talking to each other, the Anglo-Saxons and the Danes perhaps found it easier not to emphasize inflections. This probably quite unconscious development led to the decay of the inflections.

After the Norman invasion in 1066, when French was the language of the

	Singular		
	Masculine	*Feminine*	*Neuter*
Nominative	god	god	god
Accusative	godne	gode	god
Genitive	godes	godre	godes
Dative	godum	godre	godum
	Plural		
	Masculine	*Feminine*	*Neuter*
Nominative	gode	goda	god
Accusative	gode	gode	god
Genitive	godra	godra	godra
Dative	godum	godum	godum

Figure 7-1 *The Old English Declension of* Good.

aristocrats and the educated, English was left largely in the hands of the uneducated. Under their care, what was left of the inflectional system decayed rapidly. By Chaucer's time in the Middle English period, the system was much like that of Modern English.

Because the changes in inflection occurred over a long period of time, during which most speakers of English were uneducated and illiterate, they probably met with little resistance. In modern times, when most people are literate and when many educated people consider themselves to be guardians of "pure English," changes in grammar occur less frequently, and when they do, they are likely to be met with resistance. This may be true even when the change is a useful one. A case in point is the attempted rejection by linguistic purists of the progressive passive. Today, such progressive passive expressions as "My house is being built for me" are so common that it is hard to believe that the progressive passive did not even exist in English until the late eighteenth century.

In the seventeenth century, we find such expressions as "We stayed there while our house was *building*."[4] Remnants of this seventeenth century form can still be heard in the rural Eastern United States where we may hear, "The barn is a-building" for "The barn is being built." And most of us still say, "Dinner is cooking."

The seventeenth century form has limitations, however. Does "The movie is killing" mean "The movie is being killed" (perhaps by the critics), or "The movie is deadly dull"? Does "The man is calling" mean the man is being called or that he is calling someone?

To defeat such ambiguities, eighteenth-century speakers and writers shifted to the use of a form of *to be* with the participle, as in Robert Southey's, "A fellow, whose grinder *is being torn out* by the roots."[5] The shift gave us the modern progressive passive voice. Despite the utility of the new form, authorities thundered against it throughout the nineteenth century. *The North American Review* condemned it as "an outrage upon English idiom. . . ." In 1859, another scholar stated, "'The house *is being build*' for 'The house *is building*' is an awkward neologism . . . an attempt at the artificial improvement of the language in a point which needed no amendment."[6]

Despite such attacks, the new form prevailed, proving as has been proved many times that when a change is useful people will adopt it with or without the approval of the authorities.

Our rules of grammar, then, have evolved over the years to meet the needs of the users of the language. And, as we have seen, as children we master the rules of grammar that allow us to understand the language of others and to be understood when we use language. Why, then, do so many fear what we think of as grammar? The problem can be illustrated by an experience we had while on a fishing trip high in the Rocky Mountains. We were finishing a day's fishing when two men came up the trail and joined us beside the lake. The smaller of the two men served as spokesman for the two. He was a congenial, articulate man who informed us that, referring to his partner, "Me and him have fished most the lakes around here. This is one of the best."

We showed them our day's catch and chatted some more about the quality of the fishing in the area. Then, as people do, we got curious about one another.

"What do you do for a living?" the small man asked.

Glancing at one another, we reluctantly allowed that we were English teachers.

After a moment's pause, a rather thoughtful pause it seemed, the man answered, "Well, him and I, we're steel workers."

In changing from the comfortable "Me and him" of his previous conversation to the awkward "Him and I," the man revealed both a fear of English teachers and a lack of confidence in the appropriateness of his own manner of speaking. Why did he react in such a way?

The fact of the matter is, as we have seen, we learn the fundamental rules of grammar at such an early age that we have no memory of learning them, no more than we have a memory of learning how to walk. What we do remember is the schoolroom where we learned about correctness in grammar. Correctness consisted of a few rules laid over the literally thousands of rules that we already knew. We mistakenly concluded that these few rules were "grammar." What we learned in the schoolroom and what puts the fear into us is *prescriptive grammar*. In applying the rules of prescriptive grammar, it is not enough to be understood; we must also be "correct." (Prescriptive grammar tells us what we *ought* to do. Descriptive grammar tells us what we *do* do.) Where did prescriptive grammar come from, and how important is it in our lives?

Most linguists would agree that prescriptive grammar has its roots in the seventeenth and eighteenth centuries. It was a time when the speakers of modern European languages realized that their languages lacked any published references as to what was standard in grammar. There grew a desire to standardize the language, to stabilize it, and to protect it against further change. In France and Italy, this desire was achieved by the establishment of academies, groups of men who would examine the language and fix its standards. The notion of an academy in England, though proposed by some of the writers of the day, notably by Jonathan Swift of *Gulliver's Travels* fame, never succeeded. In England the desire for stability and authority in language was met by the publication of grammar books.

Despite the obvious success of English, most of the people who attempted to stabilize it by writing the new grammars assumed that the language needed improvement. Improvement in their view meant ruling certain constructions to be incorrect—*barbarous* was the frequently used term—and others correct. It seemed to most of the early grammarians that if there were a choice between two possible expressions, only one of them could be correct. For example, if "different from" was ruled correct, than "different than" had to be incorrect. With such an attitude, it is not surprising that most grammarians were prescriptive and authoritarian and obsessed with correctness. Also, because the study of linguistics did not begin until the nineteenth century, the eighteenth-century grammarians lacked even the rudimentary knowledge of linguistics that you now possess from having read this far in this chapter. Most of them had nothing to go on but personal preference and what they conceived of as the application of logic.

Perhaps the most prescriptive of the English grammarians was Robert Lowth, whose *Short Introduction to English Grammar* went through 22 editions. Lowth's views were widespread and widely accepted. His attitude was clear. He wrote

> The principal design of a Grammar of any Language is to teach us to express ourselves with propriety in that Language; and to enable us to judge of every phrase and form of construction, whether it be right or not. The plain way of doing this is, to lay down rules, and to illustrate them by examples. But besides shewing what is wrong, the matter may be further explained by pointing out what is wrong.[7]

Among the rules of correctness Lowth and his contemporaries gave us are the following:

- The distinction between *lay* and *lie*.
- The correctness of *different from* and the incorrectness of *different than*.
- The differentiation of *between* and *among*.
- The use of the comparative when only two things are being compared *(the bigger of the two,* not *the biggest of the two.)*
- The use of the nominative case pronoun after *than* and *as* (*he is taller than I,* not *he is taller than me*.)
- The abolition of the double negative on the grounds, according to Lowth, that "Two Negatives in English destroy one another, or are equivalent to an Affirmative."[8] Previously, speakers could multiply negatives to emphasize just how negative their feelings actually were.
- The distinction between *shall* and *will*.

Most of the prescriptive grammarians' notions got into school handbooks, and most of them have been there ever since. Only a few have lost ground. In the United States, for example, few people seem to worry any longer about the distinction between *will* and *shall*. More important than the specific rules themselves, however, is the fact that the prescriptive attitude in grammar has generally prevailed. The notion that some constructions must be wrong even though they are perfectly understandable in normal speech and writing binds us all.

Only a few eighteenth century grammarians, notably George Campbell and the natural scientist Joseph Priestley, spoke up for the doctrine of descriptive grammar or usage. Campbell in his 1776 *Philosophy of Rhetoric* perhaps expressed the doctrine best:

> Language is purely a species of fashion. . . . It is not the business of grammar, as some critics seem preposterously to imagine, to give law to the fashions which regulate our speech. On the contrary, from its conformity to these, and from that alone, it derives all authority and value. For, what is the grammar of any language? It is no other than a collection of general observations methodically digested, and comprising all the modes previously and independently established, by which the significations, derivations, and combinations of words in that language, are ascer-

tained. It is of no consequence here to what causes originally these modes or fashions owe their existence, to imitation, to reflection, to affectation, or to caprice; they no sooner obtain and become general, than they are the laws of language, and the grammarian's only businesses is to note, collect, and methodize them.[9]

Campbell went on to define usage as that which was "present, national, and reputable." He further defined reputable as being "whatever modes of speech are authorized as good by the writings of a great number if not the majority of celebrated authors."[10] Sad to say, although Priestley adhered to the doctrine of usage in deciding what was right, Campbell frequently ignored it and was as prescriptive as Lowth.

Were it not for the eighteenth-century prescriptive grammarians, we today might be just as comfortable with "Me and him have fished most the lakes around here" as with "He and I have fished most the lakes around here." We might even, on occasion when we really want to emphasize a negative point, state it bluntly, as in, "I don't want nothing!" But the eighteenth-century grammarians for the most part succeeded. We now have to live with the results. And the results are clear. Under many circumstances, being "correct" in grammar is highly important to us.

If you are reading this book, you are presumably a college student who aspires for the kinds of jobs that college graduates obtain. If such is the case, then you must consider correct grammar important. The grammar of educated people is supposed to be correct in the prescriptive sense. This is a concern, but perhaps not as big a concern as you might expect. Correctness but not hypercorrectness is called for. If English is your native tongue, you mastered 99 and 4/10ths percent of your grammar in your earliest years. Despite the prescriptive grammarians, very few people really worry about the use of the nominative pronoun after *than* or *as*. Even fewer worry about the use of the comparative when comparing only two things. Do worry about the double negative: "I don't want none, thank you," could lose you a job or even a desired social relationship. So could "between you and I," rather than the correct "between you and me."

Writing, a rather unnatural act compared to speaking, adds the problems of punctuation and spelling. Both were standardized during the same period that grammar was being standardized, and the same desire for correctness in these matters has been instilled in the language. Like it or not, we have to accept the fact that many people consider a misspelled word or a semicolon used for a colon as a sign of a poor education.

If you are really nervous about your grammar and writing mechanics, listen and pay attention to your English teachers and other speakers of correct English. When you read, pay some attention to how things are said and how they are punctuated. Look at the *American Heritage Dictionary of the English Language*. The publishers of that dictionary have taken Campbell's definition of reputable usage to heart and formed a usage panel of writers, including a few professors, that votes on whether a construction is correct or incorrect. For example, under the definition for *different,* a usage note tells us that *"Different from* and *different than* are both widely used, but the usage panel has a marked preference for *different from.*" So, if, in George Campbell's terms, you want to follow the usage of "celebrated authors," you should use *different from* in most instances.

Browse through the "Handbook" in this text. We cover most of the rules you are likely to need to write acceptable and correct English. In Chapter 11, "Principles of Style," we isolate particularly important rules under the heading, "Correctness" (pages 218–226). Take such rules seriously, because others will. In Chapter 12, "Conventions," we discuss punctuation and other matters of conventional usage. Your instructor may use the marking symbols listed on the inside of the back cover to refer you to particular sections you should read. Finally, in Chapter 13 we provide a "Glossary of Grammatical Terms." Despite the fact that by the age of three you were using verbs correctly without being able to define a verb, it pays to know what a verb is. It speeds up the discussion of grammatical problems in the same way that your knowledge of what a carburetor is speeds up a discussion on automotive problems.

Finally, our best advice is that although you should be serious about these matters, you should also be relaxed about them. You really do know most of the grammar you are every going to need. You have known it for years.

Exercises

1. Compare English grammar to the grammar of some other language you know. Compare such things as syntax and the use and importance of inflections. Which of the two grammars seems the simpler? If you are not familiar with another language, discuss the roles that syntax and inflection play in English.

2. From time to time, popular magazines publish articles on language and usage. Using the *Readers' Guide to Periodical Literature,* find and read several such articles. Decide if the authors are descriptive or prescriptive in their approach to language. How do they justify their positions? Are they, in your view, convincing? Prepare a review of the articles to be presented as an essay or a talk.

3. For most English speakers, the twentieth century is a time of near universal education and of rapid cultural and technological change. What effects are these circumstances having on the grammar of English and upon its vocabulary? Write an essay or prepare a talk demonstrating the causal relationships between the causes and effects you perceive.

8

Sentences

Most of us think we write clear sentences. We have an idea, think it to ourselves, and assume that what we write will be perfectly clear to others. Fortunately, our earlier reading and writing have helped us develop a feel for sentences just as we had earlier absorbed more or less unconsciously the grammar of our native language. Often, however, we don't get a sentence exactly right the first time. To help ourselves to revise wisely, we need to concentrate on the essentials of writing sentences. Sentences are the basic unit of writing.

One of the best ways to learn how to write effective sentences is to study good examples and revise bad ones. In this chapter we do that. We discuss the importance of keeping the core of the sentence together and making the verb much more important in the sentence. Chapter 9, "Paragraphs," and Chapter 11, "Principles of Style," examine sentences in the context of paragraphs and longer passages.

Keeping the Sentence Core Together

Cut to the core, ordinary English sentences consist of a subject and a predicate, as in these sentences:

Geraldine / (subject)	lost. (predicate)
George / (subject)	defeated her. (predicate consisting of the verb *defeated* and the object *her*)
Walter / (subject)	was unhappy. (predicate consisting of the verb *was* and the complement *unhappy*)

The subject is the topic to which the writer wishes to draw attention; the predicate is what the writer has to say about the subject. The typical sentence order is a subject followed by a predicate. Research shows that professional writers follow this pattern about 75 percent of the time.[1] The typical order in the predicate is a verb followed by an object or complement. The subject-verb, subject-verb-object, or subject-verb-complement is the core of the sentence. It is the main assertion of the sentence.

Although every sentence has a core, we seldom write sentences without adding information to the core. We can modify the subject:

> *The trained mechanic* repaired the engine.

We can modify the verb:

> The trained mechanic *quickly repaired* the engine.

We can modify the object:

> The trained mechanic quickly repaired the *tractor engine*.

Longer modifiers that are not so closely related to the subject, verb, object, or complement are usually set off from the core by commas. We can add information before the core:

> *Working through the night*, the trained mechanic repaired the engine.

We can add information inside the core:

> The trained mechanic, *who had recently graduated from the area technical school*, repaired the engine.

We can add information after the core:

> The trained mechanic repaired the engine, *as soon as the spare parts arrived*.

The italicized information fills out the sentences, enriching and developing the idea stated in the core by explaining and adding details.

Readers normally have little difficulty reading such expanded sentences unless too much additional information makes the subject, verb, and object or complement hard to spot.

A sentence can be hard to read because it has too many words before the core. Here is a sentence that states several conditions before the core; this makes it difficult for many readers to understand:

> If the money supply does not continue to expand, if the velocity of money does not continue to accelerate, and if the demand for credit declines, *the economy of a debt-ridden system will slump*.

A gasper like this opener delays the subject too long, forcing readers to keep too many words in mind for too long before getting to the subject. Twenty-six words and three commas coming before the core have the effect of taxing readers' ability to remember the conditions before getting to the consequences in the core. The only way to understand the sentence is to keep reading it until we memorize the conditions and the consequences. To clarify such a sentence, the writer should state the core first and list the conditions afterward:

> *The economy of a debt-ridden system will slump under the following conditions:*
> —the money supply does not continue to expand,
> —the velocity of money does not continue to accelerate, and
> —the demand for credit declines.

Long phrases and clauses inside the core can leave a subject or a verb dangling in midair. In these examples, eighteen words are too long an interruption between the italicized elements:

- Some *students*, when they receive good instruction and are given ample opportunity to practice over a long period of time, *may achieve* the ability to write well.
- Some students *may*, when they receive good instruction and are given ample opportunity to practice over a long period of time, *achieve* the ability to write well.
- Some students *may achieve*, when they receive good instruction and are given ample opportunity to practice over a long period of time, *the ability* to write well.

To improve the sentence flow, keep the core together by placing the additional information before or after the core:

- With good instruction and ample opportunity to practice over a long period of time, some *students may achieve the ability* to write well.
- Some *students may achieve the ability* to write well, when they receive good instruction and are given ample opportunity to practice over a long period of time.

Although we write most of our sentences more or less unconsciously, we don't revise unconsciously. We need to be especially careful in revising to make certain our sentences are still easy to read when we use openers that delay the sentence core or when we separate the elements of the core. Unduly delaying the core or widely separating the elements causes difficulty for readers. They may overlook or forget what belongs with what. Keeping the core together creates a clear line of thought.

Choosing the Appropriate Verb Mood

Verb mood communicates certain things about the writer's thinking and indicates the intent of the sentence—to state a fact or ask a question about a fact, to express a desire or supposition, or to make a request or give a command. The three verb moods are

- the *indicative* (for factual statements—"The shed burned down"),
- the *subjunctive* (for wishful or hypothetical statements ("The shed may burn down"), and
- the *imperative* (for commands and requests—"Burn down the shed").

As you can see, the mood of the verb causes a great difference in meaning.

The indicative mood states that what is said is true. In using it, the writer is saying that he or she is certain of the facts and can vouch for the truth of the statement.

- The radio station *receives* $22,000 of its budget from student services fees.
- Old fashioned roses *are* large bushes with long arching canes.
- The Declaration of Independence *was written* by Thomas Jefferson.
- Joe *had* a habit of keeping money in drawers all over the house.

Writers also use the indicative mood to ask about facts:

- *Is* breakfast ready?
- When *will* we *receive* the new shipment?
- *Has* Maria *asked* about me?

Frequently, though not always, we use the indicative mood in statement after statement, testifying to the factualness of what we say. Here is a passage that is part of one person's remembrance of her high-school graduation dance:

> The school gymnasium had been transformed from the old scene of basketball games and gym classes into a disco, complete with strobe lights, black and white panels, and mirrors. Kicking off our shoes and shedding our jackets and stoles, we danced to the sound of the

rock band The Frenzy Express. The beat went on until three in the morning. It was the final high-school bash, and we abandoned ourselves to celebration.

As with this passage, almost all ordinary statements and questions are expressed in the indicative mood—the most common verb mood of writing.

Far less common than the indicative mood is the subjunctive mood. We use it to state a wish or a supposition:

- I wish I *were* in Hawaii.
- Oh, if it *were* only summer again!
- If I *were* you, I would volunteer for the assignment.
- If Dana *were* chosen, she would try to do her best.
- Assuming that Pat *were* not here, who would finish the job?

Using the indicative "I wish I *was*," "if it *was*," "If I *was*," "If Dana *is chosen*," or "Assuming that Pat *was* not here" would make these sentences distinctly colloquial. In more formal writing and speech, the subjunctive *were* instead of *is* or *was* is appropriate.

The imperative mood expresses a request or a command, varying in force from a polite request to a warning.

- Please *give* this matter more thought.
- *Tell* me the capacity of the core memory.
- *Type* your paper if you can.
- *Wait* until you are used to the heat before working out hard.
- *Watch out* for power lines overhead.

The subject is usually omitted in imperative sentences: "If the artichokes are large, [you] *cut* them in half." As you can see from these examples, the imperative is not the typical verb mood of expository prose. It is used for writing instructions, as in this example that tells people how to apply a decal:

Note: *Do not moisten* the sticker.

1. Thoroughly *clean* the surface to which you will apply the decal.
2. *Remove* the protective paper by bending the decal over your index finger paper side up and peeling at the scoreline.
3. *Place* the decal on the cleaned surface.
4. Firmly *rub* the decal and edges down with your thumb.

Careful writers seldom have problems with verb mood. Novice writers sometimes do. The two most likely problems are overuse of the subjunctive mood and unnecessary shifts from one mood to another. Most of the time, writers know when to give a statement a subjunctive air. But sometimes writers state conditionally that which is better stated factually. They might write "The cell *may be defined* as the smallest unit of living matter, from which all animals and plants *may be said to be formed*," when the less tentative "The cell *is* the smallest unit of living matter, from which all animals and plants *are formed*" is appropriate. Or they might state that "The cell *could be described* as having no particular shape" instead of "The cell *has* no particular shape." The use of *may be defined*, *may be said to be formed*, and *could be described* gives a shade of meaning that suggests speculation or doubt when none is intended. Some writers carry this tendency so far as to start a letter with "I would like to thank you" instead of simply "Thank you."

Novice writers also tend to use the subjunctive mood unnecessarily to explain choices, as these examples illustrate:

- If the dial *were set* at 1, Condition Alpha *would be obtained.*
- If the dial *were set* at 2, Condition Beta *would be obtained.*

A better, more direct and concise way to describe the use of the dial is to use the indicative mood:

- The dial *is set* at 1 for Condition Alpha.
- The dial *is set* at 2 for Condition Beta.

For instructing someone how to set the dial, the imperative is the best choice:

- *Set* the dial at 1 for Condition Alpha.
- *Set* the dial at 2 for Condition Beta.

Unnecessary shifts in the mood of the verb disturb readers. Most undesirable shifts in mood occur between the indicative and the imperative. The following passage contains noticeable and awkward shifts:

> When a golfer steps up to the ball to play a shot, he first aligns the face of the club with the target. Then align yourself with the face of the club. . . .

The jarring shifts from third person (*golfer . . . he*) to second person (*yourself*) and from the indicative *steps up* and *aligns* to the imperative *[you] align* interrupt the flow of the passage and force the reader to question the intent of the passage. Is it descriptive or is it instructional?

Here are those sentences expressed consistently, first in the indicative mood (for description) and then in the imperative mood (for instruction):

- When a golfer *steps up* to the ball to play a shot, he first *aligns* the face of the club with the target. Then he *aligns* himself with the face of the club.

- When you step up to the ball to play a shot, *align* the face of the club with the target. Then *align* yourself with the face of the club.

When you are sure about what you are doing, you can shift purposely from one mood to another, as in this passage:

> The first hand tool you *should buy* is a medium-priced screwdriver [subjunctive]. *Beat* the devil out of it, then *use* it ever after for prying lids off paint cans, removing moldings, scraping, gouging, and stabbing [imperative]. Then you *will never have to wreck* any of your good screwdrivers doing these things [indicative].[2]

But be careful not to overuse the subjunctive or to shift moods carelessly. For further information, see the appropriate entries in Chapter 13, "Glossary of Grammatical Terms."

Using Active and Passive Voice

In addition to selecting verb mood carefully, we also deliberately choose between the active and passive voice when we write sentences that have transitive verbs (verbs that take direct objects, as in "The dog chased the cat" or "The moon causes tides in the ocean"). English has thousands of transitive verbs, so the choice of the active or passive voice is an important matter. Voice is the form a transitive verb takes to indicate whether the subject of the sentence acts (active voice—"The dog chased the cat") or is acted upon (passive voice—"The cat was chased by the dog.") Voice has nothing to do with the verb tense or with whether the subject is animate or inanimate (inanimate subjects can act, too), so do not confuse passive voice with past tense or automatically associate it with inanimate subjects.

- A tornado *uprooted* a tree in our backyard. (past tense, active voice)
- A tree in our backyard was *uprooted* by a tornado. (past tense, passive voice)
- We *are washing* the windows. (present tense, active voice)
- The windows *are being washed* by us. (present tense, passive voice)
- Dust *covers* everything in West Texas. (present tense, active voice)
- Everything in West Texas *is covered* by dust. (present tense, passive voice)
- The teacher *will insist* on more class participation. (future tense, active voice)

- More class participation *will be insisted* upon by the teacher. (future tense, passive voice)

As you can see, active and passive voice are well named. In the active voice, the subject acts: "A tornado uprooted." "We are washing." "Dust covers." "The teacher will insist." In the passive voice, the subject is acted upon: "A tree in our backyard was uprooted." "The windows are being washed." "Everything in West Texas is covered." "More class participation will be insisted upon." The passive is followed by some form of the verb *be* followed by the past participle of the main verb. The form of *be* depends on the verb tense: "*was* uprooted," "*are* being washed," "*is* covered," "*will* be insisted."

Although both active and passive voice are grammatically correct, we normally write and speak in the active for one good reason: we are explaining what does what to what. Therefore, in the core we place the actor before the action and the action before the object:

- The *panda ate* the *bamboo.*
- *We declined* my sister's *invitation* to dinner.
- The *Jordan Valley produces 75 percent of Israel's crops*.
- By a margin of 3 to 1, the *Senate approved* the President's *proposal*.

At times, though, the passive voice is effective—when the object of the action is more important than the actor, when the actor is obvious, irrelevant, or unknown, or when the actor should be concealed.

We find the passive voice useful in emphasizing the receiver of an action by making it the subject and in downplaying the actor by making it the object or by leaving the actor out of the sentence completely. In an article about one of Japan's major research centers, the author maintains focus on the center by using the passive voice:

> One place where Japan's fabled planning and people have not come together successfully is, ironically, Tsukuba Science City, *which was set up* precisely to catalyze the next leap forward of Japanese science.
>
> Currently the site of Science Expo '85—the fascinating high-tech world's fair demonstrating Japanese science and its applications today and tomorrow in marvelous fashion—*Tsukuba Science City was conceived* some two decades ago *by the Japanese government* to bring together some of the best minds in the public and private sector in a city devoted to scientific research and application.[3]

The italicized passive voice constructions emphasize the city and deemphasize the actors, in the first instance by leaving the actor out and in the second by making the actor the object.

Sometimes the action or the object of the action is so important and the actor is so unimportant that the actor is not indicated:

- The *results have been duplicated* in dozens of experiments.
- The *candidate has been convinced* to change her mind.
- Many *chromosomal abnormalities can be identified* before birth.
- Zacharius Jannsen is one of several Dutch spectacle makers *who is credited* with the invention of the compound microscope.
- The *letter was mailed* last week.

There are also times when the actor is unknown or irrelevant:

- My *uncle was mugged* in the airport parking lot.
- The *concentrated hydrochloric acid was poured* into the water.

As these examples show, in some cases the passive voice can be the simplest, most normal, and appropriate way of stating things. Unless the actor needs to be identified, none of these sentences would be improved if it were written in the active voice.

The chief problems with the passive voice come when the actor is not identified but should be or when the statement is awkwardly and pointlessly passive. These sentences are indirect and imprecise because the actor is not indicated:

- *Amplification* of the RF signal *is provided*.
- *Selection* of the new manager *will be made* before the end of the month.
- *A decision has been made* to require all employees to purchase parking permits.
- *It was recommended* that *a late fee of $20 would be assessed* for bills not paid by the end of the month.

The need for the identity of the actor in these sentences is easy to see. Readers can not identify who or what provided or selected or decided or recommended or would assess. We can indicate the actor either by specifying the actor in a *by* phase after the verb or by writing the sentence in the active voice, making the actor the subject of the sentence:

- Amplification of the RF signal is provided *by the FET-1 transistor*.
  The FET-1 transistor amplifies the RF signal.
- The new manager will be selected *by the district supervisor* before the end of the month.
  The district supervisor will select the new manager before the end of the month.

- A decision has been made *by the Board of Directors* to require all employees to purchase parking permits.
  The Board of Directors has decided to require all employees to purchase parking permits.
- It was recommended *by the accounting department* to assess a late fee of $20 for bills not paid by the tenth of the month.
  The accounting department recommended to assess a late fee of $20 for bills not paid by the first of the month.

As long as the actor and the object of the action are identified in the sentence, both active and passive voice express the same thing. As the grammatical subject is the most important element in the sentence, you must decide which you want to emphasize—the actor or the receiver of the action—and make it the subject. See also pages 207–208.

Avoiding Nounspeak

Less easy to see than the unnecessary passive, but perhaps even more disturbing to readers, is the awkward and pointless passive voice construction that we studied earlier:

> The amplification of the RF signal is provided by the FET-1 transistor.

The problem is the unnecessary practice of what grammarians call *nominalization*, making a verb into a noun. We actually mean the overuse of nominalization—the habitual expressing of action in nouns instead of in verbs: nounspeak. In the example, the subject *amplification* is such a noun, derived from the word *amplify*. Consider these sentences: "The FET-1 transistor amplifies the RF signal" or "The RF signal is amplified by the FET-1 transistor" is much more direct than "The amplification of the RF signal is provided by the FET-1 transistor." The first version is the easiest to grasp because it follows the what-does-what-to-what pattern. The second version, though in the passive voice, is still fairly easy to follow because the action—*amplify*—is expressed in the verb. The third version—"Amplification of the RF signal is provided by the FET-1 transistor"—is the most difficult to read for those reasons: it contains more words, it makes the verb-turned-noun *amplification* the subject (instead of the *RF signal* or the *FET-1 transistor*), and it uses the colorless and abstract *provides* instead of *amplifies* as the verb.

One of the most frequent charges against bureaucratic prose and jargon is the overuse of the passive voice, nominalization, and abstract verbs. However, their overuse can make any writing wordy, stagnant, and boring. Note the stodginess of the following sentences:

- Refinishing my grandfather's trunk is what I did last week.
- Substitution of margarine for butter should not be made.
- Announcement of Joe's arrival was provided by a note on my door.
- There is resistance among the landowners to the proposed zoning change.

The use of passive voice, nominals, and abstract verbs can be carried to such an extreme that the writer seems to lose all sense of the concrete reality being discussed. Can you imagine reading about "Provision of property protection is supplied by an electronic security system"?

Most readers find these kinds of sentences hard to read, because the action is stated indirectly. They have to identify the action of the sentence by finding the "real" verb that is masquerading as a noun and serving as the subject of the sentence. In effect, they have to change the nominal into a verb. But even when readers have little difficulty spotting the action and translating the nominal into a verb, they regard this kind of language as pretentious and overly formal. Perhaps the best guide in speaking and writing is to use the words and sentence structures that we normally use in conversation. We can make these sentences more natural and readable by changing passive voice to active, changing nominals to verbs, and getting rid of abstract verbs like *did, made, provided, supplied, occurred*, and *performed* and expletives ("dummy" subjects like *there is* and *there are*). Fortunately, these changes are easy to make.

- I refinished my grandfather's trunk last week.
- Margarine should not be substituted for butter.
- A note on the door announced Joe's arrival.
- Landowners are resisting the proposed zoning change.
- An electronic security system protects property.

These sentences now sound like they were spoken by somebody you might enjoy listening to, not by somebody reading a formal announcement to you.

Knowing what constitutes good sentence structure and effective use of verbs helps you write clear and effective sentences. As we mentioned at the beginning of this chapter, you should not be overly concerned with getting draft sentences exactly right. But when revising, you should ask these questions of each sentence:

- Is the sentence core easy to spot?
- Is the verb mood appropriate?
- Are active and passive voices used appropriately?
- Are the verbs direct and forceful?

Only when the answer to these questions is "yes" can you be sure that your sentences will be read with ease.

1. Underline the core of each sentence and identify the elements of the core that are modified.

a. While waiting for warm water, Frank brushed his teeth.

b. The temperature was 90°F, with humidity to match, as I concentrated on the target.

c. As you read your rough draft, read it aloud, so you can hear the words, the rhythm, and the tone.

d. Many Americans who otherwise support nuclear power claim that the lack of a credible waste program is, for them, the fatal flaw in the U.S. nuclear program.

e. Uncle Frank, who was a Navy pilot, collects the stamps of those countries over which he once flew.

2. Rewrite each sentence by adding information to the core. Write several versions of each sentence—one that modifies the subject, one that modifies the predicate, and at least one that modifies both.

a. They cheered.
b. Mother stood in the doorway.
c. The teacher faced the class.
d. It is still too soon to know for sure.
e. The importance of coal becomes apparent.
f. Edward VIII's coronation was scheduled for May 12, 1937.
g. My roommate could be courteous.
h. The ball popped into the catcher's mitt.
i. Lynn and I reached the bus.
j. The guests had garnered an evening full of memories.

3. The following sentences contain transitive verbs. All have passive voice verbs and some also have active voice verbs. Identify the voice of the verbs, discuss their effectiveness, and decide in what circumstances the passive or the active voice might be more effective. Rewrite ineffective passive voice verbs so they are in the active voice. Be prepared to justify your decisions in class discussion.

a. It is estimated by the American Medical Association that in the past ten years more than 10,000 nurses have gone into business for themselves.

b. V. M. Molotov served as Soviet Foreign Minister during and after Stalin's regime and was ousted from power by Nikita Khrushchev in 1957.

c. If Congress can be persuaded, a plan to establish a tall-grass prairie preserve will be approved next year.

d. Another problem is posed by the heat generated by waste canisters in salt domes.

e. If taken orally in tablet form, the drug can have serious side effects.

f. Ice cream has air whipped into it.

g. Every time Miriam was troubled by a critical review, she was bolstered by piles of fan letters from readers who had enjoyed her latest novel.

h. The streets of Belfast will be marched through by hundreds upon hundreds of men who are members of the Orange Order.

i. The tip of Manhattan Island was descended upon by nearly six million people during the relighting of the Statue of Liberty.

4. Rewrite each of the following sentences to make it more effective by doing one or more of the following:

Keeping the core together	Using active voice
Using appropriate verb mood	Avoiding nounspeak

a. If the car was repaired by Friday, we might get to Culver City by Sunday morning.

b. Clarification of the question was provided by the moderator.

c. The stock market, with a debate raging over whether the Federal Reserve Board would lower interest rates, was sharply lower.

d. The specimens are not to be shipped until approval is given by the chief technician.

e. If Overton Junior High School is closed or sold, or if it is converted into a special education center, neighborhood students would be bused across town.

f. Designation of the final sites for the nuclear waste site will be given by the Nuclear Regulatory Commission next month.

g. Students, faculty, and staff are by the Board of Regents invited to suggest amendments to the code of conduct of the college and also deletions.

h. Management of the project will be provided by the consulting firm.

i. By the Supreme Court's 7–2 ruling that administrators can suspend students for using vulgar language, a long-overdue boost was given discipline in the public schools.

j. A dozen mathematicians, some from universities generally considered leaders in mathematics and from countries such as Brazil, France, Poland, and Israel, have applied recently for visiting appointments in the university's Department of Mathematics, which is a clear recognition of the department's reputation in the mathematics community.

9

Paragraphs

The paragraph is one of the most easily recognizable conventions of writing. It is used to direct the attention of readers to the writer's grouping of related ideas and details. Centuries ago writers placed a special mark (¶ was often used) in the left margin to set off paragraphs. (The root word for *paragraph* is from the Greek *paragraphos, para* = "beside," *graph* = "to write.") Later, such marks fell into disuse, and now we generally "mark" a paragraph by indenting its first line and by ending its last line with the last word, even if it falls short of the right margin. The mark ¶ is still used as a proofreader's mark to indicate indentation for a new paragraph. "No ¶ " indicates that a paragraph indentation should be ignored.

When we compose paragraphs, we base our decisions partly on format considerations and partly on logical considerations. When we compose paragraphs based on format, we are concerned mostly with how they look on the page. In advertisements and in newspapers and popular magazine articles, where columns are narrow and readers scan the page quickly, paragraphs often run only two or three sentences long. Such short paragraphs are easy to read and look easy to read. When we shape paragraphs according to logic, we are concerned with qualifying and developing ideas and with establishing the connections among sentences in a paragraph. In formal essays and reports and in scholarly and professional books and journals, where columns are wider and readers expect fuller treatment of ideas, paragraphs are generally longer than two or three sentences but seldom longer than a dozen sentences.

There are, of course, situations in nonadvertising and nonjournalistic writing that can occasion one- and two-sentence paragraphs: when you need to separate speech of persons in dialogue, when you want to highlight a key point, when you choose to emphasize a transition from one part of a paper to another, or when you strive to create a particular rhythm more like speech rather than written prose. But when you are developing an idea or a point, most of your paragraphs should be more than two or three sentences long, because if an idea is worth introducing it is worth discussing at some length. The additional length is caused by the growth in meaningful details and use of analysis and interpretation to discuss ideas. A series of short paragraphs usually means that you have brought up points but have had little to say about them.

In this chapter, we are concerned primarily with the logical considerations of writing paragraphs that state and develop ideas—what can be regarded as "standard" paragraphs. We examine standard paragraphs as self-contained units and as parts of longer compositions. We also discuss those special occasions for the short paragraph—those containing one, two, or at the most three sentences.

The Standard Paragraph

If you study the work of any good writer, you will perceive what the standard paragraph accomplishes. Take as an example the following paragraph by John McPhee, a writer for *The New Yorker*. It illustrates how the standard paragraph is used to expand an important point, to illustrate an abstract idea, to channel thought, and to sharpen expression.

> When the Director of the National Park Service goes on a camping trip, survival in the wilderness is not an issue. His party on the Buffalo [River] consists of nine people, four of whom are professional riverman, paid to do all the work. One is a full-time cook, and he rides along in the "commissary boat," which is crammed to the gunwales with food. Mornings, the cook runs ahead, so that when lunchtime comes and the other boats catch up with him he has already set up a tent fly to create shade, a table and chairs are beneath it, and dozens of pieces of batter-dipped chicken are gurgling away in deep Ozark fat. At night, he fried multiple pork chops or big individual steaks and covers the meat with fried potatoes. His breakfasts compound cords of dark bacon with eggs and pancakes fried in bacon grease. The cook's name is Karl Hudson. He is not light on his feet. He has a mustache, and he seems to radiate anachronism. He could be a wax museum's idea of a cook in the Civil War. In fact, the whole campsite seems to be ready for Mathew Brady. The big iron skillet. The tall black coffeepot. The two wall tents. The fold cots. The canvas chairs. The tent-fly kitchen. The heavy iron skillet. The sledgehammer.[1]

Effective standard paragraphs usually resemble this one—the main idea is stated and the rest of the paragraph gets down to the particulars, the concrete examples and facts and figures that bring the idea alive. It's the way to expand a point beyond a couple of sentences. Well before the end of the paragraph the reader knows that "survival in the wilderness is not an issue," and that the director is not facing the wilderness with only a bag of nuts and raisins and a walking stick.

Two of the chief problems with an ineffective standard paragraph are that it does not carry enough detail to enable the reader to see what the writer is driving at or that it does not hang together well enough to make a unified point. Either problem is serious; both together are a menu for disaster. Here is an early draft of a paragraph on the impact of recent legislation on mainstreaming educable mentally retarded children. It shows what can happen when the writer does not provide or control the details to develop the main idea adequately.

> Regular classroom teachers and children have predominantly negative attitudes toward mentally retarded children. Class size as it relates to mainstreaming is very important. Teachers are highly skeptical about organizational aspects of the change in administrative leadership and support. Normal children cannot relate well to mentally retarded children.

Several things are wrong with this paragraph. The first sentence may be fine, but the rest of the paragraph is abstract and doesn't develop the first sentence, or at least does not clarify the relationship between the first sentence and the next three. Each sentence seems to be as general as the others, and although the sentences appear to relate to attitudes about mainstreaming mentally retarded children, the sentences seem to be isolated from one another. It is difficult to tell which way the writer should be steering. Because the paragraph begins with "Regular classroom teachers and children have predominantly negative attitudes toward mentally retarded children," the writer made a commitment to write about these negative attitudes, perhaps to specify the exact attitudes with details and to relate them more directly to the first sentence.

To find out more specifically what the draft paragraph lacks, study this revised version:

> Regular classroom teachers and children have predominantly negative attitudes toward mainstreaming mentally retarded children. Teachers are highly skeptical about how school administrators will implement mainstreaming and about how much and what kinds of support services they will receive. They are uncertain how to teach educable mentally retarded (EMR) students, believe that EMR students will disrupt their classrooms, and are concerned that EMR students will consume much valuable time in the classroom. Of particular importance to teachers is the ratio of normal children to mainstreamed children. They believe that the number of normal children in class should be reduced by several students for each mainstreamed student in class. Normal children, though less able than their teachers to state their concerns, view EMR students as different and often regard their behavior as bizarre.

The most striking differences between these two paragraphs are the specificity and unity of the revised paragraph. After reading the first draft, readers have only the vaguest notion of the issues. After reading the revised version, readers have a much better idea of what teachers and children are concerned about. The vague "Organizational aspects of the change in administrative leadership and support" is now identified as "how school administrators will implement mainstreaming and what kinds of support they [teachers] will receive." "Class size as it relates to mainstreaming" has been clarified as "the ratio of normal children to mainstreamed children." Additional specific examples have been included to explain the negative attitudes. Although this revised paragraph is no literary masterpiece, the commitment to the opening sentence and the interplay between abstract and specific ideas make it a more effective paragraph.

If there is anything resembling the gospel of the effective standard paragraph, it is that paragraphs should be unified, coherent, and developed. These three principles are the keys to writing good standard paragraphs. Unity and coherence are the opposite of disorder. Development is the opposite of incompleteness. Their contributions to the following brief paragraph are obvious:

> Changes taking place in Afghanistan are alarming in Kabul and Moscow. Glass, briquette, fruit-processing, textile, and fertilizer plants—once in full production—are now quiet due to lack of spare parts. Women, once quietly obedient behind their long veils, smuggle ammunition and gun parts past checkpoints. Bootless Afghan rebels who once earned Russian contempt for their slovenly appearance and homemade guns now drive captured Soviet armoured personnel carriers in the Hindu Kush. The main roads, which just four years ago were fine highways that linked major towns, are either closed because of sabotage or are unsafe to travel even in long, heavily armored convoys.

The first sentence states the main idea, that the changes taking place in Afghanistan are alarming to the governments in Kabul and Moscow. It is the statement to which everything in the paragraph relates, and it allows readers to know exactly what the topic is and to anticipate the nature of the supporting details to come. The paragraph has unity because the five sentences are about the idea stated in the first sentence.

The paragraph develops the main idea adequately by providing four specific examples of changes occurring in Afghanistan. Writers who really want to make a point give examples. They know that readers who can visualize something will comprehend it better and remember it longer. We have already seen how John McPhee gives us detail after detail to back up the general statement he makes at the beginning of the paragraph about the Director of the National Park Service going on a camping trip. Such details and examples make up most of a paragraph and they are probably the most interesting part of a paragraph. What brings the paragraph on changes in Afghanistan alive are the descriptions of closed plants, women smuggling ammunition and gun parts, bootless rebels driving captured vehicles, and closed highways.

The paragraph has coherence that is achieved primarily by the parallel structure of the sentences:

Subject	Predicate
"Changes"	"taking place"
"Glass, briquette, fruit-processing, textile, and fertilizer plants—once in full production—"	"are now quiet"
"Women, once quietly obedient, behind their long veils,"	"smuggle ammunition and gun parts"
"Bootless Afghan rebels"	"once earned Russian contempt for their slovenly appearance and homemade guns now drive captured Soviet armored personnel carriers"
"The main roads"	"just four years ago were fine highways that linked main towns, are either closed because of sabotage or are unsafe to travel even in long, heavily armed convoys"

The main parts of the standard paragraph are simple. They consist of several sentences organized around a controlling idea. Think of a paragraph as having three basic types of statements (according to their function in the paragraph).

- A *topic statement* that expresses clearly the main idea of the paragraph. It is called a topic statement because it states the topic or theme of the paragraph. This statement often appears at the beginning of the paragraph; it establishes logical unity by asserting the central point to be developed, proved, demonstrated, or analyzed.
- *Explanatory statements* that may do several things: clarify, qualify, restrict, or emphasize the topic statement or other statements; provide transitions or other information about how the paragraph relates to other paragraphs or how statements within the paragraph relate. These statements contribute to paragraph unity by highlighting the essence of the topic statement or by restricting the scope of the main idea. They contribute to coherence by guiding the reader through the interplay of the abstract thought of the topic statement and the varying degrees of concrete details that relate to it.

- *Illustration statements* that develop the topic sentence by presenting examples or illustrations; by citing facts, statistics, or other evidence; by quoting or paraphrasing others' comments on the idea expressed in the topic statement. These statements provide the development of the paragraph by offering the concrete material that backs up the main point of the topic statement. Most of the paragraph consists of illustration statements. Without them, the paragraph is undeveloped.

Of the three types, there may be more than one type in a paragraph. This is especially true of the explanatory and illustration statements. They may appear in any order in the paragraph but often in the order just listed—topic, explanation, illustration. We usually begin with a topic statement and then say more about it.

The simplest kind of paragraph has two levels of information: the topic statement expresses the main idea, and the illustration statements provide specific support to the topic statement. One way to write such a paragraph is to start with the "big" idea (see the italicized sentence in the example that follows) and then say more about it, like this:

> *The pressure on Japan to conform to the shifting political and economic needs of the United States has increased markedly in the last five years.* The Ford administration made explicit its desire for Japanese rearmament, and since that time a new U.S. strategic doctrine for the Pacific has evolved which casts Japan in the role of a forward maritime bastion in a new containment policy against the Soviet Union linked to the Chinese land mass. At a series of "economic summits" Japan was first persuaded to adopt policies aimed at pulling the United States and Western Europe out of a slump by increasing imports . . . then urged to salvage the inefficient industries of its trading partners by reducing its more competitive exports. In December 1979, at the beginning of the hostage crisis, the United States rebuked Japan for buying up Iranian oil at exorbitant prices. In 1980 Japan was pressed to join the United States in economic sanctions against Iran and to boycott the Moscow Olympic games.[2]

Beginning with the topic statement has advantages for both you and the reader. It keeps the main idea before you and keeps you from wandering from it. It lets readers know at once what the paragraph is about and guides them in their reading.

Even certain kinds of verse stanzas seem to follow this simple paragraph structure. For instance, when John Keats opens "The Eve of St. Agnes," he evokes the sense of coldness by stating that it was bitter cold (this is the topic statement). He then produces several images to reveal just how cold it was (these are the illustration statements):

> St. Agnes Eve—Ah, bitter chill it was!
> The owl, for all his feathers, was a-cold;

The hare limp'd trembling through the frozen grass,
And silent was the flock in woolly fold:
Numb were the Beadsman's fingers, while he told
His rosary, and while his frosted breath,
Like pious incense from a censor old
Seemed taking flight for heaven, without a death,
Past the sweet Virgin's picture, while his prayer he saith.

Keats' verse paragraph (this particular type is called a Spenserian stanza) is structured identically like the prose passages you read about alarming changes in Afghanistan and United States pressure on Japan: the main idea is stated, followed by specific details.

Sometimes you may want to place the topic statement in a position other than at the beginning. When it is withheld until the end, the topic statement may achieve the effect of climax, forcefully revealing the point of the whole paragraph. This is the case in this example:

> The financial editor worked at a desk directly behind my own. One night when I was working exceptionally late, he came in slightly unsteady from drinking. He emptied into a suitcase the contents of his locker, a few books, a batch of clippings, a pair of golf shoes. I asked in surprise if he was leaving. He said: "I've been on this paper eighteen years, son. I've just been fired by a guy I used to teach where to put commas." He staggered out, leaving me with a sick, hollow feeling in the pit of my stomach and a dark light dawning in my head. Innocence departed. Life, it seemed, was a relentless, never-ending battle; one never "arrived"; loyalty, achievement, could be forgotten in a moment; a single man's whim could ruin one. I began to take stock of the situation and discovered that the men who got to the top, no matter how long they stayed there, were nearly all men who had studied in universities, who knew something besides the routine of their own desks. *It was fear as much as anything else that drove me to college, purely personal ambition as much as curiosity about the world I lived in and what had made it the way I found it to be.*[3]

A more complex kind of paragraph has all three levels of information—usually a topic statement, one or more statements that clarify the topic statement, and statements that provide specific illustrations. This kind of paragraph is most effective when the main idea needs further comment before it is developed with specific illustrations. In these situations, the abstract thought of the topic statement and the concrete illustrations may need linking, or the reader may simply need to pause on the abstract level a bit longer than usual before moving to the particulars. Here is an example showing the three levels: the second and third sentences lobby a bit for the topic statement. The theme is that Churchill's *The*

Second World War is an autobiography, not a scientific history—an idea that the writer senses is controversial.

> Sir Winston Churchill's six-volume *The Second World War* is really an autobiographical record. He himself says it is "the story as I knew and experienced it as Prime Minister of Defence of Great Britain." Therefore it cannot be called anything like a complete history of the war. For example, Churchill tells the story of one of the crucial events of this century—the reduction of Japan to impotence and surrender by intensive bombardment culminating in what he calls the "casting" of two atomic bombs—in only eight pages, while a greater amount of wordage is devoted to a reprint of a broadcast he made to British listeners on VE day.[4]

Sometimes the unity of multiple-level paragraphs is emphasized when the writer begins and ends with topic statements, as Norman Cousins does in this paragraph:

> *Professional athletes are sometimes severely disadvantaged by trainers whose job it is to keep them in action.* The more famous the athlete, the greater the risk that he or she may be subjected to extreme medical measures when injury strikes. The star baseball pitcher whose arm is sore because of a torn muscle or tissue damage may need sustained rest more than anything else. But his team is battling for a place in the World Series, so the trainer or team doctor, called upon to work his magic, reaches for a strong dose of butazolidine or other powerful pain suppressants. Presto, the pain disappears! The pitcher takes his place on the mound and does superbly. That could be the last game, however, in which he is able to throw a ball with full strength. The drugs didn't repair the torn muscle or cause the damaged tissue to heal. What they did was to mask the pain, enabling the pitcher to throw hard, further damaging the torn muscle. *Little wonder that so many star athletes are cut down in their prime, more the victims of overzealous treatment of their injuries than of the injuries themselves.*[5]

This ten-sentence paragraph contains 194 words. It is long enough to benefit from having its underlying design emphasized. Restating the topic at the end emphasizes the logical wholeness of the paragraph and the rounded development of the main idea. Repeating the main idea at the end also punches home the most important point.

When more than one aspect of a topic is covered in a paragraph, the topic statement can be used to forecast the aspects to be developed. The following paragraph starts with a topic statement that anticipates the subsequent discussion of two characteristics of daylilies—their sturdiness and their many uses:

> The yeomen of the garden, daylilies are unbelievably sturdy and accommodating. Sun or shade, wet soil or dry, anything suits them. They don't attract pests and are never sick. Moreover they are edible, and in Asia where they originated, a veritable pharmacopoeia. The product called gum-yum or gum-tsoy, sold in Chinatowns, is daylily blossoms steamed and used like okra to thicken soups. (Fresh, they can be dipped in batter and fried.) In late spring, the tender heart of the plant can be blanched like asparagus or eaten raw, and the raw young roots are said to be excellent. Since they are also used as a diuretic (not to mention a cure for piles, dropsy, jaundice and other ailments), I have hesitated to try them. But there is something engaging about a plant with so many dimensions, so bent on giving good value.[6]

In addition to emphasizing unity by framing a paragraph with beginning and ending topic statements or with a forecasting topic statement, you will want to work carefully at creating coherence by using connecting devices to join the thoughts of the paragraph unmistakably together. Coherence in structure makes it easy for the reader to move from sentence to sentence.

Because you have already developed a sense of statement and elaboration, your topic statements and illustration of the main idea probably occur naturally in your writing. But because the connections between your thoughts are usually clearer in your mind than in the reader's, you may have to work consciously in revision to make the connections explicit. The beauty of these explicit connecting devices is that even though you have constructed them painstakingly, their effect is probably unnoticed by the reader. Nevertheless, it is they that make the paragraph easy to read. And even when the connections show, they are not useless mechanical devices. They are parts of the organizational design and content of your writing.

Among the explicit connecting devices are pronoun references, repetition of key words or phrases, transitions, parallel structure, and arrangement of details in an orderly fashion. These devices create threads of continuity that connect everything into a unified, coherent whole.

Pronouns substitute for nouns and must refer to nouns that either precede or follow them. Thus, a noun-pronoun chain naturally connects phrases and sentences. In the following paragraph, the author describes what the responsibilities of registered nurses were at the beginning of the twentieth century. Notice how the nouns *nurse* and *nurses* are connected with *she, her*, and *they*:

> In addition to the routine, workday schedule, the *nurse* was responsible for responding to all calls from the patients, and it was expected that *she* would do so on the run. *Her* rounds, scheduled as methodical progressions around the ward, were continually interrupted by these calls. It was up to *her* to evaluate each situation quickly: a sudden abdominal pain in a typhoid patient might signify

intestinal perforation; the abrupt onset of weakness, thirst, and pallor meant intestinal hemorrhage; the coughing up of gross blood by a tuberculous patient was an emergency. Some of the calls came from neighboring patients on the way to recovery; patients on open wards always kept a close eye on each other: the man in the next bed might slip into coma or seem to be dying, or be indeed dead. For such emergencies the *nurse* had to get word immediately to the doctor on call, usually the intern assigned to the ward, who might be off in the outpatient department or working in the diagnostic laboratory (interns of that day did all the laboratory work themselves; technicians had not yet been invented) or in his room. *Nurses* were not allowed to give injections or to do such emergency procedures as spinal punctures or chest taps, but *they* were expected to know when such maneuvers were indicated and to be ready with appropriate trays of instruments when the intern arrived on the ward.[7]

A second device is the repetition of key words and phrases, which, like nouns and pronouns, occur naturally in writing. In the following paragraph, the author uses several key words or synonyms to focus on the two key subjects—the pull-back dolly shot of a mobile camera and the main character of a movie about a child growing up in the wild:

The pull-back dolly is a way of revealing previously withheld information, and often it is used to establish an important detail before moving back to explore its larger implications. In Truffaut's *The Wild Child (L'enfant sauvage)*, for instance, we see a hunting party with a pack of hounds pursuing a terrified twelve-year-old child through the wilderness. The naked boy is covered with filth and weeds—more animal than human. In desperation, the creature scrambles up a tall tree to hide. Truffaut shows us a close-up of his face: panic-stricken, exhausted, his eyes darting furtively from side to side. Then the camera begins to zoom out slowly, and as it does, the boy is swallowed up by the dense foliage of the tree. The zoom stops at an extreme long shot and the boy is now a microscopic speck on the screen. In effect, the backward movement embodies eight years of history, for we later learn that the child was abandoned at the age of four, and miraculously survived, growing up virtually as an animal in the forest.[8]

The "pull-back dolly" shot is discussed further in terms of "the camera begins to zoom out slowly," "zoom stops at an extremely long shot," and "backward movement." The terms describing the wild child vary from "the twelve-year-old child," "the naked boy," "the creature," "the boy," "him," and "the child."

Transitions (from the Latin *transitio*, meaning the act of getting across) do not occur as naturally in writing as do related nouns and pronouns and repeated key terms. However, because transitions are important for showing logical relationships between sentences, you will have to insert them to help readers follow your discussion. Transitions are a little like our thumbs in that we don't realize their value until we don't have them. Study this well-written paragraph, from which we have removed the transitions:

> There is no such thing as fitness per se with regard to military service. Fitness must always be defined in terms of a particular combat situation. The armed forces find it necessary to revise the physical standards of health at frequent intervals, in order to keep them in tune with the changing requirements of military service. With propeller-driven aircraft, there were many situations in which survival depended on strength of arm and limb. The pilot of a fighter airplane in World War II had to watch for enemies in the sky by direct visual perception. His head swiveled from side to side looking to the rear. Calisthenics to develop neck muscles were part of training.

Here is the paragraph as originally written, with the transitions put back in and italicized:

> There is no such thing as fitness per se with regard to military service, *because* fitness must always be defined in terms of a particular combat situation. *In consequence*, the armed forces find it necessary to revise the physical standards of health at frequent intervals, in order to keep them in tune with the changing requirements of military service. With propeller-driven aircraft, *for example*, there were many situations in which survival depended on strength of arm and limb. *Moreover*, the pilot of a fighter airplane in World War II had to watch for enemies in the sky by direct perception. His head swiveled from side to side looking to the rear, *and for this reason* calisthenics to develop neck muscles were part of training.[9]

These transitions identify the relationship between successive thoughts. There are three cause-effect relationships in the paragraph. The first is signaled by *because* in the first sentence—it answers why "There is no such thing as fitness per se with regard to military service." The second, *in consequence* at the beginning of the second sentence, signals the cause-effect relationship between the first two sentences. The third, *and for this reason*, connects the two clauses in the last sentence. The *for example* in the third sentence lets the reader know that the sentence provides a specific detail to illustrate the thought that is contained in the second sentence. The first word of the fourth sentence, *moreover*, lets the reader know that a further example is provided and that the subject is not changing.

Good paragraphs have these kinds of transitions. Here is a partial list of transitions that you can use:

• To introduce another item in a series: *first, second, the third . . . , in the fourth place, next, then, moreover, furthermore, also, and, last.*

• To introduce an illustration or example: *for example, for instance, in particular, specifically.*

• To introduce a result or cause: *consequently, as a result of, thus, so, therefore, since, for.*

• To introduce a restatement: *in other words, that is.*

• To introduce a conclusion or summary: *in conclusion, finally, to sum up.*

• To introduce an opposing point: *but, however, on the other hand, nevertheless, on the contrary, still, in contrast.*

The fourth connecting device, parallel structure, is also used sometimes to emphasize the relationships of sentences. We have already seen on page 149 the repetition of sentence structure to emphasize the four points about changes in Afghanistan. The following paragraph, part of a passage explaining antimatter, compares the appearance and constrasts the behavior of antiwater and water:

> An atom of antioxygen linked with two antihydrogen atoms makes a molecule of antiwater. Many of them packed together will make an ocean of antiwater, and this ocean will be indistinguishable from ours. It will look the same; it will glisten in the sunlight the same and boil at the same temperature. Populated with antifish and anti-cabin cruisers, it will still look the same—until you jump in for a swim. Then both the water molecules in your body and an equal mass of antiwater will go up in an explosion that would dwarf a hydrogen bomb.[10]

To emphasize the similar appearances of water and antiwater, the writer repeats the same construction:

- "It will look the same;"
- "it will glisten in the sunlight the same"
- "[it will] boil at the same temperature."
- "it will still look the same—"

The fifth connecting device is the orderly arrangement of details. Most standard paragraphs follow a general to specific movement. However, a number of other classical writing strategies exist—among them, comparison, causal analysis, description, narration, and argument. Some of these strategies are illustrated in the sample paragraphs of this chapter, and we discuss them in more detail in Chapter 3, "Composing: Using Logic and Rhetoric." Orderly arrangement of details, along with noun-pronoun chains, repetition of key words, transitions, and parallel structure, help the writer to achieve a closely knit development of ideas and keep readers on track.

From the sample paragraphs so far, you can see that the standard paragraph has these features:

- It is formally displayed as a block of sentences. This allows readers to see it as a paragraph before reading it.
- Its central idea is expressed in a topic statement that usually comes early in the paragraph—most often in the first sentence, sometimes in the second.
- Its central idea is developed by several illustration statements. It has adequate length, usually more than three or four sentences (but seldom more than a dozen) to assure that something significant is said about the central idea.
- It contains devices that connect the sentences, allowing the thought to unfold efficiently.

Although these features suggest that the standard paragraph has a certain wholeness, this does not necessarily mean that writers always stay in the same paragraph until an idea is exhausted. Because readers concentrate on only seven to eight sentences before they start skimming, writers choose to divide a passage into several paragraphs.

The Paragraph as Part of a Larger Passage

Frequently, writers devote several paragraphs to an idea, with each paragraph making sense on its own but also serving as part of a larger passage. When this is the case, an additional feature is present—each paragraph hooks onto the paragraph before it and the paragraph after it to make the passage read smoothly.

A simple, yet effective hook is provided by a topic sentence that reminds readers of the idea that is running through several paragraphs. Notice how John McPhee divides the following passage on dermestid beetles into three paragraphs, indicating a break between what was just said and what is going to be said, yet keeping the paragraphs working as a single unit.

> Carol had about fifteen ecosystems going on at once in her twenty-by-twenty house. In the study, a colony of dermestid beetles was eating off the pelvis of an alligator. The beetles lived in a big can that once held forty pounds of mincemeat. Dermestids clean bones. They do thorough work. They all but simonize the bones. Carol had obtained her original colony from the Smithsonian Institution. One of her vaulting ambitions was to be able to identify on sight any bone that she happened to pick up. Also in the can were the skulls of a water turkey, a possum, and a coon.

The beetles ate and were eaten. Carol reached into the colony, pulled out a beetle, and gave it to her black-widow spider. The black widow lived in a commercial mayonnaise jar. Carol had found her in the basement while cleaning it up for Big Man. The spider's egg was getting ready to hatch, and when it did thousands like her would emerge into the jar. Efficiently, the black widow encased the beetle in filament gauze that flowed from her spinnerets.

Carol had fed dermestids to her turtles. She had three galvanized tubs full of cooters and sliders, under a sun lamp. "They need sun, you know. Vitamin D." She fed dermestids to her spotted salamander, and to her grey tree frog. Yellow spots, polka dots on black, the salamander's coloring was so simple and contrasting that he appeared to be a knick-knack from a gift shop, a salamander made in Japan. The tree frog lived in a giant brandy snifter, furnished with rocks and dry leaves. With his latex body and his webbed and gummy oversize hands, he could walk right up the inside of his brandy snifter, even after its shape began to tilt him backward, then lay a mitt over the rim and haul himself after and walk down the outside. He could walk straight up a wall; and he did that, while digesting his beetle. He had been with Carol three years. He was a star there in her house. He had the brandy snifter. It was all his and would be as long as he lived.[11]

This passage would communicate without its paragraph divisions, but it communicates better as paragraphed because it serves McPhee's intent well by dividing the passage into three blocks of information—each elaborating on the dermestid beetles' roles in the ecosystem in Carol's house. The *beetles* in the third sentence and *Dermestids* in the fourth sentence of the first paragraph, the *beetles* in the opening sentence of the second paragraph, and the *dermestids* in the opening sentence of the third paragraph tie in with *dermestid beetles* in the second sentence of the first paragraph to maintain a continuous focus.

In passages that present tightly organized arguments, the topic-statement hooks are even more important. In offering an interpretation of Ernest Hemingway's "The Snows of Kilimanjaro," the writer's use of topic statements in five successive paragraphs marks off the sequence of thought and controls the reader's focus on the argument. Here are the paragraph openers:

Although Caroline Gordon and Allen Tate object to Hemingway's use of snow-covered Kilimanjaro as a symbol of death, claiming it "does not operate as a controlling image" and it "seems something the writer has tacked on, rather than an integral part of the story," it is my contention that the snow-covered western summit does serve as symbol. . . .

Hemingway frequently uses whiteness in connection with the death of his central characters. . . .

In "The Snows of Kilimanjaro" whiteness again attends death; it is the whiteness of Harry's fatal infection, the unusual whiteness presented in Harry's fatal infection, and the weird aura of whiteness in Harry's reveries which officiate over his death. . . .

As Harry passes through a series of reveries toward death, whiteness appears with increasing recurrence and persistence: the more intense Harry's reveries become, the more obvious the whiteness. . . .

The many instances in which Hemingway associates whiteness with the death of his central characters, and particularly the frequent and persistent use of whiteness to accompany Harry's trip to death, make it clear that Hemingway was fully conscious of his symbolic use of the white snows of Kilimanjaro. . . .

Five major points, five topic statements, and five paragraphs. The first sentence states the main idea of the passage, exactly as a topic statement states the main idea of a paragraph. The second sentence is the topic statement of a paragraph that contains several examples of whiteness associated with the deaths of main characters in other Hemingway stories. The next two sentences are topic statements for the discussion of "The Snows of Kilimanjaro." The last sentence restates the main idea more forcefully in light of the evidence presented in the three previous paragraphs.

The techniques we have discussed so far are ways that you can achieve development, unity, and coherence in paragraphs. To conclude this chapter, we look at a very special kind of paragraph—the very short paragraph that sets off material for emphasis.

The Short Paragraph

Isolating an idea in a one- or two-sentence paragraph calls special attention to it. The structure encourages readers to stare at it for a moment. It is sort of like a bump in a smooth road: everybody notices it. The shorter the paragraph, the bigger the bump, so use the short paragraph sparingly and only for a purpose. The short paragraph can be used explicitly to indicate the topic or purpose of a passage, to provide readers with cues about how material is organized, and to emphasize or dramatize important information. It will take some trial and error to learn when to use the short paragraph, but we discuss its use and overuse with the examples that follow.

A short opening paragraph provides an emphatic way to declare purpose:

This section explains the importance of quality assurance specialists and examines the changes that may occur in the quality control field within the next decade.

This is a serviceable, if not very imaginative, short paragraph purpose statement. But it gets the job done. Better is this two-sentence opening paragraph of James D. Watson and Francis Crick's first publication announcing their work on the structure of DNA:

> We wish to suggest a structure for the salt of deoxyribose nucleic acid (D.N.A.). This structure has novel features which are of considerable biological interest.[12]

The fame enjoyed by this sparse announcement may be due to the importance of Watson and Crick's discovery of the structure of DNA. But its effectiveness is due to the simple, direct, no-frills manner in which it introduces their then controversial hypothesis. It comes straight to the point.

A brief paragraph also helps readers understand how a passage will be organized or developed. The following paragraph illustrates this use:

> In the following pages, we'll tell you about the undeniable benefits of walking, how easy it is to get started, what kinds of shoes to wear, how you can measure your success, and where to go on a walking vacation.[13]

If the context of the passage is clear or if the passage is short, don't over elaborate on the organization scheme. But if an overview is needed to find the way through the passage, provide one. Far from providing too many cues to how passages are organized or developed, we think most writers provide too few.

Another situation in which a short paragraph is valuable is in highlighting a transition from one stage of a discussion to the next, as illustrated by these two examples:

> However, if nuclear power is desirable then what to do with the waste is a question that must be answered. In the next section we examine current methods and proposed methods for disposing radioactive waste.

> In addition to the string, woodwind, and brass sections, there is one more section to an orchestra—the percussion section.

The second paragraph in the next extract is a remarkable one-line assertion by Eldridge Cleaver that serves as a pivot between two longer paragraphs:

> After I returned to prison, I took a long look at myself and, for the first time in my life, admitted that I was wrong, that I had gone astray—astray not so much from the white man's law as from being a human, civilized—for I could not approve the act of rape. Even though I had some insight into my own motivations, I did not

> feel justified. I lost my self-respect. My pride as a man dissolved and my whole fragile moral structure seemed to collapse, completely shattered.
>
> That is why I started to write. To save myself.
>
> I realized that no one could save me but myself. The prison authorities were both uninterested and unable to help me. I had to seek out the truth and unravel the snarled web of my motivations. I had to find out who I am and what I want to be, and what I could do to become the best of which I was capable. I understood that what had happened to me had also happened to countless other blacks and it would happen to many, many more.[14]

Another occasion in which a short paragraph has enormous impact is in a passage where the main point is presented at or near the end. Notice the effect Robert Pirsig achieves by setting off the last sentence of this passage as a separate paragraph.

> The real University. . . . has no specific location. It owns no property, pays no salaries and receives no material dues. The real University is a state of mind. It is that great heritage of rational thought that has been brought down to us through the centuries and which does not exist at any specific location. It's a state of mind which is regenerated throughout the centuries by a body of people who traditionally carry the title of professor, but even that title is not part of the real University. The real University is nothing less than the continuing body of reason itself.
>
> In addition to this state of mind, "reason," there's a legal entity which is unfortunately called by the same name but which is quite another thing. This is a nonprofit corporation, a branch of the state with a specific address. It owns property, is capable of paying salaries, of receiving money and of responding to legislative pressures in the process.
>
> But this second University, the legal corporation, cannot teach, does not generate new knowledge or evaluate ideas. It is not the real University at all. It is just a church building, the setting, the location at which conditions have been made favorable for the real church to exist.
>
> Confusion continually occurs in people who fail to see this difference. . . . and think that control of the church buildings implies control of the church. They see professors as employees of the second University who should abandon reason when told to and take orders with no backtalk, the same way employees do in other corporations.
>
> They see the second University, but fail to see the first.[15]

A one-sentence final paragraph has enormous impact, so the statement it contains must be important. If the idea were less important, it would not merit a separate paragraph. If an important piece of information is already clear or if a key point is already obvious, don't belabor it until the reader is no longer eager to read on.

Each of the short paragraphs in our examples could have been incorporated into another paragraph. However, when your instinct tells you that you are making *the crucial point* in a passage, be bold enough to use the technique.

Exercises

1. In each of the following standard paragraphs, identify the topic statement, evaluate the appropriateness of the examples that develop and support the topic statement, and identify the connecting devices that contribute to coherence.

A. Almost anything that an animal can employ to make a sound is put to use. Drumming, created by beating the feet, is used by prairie hens, rabbits, and mice; the head is banged by woodpeckers and certain other birds; the males of deathwatch beetles make a rapid ticking sound by percussion of a protuberance on the abdomen against the ground; a faint but audible ticking is made by the tiny beetle *Lepinotus inquilinus,* which is less than two millimeters in length. Fish make sounds by clicking their teeth, blowing air, and drumming with special muscles against tuned inflated air bladders. Solid structures are set to vibrating by toothed bows in crustaceans and insects. The proboscis of the death's-head hawk moth is used as a kind of reed instrument, blown through to make high-pitched, reedy notes.

—*Lewis Thomas, "The Music of this Sphere,"* The Lives of a Cell *(Toronto: Bantam Books, Inc., 1974) 24.*

B. But Laurel and Hardy films were far more controlled and far more tightly structured than the loose Sennett romps. Their films inevitably demonstrate the "snowball" principle that Bergson had developed in *Le Rire*. Like the snowball rolling down the mountain, the Laurel and Hardy film gathers greater and greater momentum, greater and greater bulk, as it hurtles toward the valley. Their films demonstrate the classic structure of farce—from Plautus to Feydeau: to begin with a single problem and then multiply that problem to infinity. Compared with the random movement of Sennett or the leisurely targets of Chaplin, the Laurel and Hardy films are very tightly structured indeed. If an auto gets dented in a traffic jam at the start of the film, every car on the highway gets stripped by the end of it; if a Christmas tree branch gets caught in a door at the start of a film, the tree, the house, the salesmen's car must be totally annihilated by the end of it; if the two partners have trouble with a few nails and tacks when starting to build a house, the film must inevitably end with the house collapsing into a pile of rubble. There is an insane yet perfect logic about the whole process.

—*Gerald Mast,* A Short History of the Movies, *4th ed. (New York: Macmillan Publishing Company, 1986) 119–20.*

C. Such wholesale invasions have caused the old guards in many communities to react by emphasizing the importance of ancestry. Throughout the Midwest, many of the towns staging centennial celebrations have been manipulating the occasions to exalt the families still in town whose ancestors happened to get there first. Elmstown was celebrating such a centennial during Holinghed's visit and he noticed that all the pageantry centered on old prominent families with Anglo-Saxon names. "Eventually," he says, "it became clear that the backers of the centennial were primarily interested in glorifying their own ancestry." People who had helped build the town after the pioneer era were not included.

—*Vance Packard,* The Status Seekers *(New York: David MacKay Company, Inc., 1959) 51.*

D. High-level waste can be divided into two main radioactive categories. Short-lived fission products are caused by the breakdown of uranium nuclei and are hazardous primarily for the first 1000 years of waste isolation. The long-lived transuranics (like plutonium, americium, and neptunium) are formed when the uranium nuclei absorb stray neutrons, and pose a problem for hundreds of thousands of years (see Figure 4-2). Though the transuranics are responsible for the long-term hazards of nuclear waste, the fission products account for most of the intense radiation and heat generated by the waste in the first few hundred years. When spent fuel is reprocessed, significant amounts of the transuranics are extracted, leaving the balance of the transuranics and the short-lived fission products as waste.

—*Michio Kaku and Jennifer Trainer,* Nuclear Power: Both Sides *(New York: W. W. Norton & Company, 1983) 112.*

E. What he found in that desert camp, that dry, hard land, set the anthropological world back on its collective ear. What his scale and his wristwatch and his systematic scribbles showed was that we were fooled, that we had it all wrong. To be a hunter and gatherer wasn't that bad after all. They didn't work that hard even in this land of thorns. For an adult it came to less time than a nine-to-five office worker puts in on the job. They lived a long time, too, didn't wear out and die young but odd-looking, as we had always thought. Even in this camp, the camp with the good hunting dogs, it was plants, not meat, which provided the staff of life. Women walked through the nut groves and collected nuts with their toes, dug in the molapos and sang to each other through the bush. Unlike the game, which spooked so easily and followed the unpredictable rains, the nuts, roots, and berries were dependable, there in plenty, there for the picking. Another distinguished anthropologist, Marshall Sahlins, terms those DBC 12 people "the original affluent society"—something quite different from the traditional conception of hunting and gathering as a mean, hard existence half a step ahead of starvation and doom.

—*John Yellen, "Bushman,"* Science 85 *May 1985: 44–45.*

2. In short papers the standard paragraph is the basic unit for developing one aspect of a thesis. It often has an opening that states the topic, several sentences that develop the topic statement, and sometimes ends with a wrap-up sentence. In these respects, the structure of the standard paragraph is similar to that of an entire paper. In this exercise we ask you to write a one-paragraph essay on one or more of the following topics as a way to improve your writing of both paragraphs and papers:

- The personality of my roommate
- Why I watch (or don't watch) Sylvester Stallone movies
- How to survive preregistration (or registration)
- The best (or worst) thing about the student center (or the library, dorm, or other facility on campus)
- Why I want to take an elective course in ____________

Write a topic sentence, and then develop it into a one-paragraph essay of approximately 250 to 400 words.

3. Choose one of the topic statements that you developed in Exercise 2 and regard it as a thesis for a short essay on the same topic. Write individual topic statements for three or four paragraphs that could be used to develop the topic.

10

Format

Format has three aspects:

1. the physical appearance of a paper—the shape, size, and general layout of material on the page;
2. the general arrangement of a paper into preliminary elements (title page, table of contents, and so on), main elements (introduction, body, and conclusion, headings quotations, and so on), and back elements (appendixes, references, and so on); and
3. the form of documentation and graphics.

We discuss these three aspects of format in this chapter. Our suggestions and models—along with directions from your instructor—will help you prepare a paper that gives the impression that you care about your work and its appearance.

In creating attractive and useful format, you must pay particular attention to neatness, consistency, and detail. An attractive and useful format is important, because as a general rule readers consider sloppy, crowded, error-ridden manuscripts that have no discernible beginning, middle, and end indicative of sloppy, ill-conceived writing. Give your readers clean, double-spaced papers that are consistent and that highlight important information.

Physical Appearance of Your Paper

We recommend that you type or word process and print your out-of-class papers and reports. The mechanics of the typewriter and printer simplify such format matters as evenness of the left margin, the spacing of lines and words, and the shapes of letters and numbers. If you write out your papers by hand, achieving consistency and neatness in these matters is more difficult. However, if you do submit handwritten copy to your readers, you don't need to hand print the copy;

but be sure that your handwriting is legible and that the appearance of your papers approximate the format requirements discussed in this chapter. The items that must be considered in the physical appearance of your paper are the choice of paper, ribbon, and type, the margins of the page, the spacing and indenting of material, and the pagination.

Paper, Ribbon, and Type

The contrast of black text on white paper and clean, clear type contribute to easy reading. Faint type produced from a worn ribbon contributes to eye fatigue.

- Use white, unlined, 20 pound, 8½″ by 11″ paper.
- Use the same size sheets for all pages.
- Use the same typewriter or printer or at least the same type size and style for the entire paper.
- Use black type and a fresh ribbon.
- Do not use script or other unusual type.
- Make sure that the type is clean.
- Use a typewriter or printer that is in good working condition.
- If you use a dot matrix printer, be sure that the print is easy to read.

Margins

Ample margins (see Figure 10-1) frame the text with a border of white space, reducing peripheral distractions and allowing the paper to avoid an overcrowded appearance.[1]

- Leave one-inch margins at the top, bottom, and right and either a one-inch or one-and-a-half-inch margin at the left.
- Keep graphics within the page margins.
- The right margin does not need to be justified. If your typewriter or printer does not adjust space between words well, right justification can cause the page to have "rivers and lakes" of white space.

Spacing and Indenting

Along with faint type and excessively narrow margins, single-spaced text contributes to eye fatigue. Single-spaced text is crowded text, and it is nearly impossible for you or your teacher to edit. See Figure 10-1 for spacing and indenting requirements.

- If your typewriter or word processor has variable pitch (*pitch* refers to the number of characters per inch), for eye ease use 10-point pitch (that produces 10 characters per inch).

This is 10-point pitch.

This is 12-point pitch.

This is 15-point pitch.

If you are using a typewriter, use pica spacing (10 characters to an inch) instead of elite spacing (12 characters to an inch).

- Double-space throughout the paper, including titles, headings, quotations, and references.
- Begin paragraphs by indenting the first line five spaces from the left margin.

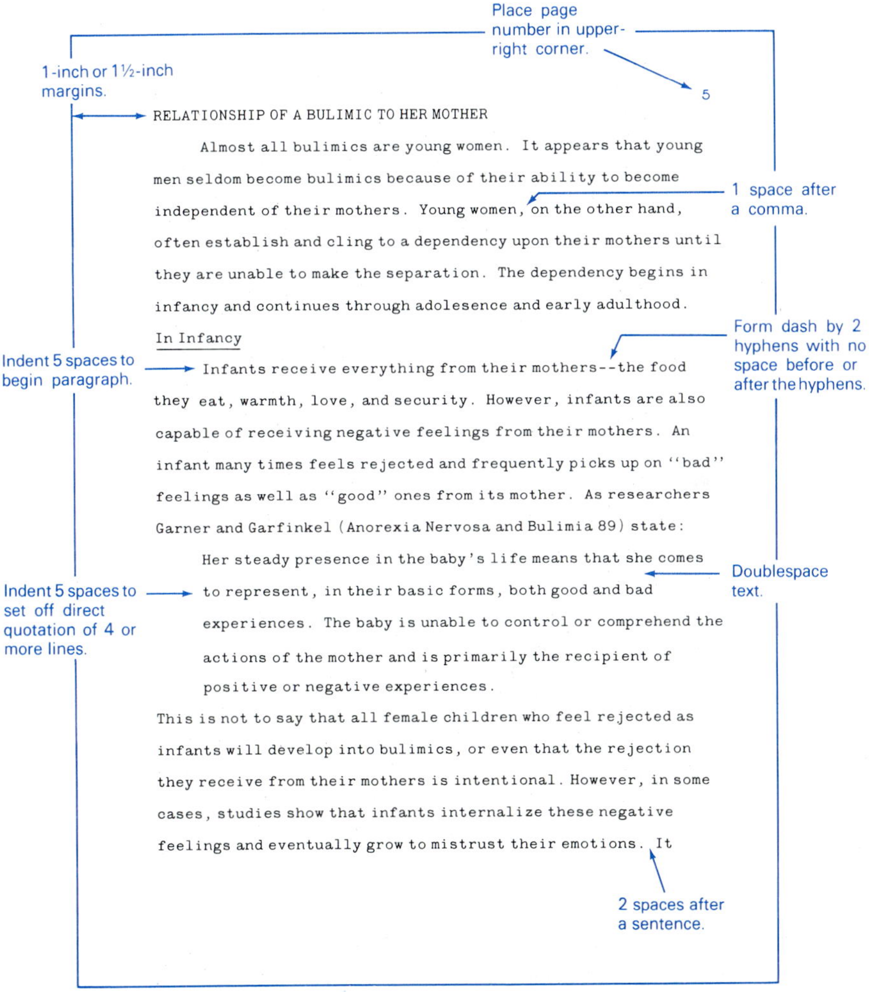

Figure 10-1 *Sample Page Format.*

- Set off lists by indenting five spaces from the left margin.
- Set off quotations longer than four lines by indenting ten spaces from the left margin. If the quotation begins a new paragraph, indent an additional three spaces. For emphasis, you may also set off shorter quotations in this way.
- Leave one space after a comma and after the period following a person's initials.
- Leave two spaces between sentences and after a colon and semicolon.

Pagination

Number each page, starting with the second page, to make cross-referencing easy and to prevent confusion in case the pages get out of order. (Count the first page, but it is not necessary to place the number "1" on it.)

- Place the page number—in arabic numerals—in the upper righthand corner of the page, one inch down from the top of the page and even with the right margin. See Figure 10-1.
- Number the pages consecutively to the end of the paper, including the appendix or appendixes and references (if your paper includes them).
- If your paper has preliminary pages (such as a title page and table of contents), number them in small Roman numerals (ii, iii, iv, and so on). The title page, if included, is counted as page i although it is not numbered. Center the page number for all other preliminary pages at the bottom of the page, two lines below the last line of type. See Figures 10-2, 10-3, and 10-6.

General Arrangement of Your Paper

As discussed in Chapter 4, "Composing: Planning, Writing, and Revising," overview statements, topic statements, transitions, and other devices display the organization of material and provide easy access for readers. Papers may also have these additional elements:

- Preliminary elements that serve as a guide to the contents and purpose of the paper, such as a title page, table of contents, and an abstract or synopsis;
- Main elements of the paper itself—introduction, body, and conclusion, and headings, quotations, and equations;
- Back elements that include a list of works cited and appendixes.

Check with your instructor to learn what is required.

Preliminary Elements

The preliminary elements that precede the main body of the paper include the title page, the table of contents, the list of illustrations, and the abstract. They appear in the order listed.

Title Page. A title page (Figure 10-2) shows the title of the paper, the author's name, and the date. It is counted as page i, but the number does not appear on the page.

Table of Contents. A table of contents (Figure 10-3) lists the sections and subsections of the paper. It is equivalent to an outline of the paper, but it gives the page number for each entry. Every heading in the paper appears in the table of contents in the same wording, capitalization, and punctuation (if any) as in the paper.

List of Figures or List of Tables. A list of figures or a list of tables should be included if more than three or four figures or tables are in the paper (Figures 10-4). A list of illustrations may be used to show the location of both figures and tables, if you subdivide the list into figures and tables (Figure 10-5). The wording, punctuation, and capitalization of each title in the list should agree with what is found on the illustration itself. The use of leader lines (the spaced periods leading from the title of each entry to its page number) aids the reader.

Abstract. An abstract, sometimes called a synopsis, is a very short summary of the paper (Figure 10-6). An abstract or synopsis condenses the essence of the paper so that the reader can understand the purpose and main ideas from reading the abstract alone.

Main Elements

The paper itself follows the preliminary elements and has an introduction, body, and conclusion and format devices that help package the material into easily readable form. In Chapter 4, we explain how to write the introduction, body, and conclusion (see pages 81–84). Now we consider format in handling headings and subheadings, quoted material, and equations and formulas. In later sections we explain the forms of documentation and graphics.

Headings and Subheadings. Headings and subheadings are labels within the text that allow readers to tell what is contained in a section or subsection. If you plan to use headings and subheadings, determine how many levels you need and be sure to give identical arrangement to headings of equal importance. If you include a table of contents, all headings must correspond exactly with the table of contents entries. (See Figure 10-7).

BULIMIA: THE SILENT EPIDEMIC

Submitted to

Dr. Don Rude

English 1302

by

Elizabeth Strickland

Theatre Major

December 9, 1985

Figure 10-2 *Sample Title Page.*

CONTENTS

ii

Figure 10-3 *Sample Table of Contents.*

LIST OF FIGURES

iii

Figure 10-4 Sample List of Figures.

LIST OF GRAPHICS

iii

Figure 10-5 *Sample List of Graphics.*

ABSTRACT

Bulimia is an emotional and psychological disorder suffered by young women victimized by America's cultural emphasis on thinness. Researchers find that the psychological make-up for a bulimic can begin to develop, in some cases, as early as infancy. These tendencies are nurtured into adolesence and eventually into adulthood, as women are subjected to a society that equates female worth with physical beauty and physical beauty is characterized by thinness. Hospitalization and outpatient therapy are usually the only means of rehabilitating victims.

iv

Figure 10-6 *Sample Abstract.*

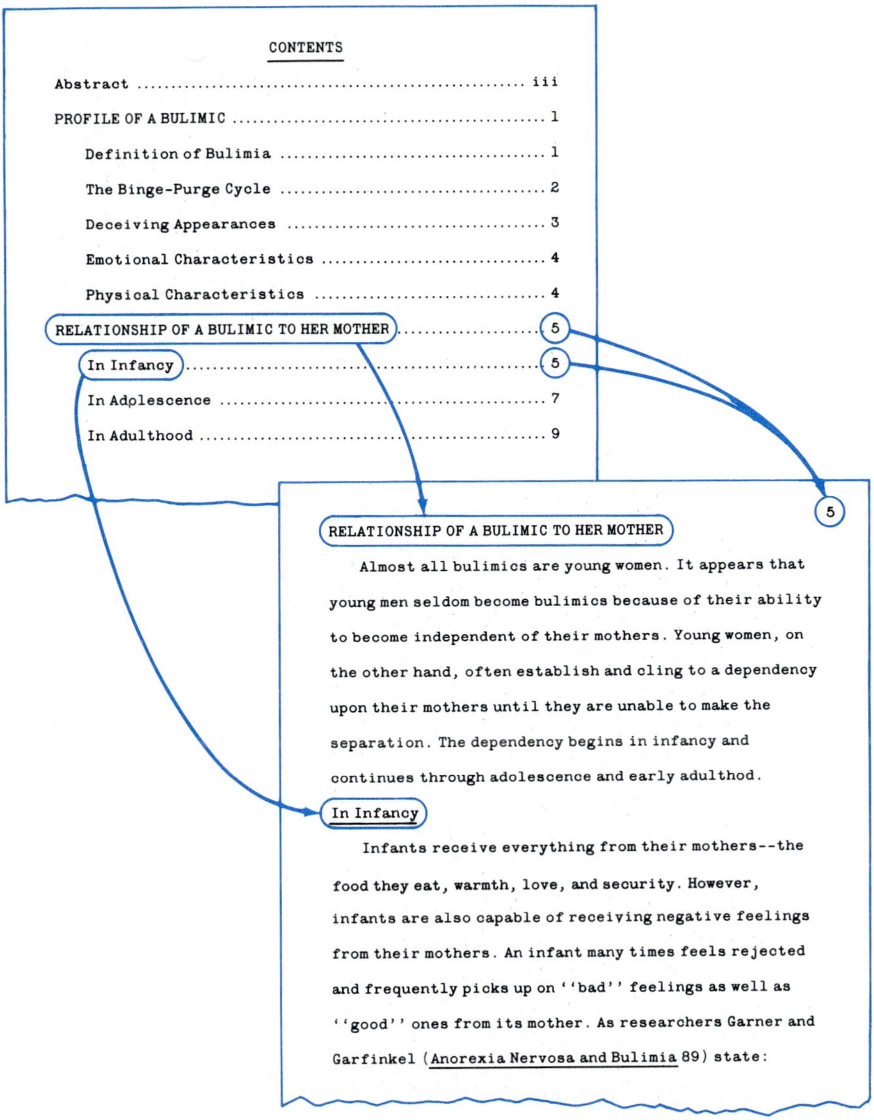

CONTENTS

Abstract iii

PROFILE OF A BULIMIC 1

Definition of Bulimia 1

The Binge-Purge Cycle 2

Deceiving Appearances 3

Emotional Characteristics 4

Physical Characteristics 4

RELATIONSHIP OF A BULIMIC TO HER MOTHER 5

In Infancy 5

In Adolescence 7

In Adulthood 9

5

RELATIONSHIP OF A BULIMIC TO HER MOTHER

Almost all bulimics are young women. It appears that young men seldom become bulimics because of their ability to become independent of their mothers. Young women, on the other hand, often establish and cling to a dependency upon their mothers until they are unable to make the separation. The dependency begins in infancy and continues through adolescence and early adulthood.

In Infancy

Infants receive everything from their mothers--the food they eat, warmth, love, and security. However, infants are also capable of receiving negative feelings from their mothers. An infant many times feels rejected and frequently picks up on ''bad'' feelings as well as ''good'' ones from its mother. As researchers Garner and Garfinkel (Anorexia Nervosa and Bulimia 89) state:

Figure 10-7 *Agreement of Table of Contents Entries and Headings in Text.*

- Center and type in all capital letters the title of your paper.

```
                    RADIATION RISKS IN PERSPECTIVE

     The average exposure received by nearby

inhabitants in the area of Three Mile Island. . . .
```

- Place first-level headings on the left margin and type in all capitals.

```
RADIATION RISKS IN PERSPECTIVE

     The average exposure received by nearby

inhabitants in the area of Three Mile Island. . . .
```

- Place second-level headings on the left margin, underlined. Capitalize important words and leave prepositions and articles in lower case.

```
Radiation Risks in Perspective

     The average exposure received by nearby

inhabitants in the area of Three Mile Island. . . .
```

- Indent five spaces for third-level headings and type in normal upper case and lower case, underlined. Place a period after the sub-heading and begin text of sub-subdivisions on the same line.

```
     Radiation risks in perspective. The average

exposure received by inhabitants in the area of Three

Mile Island. . . .
```

Quotations. Quotations of fewer than four typed lines are normally run into the text and enclosed in quotation marks.

```
     The "most orthodox article of literary faith,"

Macaulay announced in his essay on Milton, is the

belief that "the earliest poets are generally the best"
```

(_Essays_ 1: 206). Earlier, writing on Italian literature, he anticipated this announcement by claiming that "a rude state of society is that in which great original works are frequently produced" ("Criticisms on the Principal Italian Writers. No. I. Dante" 62). Macaulay's notion was that the imagination was strongest in rude or half-civilized societies and that poetry developed rapidly, reaching its height very early in a nation's cultural history, and then began to decline.

When a quotation of four or more typed lines is included in the text, set it off by a three-line space above and below the quoted material, indent ten spaces, and type it double-spaced without adding quotation marks.

The visual qualities of language were important to Macaulay because he regarded poetry as a visual affair. Great poetry was possible for him only with a relatively rude state of langugage, and, as he wrote in "Milton," it was inevitable that poetry would be more difficult to create as language developed:

> The progress of language, which was at first so favorable, becomes fatal to it, and instead of compensating for the decay of the imagination, accelerates that decay, and renders it more obvious (_Essays_ 1: 208-209).

Abstraction leads to what Macaulay called "philosophical" vocabulary that achieved the "generalisation . . . necessary to the advancement of knowledge" (Essays 1: 207).

Shorter quotations that are given special emphasis are formatted the same way.

Macaulay's close ties with the Whig party did not escape the notice of reviewers writing for Blackwood's, Fraser's, and The Quarterly Review or the Tory correspondents for The Times. Most of them wrote in essence what Leslie Stephen was to say later:

To define a Whig and to define Macaulay is pretty much the same thing (567).

When quoting two or more paragraphs, indent the first line of each paragraph.

John Clive, in an interesting discussion of what he calls Macaulay's "propulsive imagination," characterizes Macaulay's method of writing history as the "instinctive ability to propel inert facts into motion" (25) or propel himself into the historical context of his research. Two consecutive entries from Macaulay's journals for June 28 and June 29, 1849, record this ability:

After breakfast at the Museum, and sat till three, reading and making extracts. I turned over three volumes of newspapers and tracts--Flying Posts, Postboys, and Postman. I found some curious things which will be of direct service; but the chief advantage of these researches is that the mind is transported back a century and a half, and gets familiar with the ways of thinking, and with the habits, of a past generation.

The reign of William the Third, so mysterious to me a few weeks ago, is beginning to take a clear form. I begin to see the men, and to understand all their difficulties and jealousies.

For additional information about handling quotations—especially on the use of quotation marks with other punctuation, quotations within quotations, and ellipses to indicate omitted material—see "quotation marks" and "ellipses" in Chapter 12, "Conventions."

Equations and Formulas. Equations and formulas are symbolic representations of chemical or physical processes and mathematical relationships. Because they are specialized abstract statements, they should be used only if readers can understand them or if they are thoroughly defined.

Simple ones, such as these at the end of the following passage, are often run in the line of text:

> Galileo's plan may be clarified by an example. In the simple situation in which a ball is dropped from a person's hand one might speculate endlessly on *why* the ball falls. Galileo advised us to do otherwise. The distance the ball falls from its starting point increases as time elapses from the instant it is dropped. In mathematical language, the distance the ball falls and the time that elapses as it falls are called *variables,* because both change as the ball falls. Galileo sought some mathematical relationship between these variables. The answer he obtained is written today in that scientific shorthand known

as a formula. For our example, this formula is $d = 16t^2$. This formula states that the number of feet (d) that the ball falls in t seconds is 16 times the square of the number of seconds. For example, in 3 seconds the ball falls 16×4^2 or 256 feet, and so forth.[2]

Sometimes, for emphasis, simple equations or formulas are set off from the text:

He [Kepler] followed this lead, and after an amazing combination of mathematical and musical arguments, arrived at the law that if T is the period of revolution of any planet and D is its mean (or average) distance from the sun then

$$T^2 = kD^3$$

where k is a constant that is the same for all planets. (Note that the correct value of D is actually the semimajor axis of each elliptical path.)[3]

A sequence of important equations is set off from the text, and each equation is numbered in parenthesis or brackets flush with the right margin for later reference.

He [Galileo] discovered that if air resistance is neglected, all bodies falling to the surface of the Earth have the same constant acceleration a; that is, they gain velocity at the same rate, 32 feet per second each second. In symbols,

$$a = 32 \tag{1}$$

If the body is dropped—that is, merely allowed to fall from the hand—it will start with zero velocity. Hence at the end of 1 second its velocity is 32 feet per second; at the end of 2 seconds its velocity is 32 times 2 or 64 feet per second; and so forth. And the end of t seconds its velocity v is $32t$ per second; in symbols

$$v = 32t \tag{2}$$

This formula tells us exactly how the velocity of a falling body increases with time. It says, too, that a body that falls for a longer time will have a greater velocity. This is a familiar fact, for most people have observed that bodies dropped from high altitudes hit the ground at higher speeds than bodies dropped from low altitudes.

We cannot multiply the velocity by the time to find the distance that a dropped body falls in a given amount of time. This would give the correct distance only if the velocity were constant. Galileo proved, however, that the correct formula for the distance d the body falls in t seconds is

$$d = 16t^2 \qquad (3)$$

where d is the number of feet the body falls in t seconds. For example, in 3 seconds, the body falls 16×3^2 or 144 feet.

By dividing both sides of formula (3) by 16 and then taking the square root of both sides, we find. . . .[4]

For more information on specific methods of expressing equations and formulas, see a standard style guide, such as *The Chicago Manual of Style*[5] or *Mathematics into Type*.[6]

Back Elements

Back elements, which follow the main elements of the paper, may include a list of references and supporting material that is too detailed to include in the body of the paper. A list of works cited is illustrated in Figure 10-8. Material in appendixes may include a glossary (Figure 10-9), graphics, copies of correspondence, questionnaires, or other material that is an integral part of the paper but that is so detailed or long that it interrupts the flow of the paper. Graphics should closely pertain to the discussion they illustrate. However, long lists of information and tabulated data probably should be placed in appendixes. Designate multiple appendixes Appendix A, Appendix B, and so on.

Documentation

There are two major ways to document material derived from another work: (1) by numbered notes and (2) by parenthetical in-text citations and a list of works cited at the end of the paper. The second method is commonly used in short papers and in term papers. If you are not required to use a particular method, we suggest that you learn the forms based on *The MLA Style Manual*.[7] We use the first method in our own documentation for this book. The numbered notes are gathered together in "Chapter Notes" on pages 287–291. In this present section, we explain and give examples of the second, which consists of

- In-text citations, which identify the sources specifically so the reader can find full publication information in the list of works cited.
- A list of works cited at the end of the paper. These are arranged alphabetically, which provides the information necessary for the reader to locate each source cited.

19

WORKS CITED

Beumont, P.J.V. et al. "Body Shape Perception and Its Disturbance in Anorexia Nervosa." British Journal of Psychiatry 144 (1984): 167-71.

Cassino, T. and E. Sanger. "Eating Disorders: Avoiding the Power Struggle." American Journal of Nursing Jan. 1984: 31-33.

Cooper, P.J. and C.G. Fairborn. "The Clinical Features of Bulimia Nervosa." British Journal of Psychiatry 144 (1984): 238-46.

Garfinkel, P.E. and D.M. Garner. Anorexia Nervosa and Bulimia. New York: The Guilford Press, 1985.

---. Anorexia Nervosa: A Multidimensional Perspective. New York: Brunner/Maxel, Inc., 1982.

Katzman, M. and L. Weiss. "Group Treatment for Bulimic Women." Arizona Medicine: Psychiatric Disorders 41 (1984): 100-04.

Marks, R.G. "Anorexia and Bulimia: Eating Habits that Can Kill." R.N. Jan. 1984: 44-47.

Potts, N.L. "Eating Disorders: The Secret Patterns of Binge/Purge." American Journal of Nursing Jan. 1984: 32-35.

Roth. G. Feeding the Hungry Heart. New York: New American Library, 1983.

Wilson, C.P. "The Family Psychological Profile of Anorexia Nervosa Patients." The Journal of the Medical Society of New Jersey 77 (1980): 341-44.

Figure 10-8 *Sample List of Works Cited.*

21

GLOSSARY

Anorexia: The technical term for loss of appetite. Victims of anorexia nervosa actually fear the consequences of satisfying their appetite, fearing that they will become fat.

Basal metabolic rate: The rate at which energy is used in the body at complete rest, 12 to 14 hours after a meal. The energy used is needed primarily to maintain heartbeat, respiration, body temperature, etc.

Bulimia: The technical term for eating large quantities of food at one time, commonly referred to as "binge-eating" or "stuffing."

Digestibility: The proportion of food absorbed from the digestive tract into the bloodstream, normally 90 to 95%.

Evian water: A slightly mineralized water used as a diuretic.

Nutritional balance: That point in a diet in which the intake and output are balanced, e.g. nitrogen balance, calcium balance, etc.

Reference woman: An arbitrary physiological standard, defined as 25 years of age, 55 Kg weight, engaged in general housework, office or light industry work, using 2,300 calories per day, living in a temperature zone at a mean annual temperature of 10° C.

Figure 10-9 *Sample Glossary.*

When you cite works in your text, you must key them to the list of works cited at the end of your paper.

In-Text Citations

Here are examples of various types of in-text citations.

One Work by a Single Author. When the author's name appears as part of your sentence, cite only the page number or numbers in parentheses:

Williamson (114) studied the amount of time . . .

In pointing out the inadequacy of epidemiological studies of bronchogenic cancer risk in workers exposed to plutonium, Williamson states that "Unfortunately, the follow-up of workers following termination of employment in plutonium work has been limited to only a few special situations" (114).

Otherwise, place both the name and page number or numbers in parenthesis:

A recent study (Williamson 114) showed that. . . .

One Work by Two or Three Authors. When a work has two or three authors, cite all names:

Overcoverage by the media has contributed to the public perception that radiation is a major threat to its safety (Soo and Cartwright 74-75).

The only scientific evidence on the subject is a recent paper (Mitchell, Oglethorpe, and Robinson 13) that offers. . . .

One Work by More than Three Authors. When a work has more than three authors, include only the name of the first author followed by "et al." or "and others" for the others:

```
In a detailed study (Jenkins et al. 96-124)
commissioned by. . . .
```

Work by a Corporation or Organizational Author. When a work has a corporation or organizational author, cite the name of the corporation or organization as the author:

```
Wisconsin Power and Light Company (109) states. . . .
```

```
Further evidence (Institute for Energy Analysis 247-
250) shows that at least fifty percent. . . .
```

Work with No Author. When a work has no identifiable author, cite the title of the article or book as the author:

A simplified model will help explain this random

process ("Population Dose and Health Impact of the

Accident at Three Mile Island Nuclear Station" 88).

Critics of nuclear power (<u>Radiation and Humans</u> 573-792)

have charged. . . .

Authors with the Same Surname. If the list of works cited includes publications by two or more authors who have the same surname, include the author's initials in all in-text citations:

```
The Council on Economic Priorities (B. L. Cohen 82)
relies solely on industry performance data.
```

```
B. L. Cohen et al. (90) and G. I. Cohen (8-9) report
that the average capacity. . . .
```

Two or More Works within the Same Parentheses. Order the citations of two or more works in the same parentheses by following the same order in which they appear in the reference list. Separate the works by semicolons.

Several studies (Davis 125-135; Jones 45-52; Killingsworth 33-38) have called into question. . . .

Two or More Works by the Same Author(s). To cite one of two or more works by the same author(s), add the title of the work and the relevant page numbers:

Steadman ("Dosage Monitoring" 88-92) recommends. . . .

A recent study suggests . . . (Steadman, "Dosage Monitoring" 88-92).

Multivolume Works. When referring to a volume of a multivolume work, cite the volume number, followed by a colon, a space, and the appropriate page number or numbers:

The Nonproliferation Treaty is widely viewed by Third World countries as a hoax (Murillo 1: 60).

Personal Communications. Because personal communications such as telephone conversations, interviews, and personal correspondence normally are not included in the reference list, provide full information in the parenthetical citation:

The developers of nuclear power had too narrow a view of their task (J. W. Gofman, telephone interview, 5 April 1986).

However, a review of the accident also revealed that no one was injured (Mary Stevenson, letter to author, 21 May 1985).

List of Works Cited

The list of works cited at the end of your paper documents every work cited and provides the information necessary for the reader to retrieve each work. Each reference cited in your paper must appear in the works-cited list, and each entry in the works-cited list must be cited in your paper. In this section we explain the correct form and arrangement of entries in a list of works cited.

Book by One Author.

Taylor, L. S. *Radiation Protection Standards.* Boca Raton, FL: CRC Press, 1970.

If the book has no apparent author or editor, begin with its title:

Report of the President's Commission on the Accident at Three Mile Island—the Need for Change: The Legacy of TMI. Washington, DC: U.S. Government Printing Office, 1979.

Book by Two or Three Authors.

Beyea, J., and F. von Hippel. *Nuclear Reactor Accidents: The Value of Improved Containment.* Princeton: Princeton UP, 1980.

Knowles, P. F., D. Marsh, and H. W. E. Rattle. *Magnetic Resonance of Biomolecules.* New York: Pergamon Press, 1976.

Book by More than Three Authors.

Schurr, S. H. et al. *Energy in America's Future.* Baltimore: Johns Hopkins UP, 1979.

Book by Corporate or Organizational Author.

Panel on Energy and Climate, National Academy of Sciences. *Energy and Climate*. Washington, DC: U.S. Government Printing Office, 1977.

Book with Editor.

Bishop, W.P., ed. Essays on Issues Relevant to the Regulation of Radioactive Waste Management. Washington, DC: The Nuclear Regulatory Commission, 1978.

Multivolume Book.

Moore, J. G., ed. Scientific Basis for Nuclear Waste Management. Vol. 3. New York: Plenum Press, 1981.

Parts of a Book.

Blonke, J. O. "Management of Radioactive Waste." Nuclear Power Safety. Ed. L. E. Weaver. New York: Pergamon Press, 1976. 255-279.

Book in Other than First Edition.

Slichter, C. F. Principles of Magnetic Resonance. 2nd ed. New York: Spring-Verlag, 1980.

Article in Journal with Continuous Pagination.

Loewe, W. E., and E. Mendelsohn. "Revised Dose Estimates at Hiroshima and Nagasaki." Health Physics 41 (1981): 663-666.

Article in Journal that Pages each Issue Separately.

Bingham, Roger. "The Politics of Mistrust." Science 85 6.10 (1985): 34-40.

(After the volume number, add a period and the issue number without any intervening space. The article cited appeared in volume 6, issue 10.)

Popular Magazine Article.

Nader, R. "Are Nuclear Side Effects Hazardous to Your Health?" Family Health Jan. 1977: 53.

Newspaper Article.

Burnham, D. "GE Warns of Halt of Making Reactors." New York Times 15 May 1977: 1.

Article in a Reference Book.

"Nuclear Molecule." McGraw-Hill Encylopedia of Science and Technology. 5th ed. 1982.

Unpublished Documents.

Komanoff, C. "A Comparison of Nuclear and Coal Costs." Testimony before the state of New Jersey, Board of Public Utilities, Phase III, 9 October 1978.

Hyman, L. "The Impact of Regulation on Utilities." Speech before the Pennsylvania Power Conference, 30 April 1980.

Entries in the list of works cited are arranged in alphabetical order by the surname of the first author or editor (see Figure 10-8). A work that has a corporation or organizational author is alphabetized by the first word of the corporation or organization (excluding *A, An,* or *The*). A work that has no identifiable author is alphabetized by its title (excluding *A, An,* or *The*).

When there are two or more works by the same author, arrange them in alphabetical order. Give the author's name only in the first entry. For subsequent entries, type three hyphens and a period, skip two spaces, and cite the title.

Cohen, B. L. "The Cancer Risk from Low Level Radiation." Health Physics 39 (1980): 659.

---. "Hazards from Plutonium Toxicity." <u>Health Physics</u> 32 (1977): 359.

---. "Impact of the Nuclear Energy Industry on Human Health and Safety." <u>American Scientist</u> 64 (1976): 550.

---. <u>Nuclear Science and Society</u>. New York: Anchor Books, 1974.

List single-author entries before multiple author entries beginning with the same surname. Repeat the author's surname; do not use the three hyphens:

Cohen, B. L. "Hazards from Plutonium Toxicity." <u>Health Physics</u> 32 (1977): 359.

---. "The Cancer Risk from Low Level Radiation." <u>Health Physics</u> 39 (1980): 659.

Cohen, B. L., and H. N. Jow. "A Genetic Hazard Evaluation of Low Level Waste Burial Grounds." <u>Nuclear Technology</u> 41 (1978): 381.

Cohen, B. L., and I. Lee. "A Catalog of Risks." <u>Health Physics</u> 36 (1979): 707-722.

Simple Graphics

When carefully prepared, graphics can clarify or reinforce a point or concept. For instance, a writer discussing international terrorist activities during 1985 might use a bar chart to provide a perspective on the problem as illustrated in Figure 10-10. Presenting the annual number of international terrorist attacks in a bar chart enables readers to find the information easily, makes the comparison between years more visible, and dramatizes the trend without distorting it.

As you develop your paper, you should consider whether displaying information graphically would be more effective than conveying it in prose. In the rest of this section, we explain how to prepare two basic types of graphics—tables and figures.

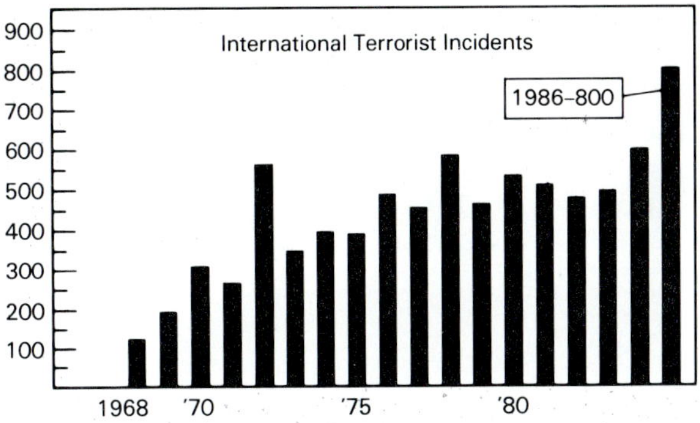

Figure 10-10 *Sample Bar Chart.* (Source: *U.S. State Department.)*

Tables and figures are easy to read, if you follow these six practices:

1. Size tables and figures to fit on the page where they are first mentioned or on the page that immediately follows. Make them compact, but not crowded. Present them large enough to be read easily, but do not spread them out to the point that their elements appear to be floating in space.
2. Keep tables and figures inside the regular margins of the page.
3. Label the elements of tables and figures—the variables, the numerical values, the units of measure, and so on.
4. Except for drawings and sketches, use a rule to draw straight lines, a compass to draw circles and arcs, a protractor to lay down angles, and a French curve to connect individual points with a smooth curve.
5. If the tables and figures are formal, provide a number and title for each. Number the table with an arabic or uppercase roman numeral, according to its appearance in the paper. The first table is Table 1 (or I), the second is Table 2 (or II), and so forth. Number the figures with an arabic numeral, according to its appearance in the paper. The first figure is Figure 1, the second is Figure 2, and so on. Furnish each table and figure with a title that identifies what the table or figure is about. Here is an example:

```
Table I. Estimated Generating Costs for Coal-Fired

Power Plants by Year of Commercial Operation.
```

or

```
Figure 1. The Nuclear Fuel Cycle.
```

The number and title of a table goes above the table. The number and title of a figure goes below the figure.

6. Introduce tables and figures before readers get to them. Refer to them these ways:

```
Table I shows . . .

  . . . as shown in Table I . . .

  . . . (see Table I) . . .

  . . . (Table I) . . .

Figure 1 shows . . .

  . . . as shown in Figure 1 . . .

  . . . (see Figure 1) . .

  . . . (Figure 1) . . .
```

If the table or figure is not on the same page where it is mentioned, include its location in the reference, as in these examples:

```
France and the USSR are now the world leaders in the
generation of nuclear energy (see Table IV on page 8).

The Northeastern states lead the country in the
consumption of nuclear energy (Figure 3 on page 4).
```

Tables

A table is a compact display of information plainly separated into columns and rows, as shown in Figure 10-11. Tables are sometimes just informal lists incorporated into a paragraph. Informal tables are not set apart by lined boundaries and are not identified by a table number or title (see Figure 10-12). Sometimes, though, a table is constructed so that it may be read without immediate reference to the accompanying discussion. Such a table is regarded as a formal table and may be set apart from the text by a lined boundary and is identified by a number and title. A formal table is shown in Figure 10-11.

Figures

Everything tabular is a table. All other graphics—photographs, drawings, maps, and charts—are figures. Figures, like tables, present statistical information

No. 991. Wood energy consumption, by region and sector: 1980 ro 1983
(In trillions of Btu, except percent)

Year	Total	Percent of total energy consumption	Region				Sector			
			Northeast	Midwest	South	West	Residential	Industrial	Commercial	Electric utilities
1980...	2,483	3.4	386	329	1,380	388	859	1,600	21	4
1981...	2,495	3.5	395	335	1,349	416	869	1,602	21	3
1982...	2,478	3.5	358	343	1,392	385	937	1,516	22	2
1983...	2,640	3.6	380	323	1,526	411	925	1,690	22	3

Source: U.S. Energy Information Administration, *Estimates of U.S. Wood Energy Consumption*, 1980–1983.

Figure 10-11 *Example of a Formal Table.* (Source: *U.S. Bureau of the Census.* Statistical Abstract of the United States, *106th ed. Washington D.C.: U.S. Government Printing Office, 1986.)*

Many people still believe that some foods have particular properties that promote health or that will not cause them to gain weight. The development of the science of nutrition has given us our first scientific basis for using dietary advice. The best sources for dietary information are professionals who have the scientific and technical education that qualifies them to devise diets.

Sources of Information about Nutrition

Professionals	Non-Professionals
nutritionists	advertisers
dieticians	health food stores
physicians	relatives
dentists	neighbors
home economists	friends
nurses	

No diet should be followed without the advice or supervision of a physician, who will seek the advice of a qualified dietician when necessary.

Figure 10-12 *Example of an Informal Table.*

in compact form. Like tables, figures may be informal or formal. An informal figure is part of the information of the paragraph and is not set apart or identified by a title and number. Any formal figure is designated as such with an arabic numeral. Some of the more common types of figures are bar charts, line charts, and pie charts.

Bar Charts. Bar charts are used to compare similar items at different times (see Figure 10-10) or to compare different items at the same time (see Figure 10-13). Figure 10-10 shows the number of international terrorist incidents (the similar items) from 1968 through 1985 (at different times). Figure 10-13 shows the age of new job applicants and placement (different items) for 1986 (the same time). Bar charts have these particular features:

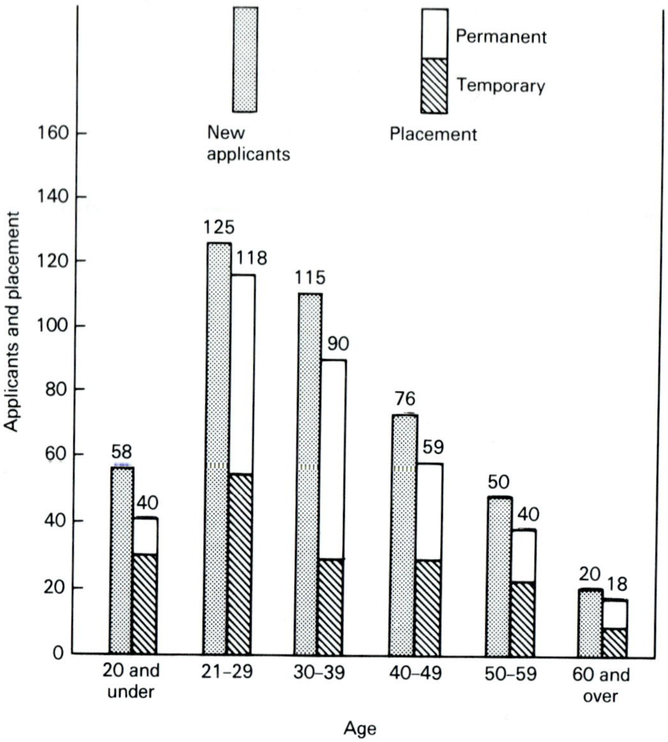

Figure 10-13 *Bar Chart Used to Compare Different Items (Number of New Applicants and Age and Number of Placements) at the Same Time (1986).*

- The bars are the same width and are separated by a space at least equal to their width.
- The heights of the bars reflect the numerical values.
- The independent variable runs across the horizontal scale, the dependent variable runs up the vertical scale.
- The bars are shaded to make them stand out against the white background of the chart.

Line Charts. Line charts, like bar charts, are used to show trends (see Figure 10-14). But a line chart reports a trend better, because it uses a line to connect the quantities shown at given points. As long as the lines are distinct, several items can be compared in a single chart—perhaps as many as three or four as shown in Figure 10-15. In addition to the elements explained on pages 191–192, line charts have these features:

- The independent variable runs across the horizontal scale, the dependent variable up the vertical scale.

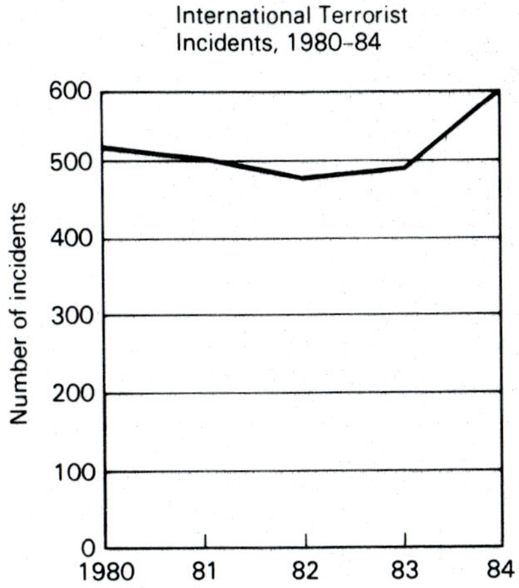

Figure 10-14 *Line Chart. (*Source: *U.S. Department of State.* Patterns of Global Terrorism: 1984. *November, 1985: ii.)*

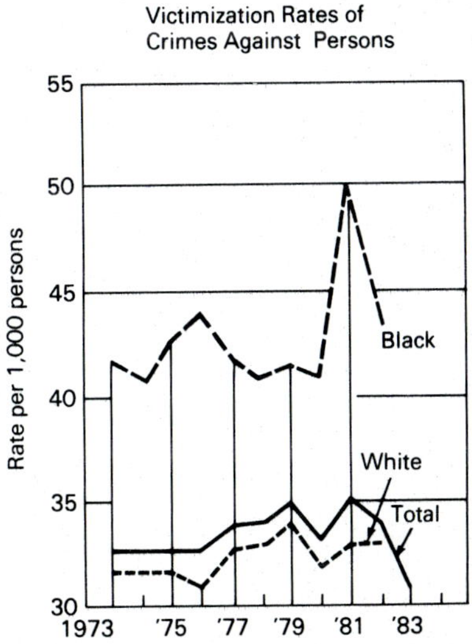

Figure 10-15 *Line Chart Used to Compare Three Trends. (*Source: *United States Bureau of the Census.* Statistical Abstract of the United States, *105th ed. Washington, D.C.: U.S. Government Printing Office, 1985, xx.)*

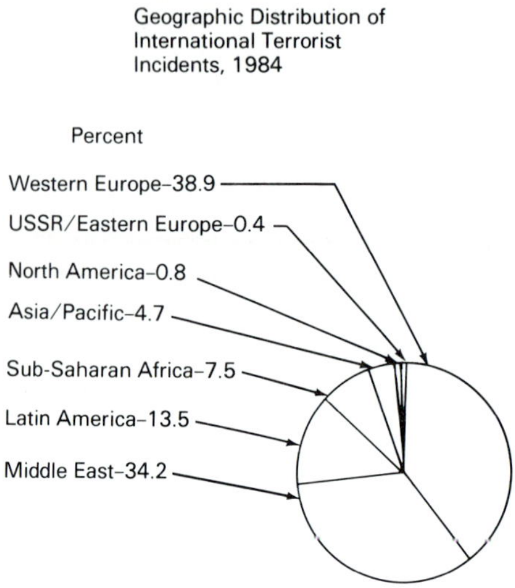

Figure 10-16 *Circle or Pie Chart. (*Source: *U.S. Department of State.* Patterns of Global Terrorism: 1984. *November 1985: ii.)*

- The items plotted on the chart are represented by captions or by different types of lines (solid lines, broken lines, dotted lines, lines with dots and dashes, and so on).

Circle or Pie Charts. A circle or a pie chart (see Figure 10-16) is used to show how parts of a whole are distributed. It is a circle that is divided into segments by straight lines within the circle. The circle represents the whole (100%). Each segment of the circle represents a proportion of the whole. In addition to the elements mentioned on pages 191–192, pie charts have these features:

- Zero on the scale is at the 12 o'clock position.
- The segments decrease in size clockwise (although any "miscellaneous" segment appears last).
- Any "miscellaneous" segment should be defined.
- Segments may be shaded to make the chart stand out against the surrounding white space. Each segment should be shaded differently to distinguish it from the others.

Exercises

1. Select a chapter of this textbook and identify as many format elements as possible. Although this textbook is typeset and uses such elements as bold print, different type styles and sizes, try to relate these features to the elements presented in this chapter. Do the same for a textbook in another course that you are taking this term. Are there any variations or departures in either textbook from the elements discussed in this chapter?

2. Arrange the following sources as if they were a list of sources cited. Use the format of *The MLA Style Manual*.

- An article by G. Harris titled The Globalization of Advertising, which was published in the International Journal of Advertising on pages 223 through 234 of the third issue of volume 3, 1984.
- A book titled Television Coverage of International Affairs, published in 1982 by the Ablex Publishing Corporation of Norwood, New Jersey. The author is W. C. Adams.
- An article titled MacBride: The Report and the Response, cowritten by K. Singh and B. Gross, which appeared in the Journal of Communication on pages 104 through 117 in 1981, volume 31, issue number 4.
- An unpublished paper titled The Third World and the Fourth Estate, written by E. T. Pinch and presented at the U.S. Department Senior Seminar in Foreign Policy on April 9, 1977, in Washington, D.C.
- A chapter titled Television as a Source of International News: What Gets Across and What Doesn't, written by H. Sahin, D. D. Davis, and J. P. Robinson, which appeared in an edited book titled Television Coverage of International Affairs, pages 229–243. The editor of the book is W. C. Adams. The book was published in 1982 by Ablex Publishing Corporation of Norwood, New Jersey.
- An article by I. W. Hill titled U.S. Battles to Prevent Third World News Control, which appeared on page 24 of the August 4, 1979 issue of Editor & Publisher.
- An article appearing in 1982 in Journalism Quarterly titled Television Use and Social Stereotypes, volume 59, pages 119 through 122. The author is A. Tan.
- A book published in 1978 by the University of California Press in Berkeley, California, written by B. Bagdikian and titled Conglomeration, Concentration, and the Flow of Information.
- A book titled The Information Machines written by B. Bagdikian, published in 1972 by Harper & Row of New York.
- A newspaper article titled West's News Organizations Vow to Fight UNESCO on Press Curbs, written by P. Lewis, which appeared on page 11 of the May 18, 1981 issue of the New York Times.
- A paper presented at the Conference on the International News Media and the Developing World, which was held at Cairo University in Cairo, Egypt. The author of the paper is W. Schramm, and the paper was presented on April 3, 1978.
- A newspaper article by P. Lewis titled Gloves Come off in Struggle with UNESCO, which appeared in the New York Times, page E3 of the May 24, 1981 issue.

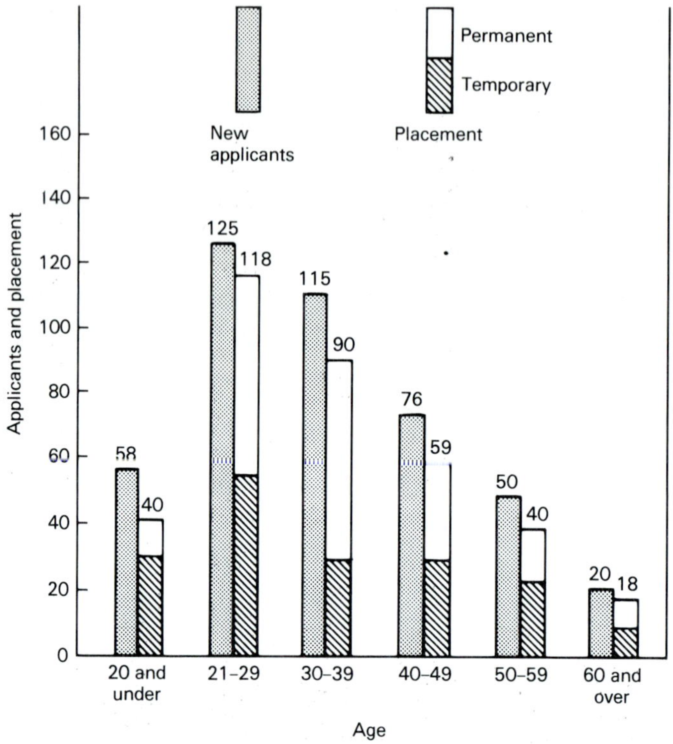

Figure 10-13 Bar Chart Used to Compare Different Items (Number of New Applicants and Age and Number of Placements) at the Same Time (1986).

3. Use the above repetition of Figure 10-13, and answer the following questions.

A. Why are the number of applicants and placements and the age groups arranged the way they are?

B. Which age group had the most applicants?

C. Which age group had the fewest permanent placements?

D. Which age group had the most placements?

E. Which age group had the most permanent placements?

F. Which two age groups had the fewest applicants?

G. Which age group had the second highest number of applicants?

H. Which two groups had equal number of temporary placements?

I. Which age group had the highest percentage of placements?

J. Which age group had the lowest percentage of placements?

K. Which age group had the highest percentage of permanent placements?

L. Why should a line chart be inappropriate for reporting this data?

M. How do you know the number of placements for each age group?

N. How do you know the number of permanent placements for each age group?

O. Suppose that you were going to make a circle or pie chart of the data in this bar chart. Why might you choose to report the data in a circle chart? What would you have to do to convert the data into useful circle chart format? How many segments would your circle chart have? Could you report all the information in a single circle chart, or would it be better to use more than one?

4. Convert the data in this formal table into a formal line chart.

Table I
Percent of Capacity Leased
Aardvark Rentals, 1982—1986

Year	Percent	Location
1982	62	Broken Arms Apartments
	80	Brookside Manor
1983	75	Broken Arms Apartments
	90	Brookside Manor
1984	70	Broken Arms Apartments
	90	Brookside Manor
1985	62	Broken Arms Apartments
	88	Brookside Manor
1986	60	Broken Arms Apartments
	88	Brookside Manor

5. In Chapter 1 we discussed using classification to organize the books in your personal library so you could find them more easily. The categories we suggested included fiction, poetry, history, reference, mathematics, science, and so on. Use that classification or a similar one to organize your books, and report the total number of books in your personal library and the number in each category three ways: (1) in a table, (2) in a bar chart, and (3) in a circle or pie chart.

III

Handbook

11

Principles of Style

Style in writing is a very personal thing, as personal as the clothes we wear, the food we eat, the friends we favor. Some writers are naturally rather informal in tone; others are more restrained and formal. But even after considering these individual differences, most rhetoricians agree that a good style is clear, appropriate to the audience and situation, and correct. The principles we present in this chapter are meant to help you achieve those three goals.

In this chapter and throughout the rest of Part III, "Handbook," we provide several aids that should make the Handbook more useful. Whenever we use a term that we have defined in Chapter 13, "Glossary of Grammatical Terms," we note that term by italicizing it and marking it with an asterisk. When explanations elsewhere in the book help explain a principle further, we provide cross references to the helpful sections. Finally in this chapter and in Chapter 12, "Conventions," we have furnished a system of marking symbols. These symbols are listed inside the back cover, where they provide a handy index to the contents of the two chapters. Your teacher may use the symbols to help you isolate some ways to improve your style.

Clarity

Readers are likely to consider your style clear if they can follow your organization easily, read your sentences without hesitation, and understand your vocabulary. In this section we provide advice in these three areas.

Organize Your Paper Carefully (Org)

Organize your paper using hierarchies that best suit your purpose, material, and audience. Remember the four major purposes for writing:

- To present and explain knowledge and to define terms
- To explain and defend a thesis
- To present an evaluation of something
- To present and support a recommendation

To suit these purposes, there are such hierarchies as classification, generalization, topical order, comparison, causal analysis, description, narration, and argument. Normally, you will have one governing hierarchy, but within the piece you may very well choose a subordinate hierarchy for a particular section or paragraph. You may, for example, have paragraphs of description within a narration, or paragraphs of narration within an argument. See Chapter 3, "Composing: Using Logic and Rhetoric," and pages 76–81.

Display Your Organization (DYO)

From start to finish, your top priority should be to guide your readers through your work. Don't let your readers get lost.

Begin with an introduction. As obvious as that sounds, we have read countless student essays and business reports that failed precisely because readers were plunged without guidance into a mass of information. Short pieces may need little more than a topic sentence that makes subject and purpose clear. Longer pieces may need an introduction that shows subject and purpose and provides an overview of what is to come. Provide whatever is needed.

Your work may be divided into several sections. Supply introductions to each section. Again, the introduction may be a full one or only a topic sentence, depending on the length and complexity of what follows.

Sections may be divided into paragraphs. Provide topic sentences for your paragraphs; these sentences introduce the subject of the paragraph. If the connection of the paragraph to the preceding paragraph is not obvious, provide the connection. Keep your readers informed about where they are.

Link together the sentences in your paragraphs. Normally, if you are sticking to your subject as you should be, little linkage will be needed, beyond perhaps the purposeful repetition of key terms (such as *link* and *linkage* in this paragraph). But sometimes the linkage needs to be shown. You may have to clarify for your readers what the next sentence is doing. That is, is the next sentence meant to contradict the previous one? Or does it provide an example for it, or extend its idea? To provide such linkage, you need to use words with which you are perfectly familiar. Such words include *however, nonetheless, but, for example, for instance, furthermore, also, next,* and so on. Don't be too heavy handed about it, but keep your reader's eye on your object.

The pattern, we hope, is clear. From start to finish, introduction to conclusion, you must help your readers follow your organization. No other principle in this chapter will do as much for clarity as this one. For more information about showing your organization, see pages 86–90 and 168–176.

Extend Your Sentences Sensibly (Sentence)

You have many constructions available to you for extending your *sentences**: *absolutes**, *appositives**, *adverbials**, and *clauses** and *phrases** of various types. You can write *simple sentences**, *complex sentences**, *compound sentences**, and *compound-complex sentences**. Chances are that you already use most of these constructions. However, it might be a good idea if you looked them up in Chapter 13, "Glossary of Grammatical Terms." With a more definite knowledge about what these are, you might use them more frequently. When you do extend your sentence, remember to respect the integrity of the core of your sentence.

The core of your sentence is its *subject** and *predicate**. We can and do insert information between subject and predicate:

> These related disciplines—*literature, history, art, philosophy,* and *language*—constitute what we know as the humanities.

Such constructions are useful, but they can be overdone. Readers want to know what statement you are making about the subject. If you hold off the predicate too long, they grow impatient or confused. Therefore, use such constructions infrequently and take care that those you use are not too long.

More commonly than inserting material between subject and verb, we place material before the subject:

> *Literature, history, art, philosophy,* and *language*—these related disciplines constitute what we know as the humanities.

Or

> *In addition to the humanities,* I wish to discuss the roll of science in a liberal education.

Professional writers place material before the subject about 25 percent of the time. To do so is a common construction, one you should feel comfortable using. However, do not overdo such constructions. As is the case with interrupting the subject and predicate, you will confuse or annoy your readers if you hold off the subject too long. That is the problem with the following example:

> *If you are a high school graduate or between the ages of 18 and 65, are a resident of the city, have been previously employed for at least six consecutive months, and are currently unemployed,* you are eligible for financial assistance.

Such a sentence is better presented as a list:

You are eligible for financial assistance if you meet all these conditions:

—You are a high school graduate or between the ages of 18 and 65
—You are a resident of the city
—You have been previously employed for at least six consecutive months
—You are currently unemployed

In general, a long sentence will be read more easily if most of its words come after the verb rather than before. For instance, the last sentence is read more easily than this altered version:

In general, if most of the words come after the verb rather than before, a long sentence will be read more easily.

See also pages 132–135.

Avoid Nounspeak (NS)

Nounspeak[1] is a term referring to two stylistically clumsy ways of using nouns: creating nominalizations and piling up nouns in front of other nouns to modify them. A nominalization is a *verb** turned into a *noun**—for instance, *decision* from *decide* and *consideration* from *consider*. Used correctly, nominalizations can be quite useful. Writers frequently use a nominalization to refer to an idea stated in a previous sentence or to common concepts:

We *decided* to leave the party early. This *decision* prevented our losing a good deal of sleep.
Correctness, not *hypercorrectness,* should be the goal of the accomplished speaker and writer.

However, we use nominalizations unwisely when we substitute them for ideas that would be better expressed as verbs:

We *gave consideration* to all the factors involved.

Instead of

We *considered* all the factors involved.

Or

It is our *intention* to make a full *exploration* of all the factors involved.

Instead of

We *intend to explore* fully all the factors involved.

See pages 141–142 for more information about nominalizations.

In the second type of nounspeak, nouns are piled up in front of other nouns to modify them (see *Modifier**). *Consumer information seeking behavior* and *option period rates* are examples of such constructions. The trouble with such constructions is that the reader is never quite sure which noun modifies which noun. Does *option period* modify *rates* or does *option* modify *period rates?* We can clarify the statement and get rid of the nounspeak by breaking up the string of nouns in a way that shows the desired modification. for example:

rates for the option period
consumers' behavior in seeking information[2]

Note that there is nothing wrong with using a noun to modify another noun. This type of common construction occurs in words like *sugar cake* and *mail carrier*. Confusion results when several nouns are piled up as modifiers. This creates nounspeak.

Choose the Proper Voice (Voice)

You have two choices of *voice*:* active and passive. In most instances, use the active voice. Good writers fill page after page with active voice, as in this paragraph:

> First, the humanities and the arts confront a great challenge, in that the values and approaches to knowledge that they embody often appear to be at odds with the dominant mode of thinking in our society today: that of science and technology. During the past century or so science has made rapid and spectacular progress in expanding our knowledge of the physical world, from the chemical basis of life to events explicating the origins of the universe. Technology, the practical application of scientific knowledge, has made a more visible—if not a more profound—revolution in modern life, in how we live, the foods we eat, the health care we receive, the products we consume, and how we regard ourselves and the world. But it is also true that the great prestige of science has, wittingly or unwittingly, encouraged a tendency to devalue other kinds of knowledge sought, sifted, and secured by less empirical means.[3]

In every sentence of this passage we know the agent of action: "the humanities and the arts," "science," "technology," and "the great prestige of science."

Most editors reject the excessive use of passive voice on the grounds that it makes writing dull and wordy and frequently confusing. Passive voice is particularly deadly when combined with nounspeak:

> Consideration was given to the workers' protests, but no explanations were forthcoming.

Such a sentence lies lifelessly on the page. Furthermore, we don't know from it who did the considering and from whom the explanations should have been forthcoming. In active voice, the pace picks up, and the agents are identified:

> Management considered the workers' protests but offered no explanations.

Although you will use the active voice far more often than the passive, the passive does have its uses. It emphasizes the receiver of the action when that is your goal:

> By 1950, the stage was set for mass culture and overconsumption.

Use the passive when the agent of the action is unknown or unimportant or when you have a strategic reason for ignoring the agent:

> Two of my trees were cut down last night.
> The condemned man was given a hearty meal.
> The situation was mishandled in the past, but now we are ready to move forward.

You can also use the passive to link the concept in a preceding sentence to the concept expressed in the next sentence:

> Hormones were being extracted from animal endocrine glands, and changes in blood pressure, volume, and circulation were considered legitimate objects of study. *The whole process was remarkably accelerated by World War II. . . .*[4]

See also pages 138–141.

Choose the Proper Mood (Mood)

You will use the *indicative mood**, in some combination of active and passive *voice**, in most of your writing. This is the *mood** in which you state facts and ask questions:

> What do students in our nations' schools do all day? Most of them are clearly not spending their time reading the classics, learning

> math, or studying the physical sciences. It is likely that, along with photography workshops, keeping journals, and perhaps learning about computers, students spend most of their day in moral education classes. But these classes are not, as one might expect, designed to acquaint students with the Western moral tradition. Professional theorists in schools of education have found that tradition wanting and have designed an alternative, one they have marketed in public schools with notable success.[5]

Use the *imperative mood** primarily for making requests and giving instructions:

> Please pass the salt.
> Roll out the thinnest sheet of pasta that you can. Fold the sheet into a loose roll and cover it, leaving just a few inches exposed. Cut this exposed part into 1½ inch squares.[6]

The imperative mood in instructions is concise and clear. The example that tells how to roll pasta would become cumbersome if expressed in the *passive voice**.

> A sheet of pasta is rolled out as thin as you can. The sheet is folded into a loose roll and covered, leaving just a few inches exposed. This exposed part is cut into 1½ inch squares.

The instructions grow even more cumbersome if the *subjunctive mood** is used in either active or passive voice.

> You should roll out the thinnest sheet of pasta that you can. You should roll the sheet into a loose roll. . . .
> The thinnest sheet of pasta you can should be rolled out. The sheet should be folded into a loose roll. . . .

Save the subjunctive mood for those few times when you truly wish to express that something is conditional. "You may make the pasta by hand or by machine" implies a clear choice that is up to the reader. "You should make the pasta by hand rather than by machine" implies that a choice can be made but makes clear that the hand method is the better choice.

See also pages 135–138.

Get People into Your Writing (People)

We all understand concepts and instructions better when we can relate them to people. We all like to feel we are part of the action. You will write more effectively if you get people into your writing as often as it is appropriate.

The simplest way to get people into your writing is with the use of personal *pronouns**. These are the words *I, she, they, you, we,* and so on. Notice that in this book we refer to ourselves as *we* and to you as *you*. You probably relate more directly to such expressions. If we did not use them, we would have to resort to *passive voice** and clumsy expressions like *your authors* and *the reader*.

Particularly in instructions and explanations, get the reader into the action through the use of personal pronouns. The St. Paul Insurance Company found they could clarify their policies greatly by substituting personal pronouns and simpler sentence structures for what had been typical insurance legalese:

> **Before**
> This Policy and its Insuring Agreements shall be void if the Insured has concealed or misrepresented any material fact or circumstance concerning this insurance or the subject thereof or in case of any fraud, attempted fraud or false swearing by the Insured pertaining to this insurance or the subject thereof, whether before or after a loss. However, unintentional errors or omissions on the part of the Insured shall not operate to prejudice the rights of the Insured under this Policy and its Insuring Agreements.
>
> **After**
> This policy will be void if you or any other protected person hides any important information from us, misleads us, or attempts to defraud or lie to us about any matter concerning this insurance—either before or after a loss. Of course, everyone makes mistakes. Unintentional errors or omissions won't affect your rights under this policy.[7]

The St. Paul Company (and now many other companies) has gone so far as to insert narrative examples in its description of policies, in order to get people into the action. Note this instance:

> We'll cover the interest on any loan you have to take out because you can't collect your receivables and need money while you're waiting for payment of your claim. For example: *Your records are destroyed and the losses are covered by us. You need ready cash to pay the rent, so you take out a short term bank loan. We'll pay the interest on the loan.*[8]

Perhaps you feel uncomfortable using *I*. Don't feel this way. Most magazines and journals today encourage, even insist upon, the use of *I* by their authors. Here are several quotations taken at random from *The American Scholar,* a scholarly and dignified journal, that sees no harm in using *I:*

> I did not get to meet Lehrer until a few years later, when I began taking graduate courses in mathematics.[9]
> It is this perspective that I wish to question here. In particular I will

> challenge the view, widespread among democratic theorists, that as "community" requires "participation," so "participation" breeds "community."[10]
>
> In 1966 when I was a medical resident and first went to a medical meeting in Atlantic City, clinical investigation in American medicine was at its zenith.[11]

Any time you deal with human action, you will raise reader interest and understanding if you put people into the action. In the next passage we quote, the author is describing some of the planning involved in developing a building site. The author could have described the planning in a passive, abstract way, but notice how he uses people instead:

> "First of all, to do anything on the scale we've done, you need a very large piece of land," says Jim Toepfer, the president of Mission Viejo's Colorado Division. "And it has to be in a place where people want to settle and live. An opportunity like we had, to buy 22,000 acres near a booming area like Denver is rare." But, stresses Toepfer, his firm did a lot of homework on the Highlands Ranch property before buying it. "We tested the soil," he says. "We did studies of the available water. We studied the ecology of the area to make sure it wouldn't be adversely affected if we wanted to build a sewage treatment plant for the town. We did mineral and agricultural analyses of the land, checked its drainage, looked into existing zoning. In short, we asked ourselves, 'Could we build on this land and have it make good business sense?'"[12]

When you place people into your writing, either through the use of personal pronouns or by describing the actions of real people, you quite naturally fall into the use of *active voice** and, when appropriate, the *imperative mood**. By introducing people, you prevent your writing from being flat, passive, overcomplicated, and uninteresting.

Stay Close to Reality (Reality)

Words are necessarily abstractions from things themselves. The word *pencil* is not the instrument of wood, paint, and graphite that we write with—it is the symbol for the real thing. But there are many levels of abstraction. We can abstract so that we can get further and further away from reality. *Pencil* is close to the real thing. *Writing instrument* is further removed. *Instrument* is yet further removed, *tool* still further, *asset* further yet, and so on. Often we need to generalize, to include many things under one heading. We need at times to discuss tools in general, as in "a carpenter needs a wide variety of tools." But at other times we need to be precise: not "drive nails with a tool," but "drive nails with a hammer."

All this would seem obvious and not worth mentioning, except that many people do, indeed, write so abstractly that we have difficulty knowing what it is that they are actually saying. The writer who is too abstract substitutes "His behavior was very supportive" for "He lent me his car and twenty dollars for gas." High-level abstraction, particularly when combined with the *passive voice**, produces writing that says little. The writer who produces a sentence such as, "The trip to Chicago was enjoyed," leaves the reader wondering what was enjoyed and by whom.

Bureaucrats are particularly prone to working with higher abstractions. They "institutionalize" people—leaving us to wonder what kind of institution—rather than "jail" them. Some of this abstraction comes from a lack of knowing how to express reality, some from a mistaken belief that such language lends dignity to writing. But some abstract statements may result from a deliberate attempt to cloud an issue. Notice how the combination of high-level abstraction and passive voice produces the following empty statement from the Soviet Press Agency *Tass* concerning the Russian nuclear accident that occurred at Chernobyl in May of 1986:

> An accident has occurred at the Chernobyl nuclear power plant as one of the reactors was damaged. Measures are being taken to eliminate the consequences of the accident. Aid is being given to those affected. A government commission has been set up.[13]

If you put people into your writing, as we advise you to do in the preceding section, you will get close to reality. But even when you are writing about things and concepts, get as close to reality as you can. Never be any more abstract than you have to be.

Use Precise Expressions—Usually the Familiar Ones (Exp)

To write well, we must choose the precise word or expression that says what we mean. But English is full of synonyms and near synonyms: *freedom* and *liberty; fire, flame,* and *conflagration*. Because we have such a huge word stock, our lives can be complicated by the need to make choices among words and expressions. We base our choices on several factors. One certainly has to be audience. If you wish to express the notion that a large amount of space is available, you might have to choose between *roomy* and *capacious*. If your readers are likely not to be familiar with *capacious,* choose *roomy*. If your audience can understand *capacious,* it might be enjoyable for you and your audience to see this word.

Likewise, you might enjoy writing about a *fortuitous* event rather than an *accidental* one. The term *fortuitous* may even be more accurate. To speak of a house *in flames* would likely be more precise, and certainly more descriptive, than saying the house is *on fire*. But to speak of a small fire as a *conflagration* would be a mistake unless you were deliberately being ironic or satirical. Such choices make for interesting writing and precision, too, so long as you don't overdo the elegant choices and get pompous and hard to understand.

When you develop a professional vocabulary, you may find that there are no common words to substitute for professional terms, except for circumlocutions. When discussing *genes* and *chromosomes,* you have little choice about using the two terms. Just be sure, if your readers are likely to be unfamiliar with such terms, to define them on a level your audience can comprehend.

Nevertheless, after making allowance for the use of elegant, precise, and professional words, we advise you to choose the most *familiar* precise expression on most occasions. It will gain you little to choose *utilize* over *use, initiate* over *begin, this point in time* over *now, due to the fact that* over *because, per annum* over *a year, represent* over *is,* and so forth. Such choices add nothing in the way of precision, but they *will* add a good deal of difficulty and pomposity. Sometimes, indeed, choosing the most precise expression may lead the writer into what some may think is the *too* familiar. However, the editors of *The American Scholar* were apparently not disturbed by the author's use of *flat out* in the following sentence:

> Before going into corroborative detail, let me state, flat out, that Douglas Bush was recognized as the world's outstanding authority on Renaissance English literature and on Milton.[14]

See also the entries under *Tone,* pages 213–216.

Tone

Many tones are available to you, from the colloquial to the highly formal. The tones you choose depends on your purpose, audience, and material. Just as you wear jeans and jogging shoes to class and someday will wear a suit to a job interview, you must choose a tone to fit the situation. In this section, we discuss appropriate tone and also connotation, clichés, and euphemism. To get the tone right, it is essential to use words with the right connotations. Clichés can ruin tone at any level. Euphemism is usually to be avoided, but sometimes an audience or a situation may demand it to some degree.

Choose the Appropriate Tone (Tone)

Good writing can range along a continuum from casual to formal. The following introduction to a magazine piece is chatty and informal, acceptable, but, because it's intended for an adult audience, maybe just a step away from being too much:

The dinosaurs are back! No kidding, it's true. It may be hard for some grownups to believe, but we have it from reliable sources that a certain Professor Jones, a heretofore unknown paleontologist (they study dinosaurs), has uncovered a miraculous method of bringing these mammoths back to life. The secret—and don't spread this around—involves some magic dinosaur bones, a generous helping of good ol' rock and roll, and a good sprinkling of imagination.[15]

Further along the continuum is this introduction to a piece on Boston Red Sox star, Carl Yastrzemski:

In 1967 the Boston Red Sox won the American League pennant and went to the World Series. I, who grew up in Boston, was just turning seven years old, which was exactly the right age to be marked for life as a Red Sox fan. That same year a loan Boston Red Sox outfielder named Carl Yastrzemski won the batting Triple Crown, leading all other American League hitters in batting average, home runs, and runs batted in. Hooked, you might say, and double hooked: I had a team and I had a hero. I have been a Red Sox fan all my life; I expect to go to my grave a Red Sox fan; and through all these years, the Red Sox have seemed to me best represented by the spirit and quality of Carl Yastrzemski, or Yaz, as he is known in the press and to all Red Sox diehards like me. This spring for the first time in twenty-four years, Carl Yastrzemski is not in a Red Sox uniform, and the feeling is strange, even a little eerie.[16]

The tone is still personal, but the chatty asides—"No kidding, it's true" and "don't spread this around"—are gone. There is a more conscious effort at graceful writing, shown, for example, in the parallelism of "I had a team and I had a hero" and "I have been a Red Sox fan all my life; I expect to go to my grave a Red Sox fan. . . ." Colloquial terms like "hooked" and "double hooked" go side by side with the fairly formal language and rather formal construction of "This spring for the first time in twenty-four years, Carl Yastrzemski is not in a Red Sox uniform, and the feeling is strange, even a little eerie."

Nearing the formal end of the continuum, we have this introduction to a book review:

The images are frightening and familiar: World War I propaganda prints of Germans hordes sweeping toward France, raping nuns and bayoneting Belgian infants; Parisian taxis rushing troops Northeast to the Battle of the Marne, lush forests along a strip of European landscape running from the North Sea to the Swiss border turned into an arid moonscape by countless bombs; picture post cards sent by barely literate trench soldiers to mothers and sweethearts in Brittany or Provence. Then another war and occupation with even more familiar images (thanks to, among other things, more cameras): Hitler posed like any tourist on the terrace of the Palais de Chaillot, the Eiffel Tower rising in the background; luxury hotels—the Meurice, Prince de Gulles, Continental—draped with swastikas and requisitioned by a new elite; uniformed sightseers visiting the Tuileries by day, ogling gartered thighs at the Moulin Rouge by night. And the most familiar image of all: the Champ-Elysees, from the Arc de Triomphe to the Place de la Concorde, a majestic view sullied by memories of German troops goosestepping past the vanquished French. Some Parisians turn their backs in defiance, others look on stunned or weeping, still others seem quietly relieved that, after years of political chaos and violent conflict at home, a resolution is at hand.[17]

The paragraph and the sentences are long. There is a very conscious parallelism of the images of the two wars. The closing sentence balances the actions of the "vanquished French" in a well-constructed series: "Some Parisians turn their backs in defiance," and so forth. The personal touch of the first two samples is missing, and there is no use of colloquial language. The French are *vanquished,* not *beaten*.

Often, tone depends on the publication in which your work would appear. Consider this paragraph, taken from an article published by the Brooklyn Botanic Garden:

Sometimes confused with pleaching, pollarding of trees and shrubs consists of the annual cutting back of branches to the trunk, in order to induce new growth to appear. Sometimes this is done with decorative intent, as in the pollarding of catalpas to keep the head of foliage low and small. More often it is done for a craftsman's purpose, as when willows are cut back to force the growth of slender branches for basket-making. Pollarded trees are frequently seen bordering farms in Europe, also on streets in Tokyo.[18]

On the face of it, it seems unlikely that the editors at the Brooklyn Botanic Garden would accept an article that began, "No kidding, pollarding is back! The secret to pollarding—and don't confuse it with pleaching—is snipping the branches back to the trunk every year."

Most good writing that you see in books, magazines, and newspapers probably rests in the middle of the continuum. Most good business writing also occupies the middle ground. It is writing that is clear without being heavy, courteous without being obsequious, simple without being simplistic. But from time to time you'll need to try your hand at a more casual or a more formal tone. When you do, be careful. The danger of the too casual tone is that it can become strained and ludicrous:

Turing's Man is a great—Hey, I mean really great—tome. (Get that word, *tome;* that's Greek, for *book,* well, OK.) Anyway, Dave Bolt, the author of *Turing's Man,* has this thing about computers and AI (artificial intelligence to you). He thinks they can put culture right down the old tube, whoosh, just like that.

The danger of the too formal is that it can become pseudo-formal, artificial, and pompous. There can be a straining for effect that is just as ludicrous as the too casual, and probably even harder to read. In pompous prose, things are never *done;* they are *implemented.* Trains don't come into the station; they *platform.* Things don't *affect* other things; they *impact* them. People don't have children; they *parent* or *are parenting.* People don't talk to each other; they *dialogue* or *interface.* In pompous prose, the words are abstract, the sentences are complex, and the thought is fuzzy—as in this example, spoken by a Pentagon admiral:

> We were not micromanaging Grenada intelligencewise until about that time frame.[19]

That is, "Up till then, we hadn't paid much attention to spying on Grenada."[20] It is not merely that the admiral's statement about Grenada is fuzzy, it's that words like *micromanaging* and *intelligencewise* irritate or amuse sensible users of language. Avoid the extremes.

Getting the right tone for a piece of writing is always worthwhile. Sometimes it is hard to achieve. Chapters 1, "Discovery: the Beginning of the Writing Process," 6, "Words," and 7, "Sentences," supplement the information presented here. But certainly, a sensitivity for tone is best achieved through reading.

Get the Connotation Right (Connotation)

The connotation of words plays an important role in tone. Be aware of the emotional overtones of the words you use. Not knowing connotations can lead to disaster; being conscious of them can enrich your language. Poets and advertising writers are well aware of the connotations of words. When Edmund Waller wrote

> Go, Lovely Rose—
> Tell her that wastes her time and me
>   that now she knows,
> When I resemble her to thee,
>   How sweet and fair she seems to be.

he knew his audience would have pleasant associations of love and romance from the word *rose.* These connotations went far beyond the denotative meaning of "a plant or flower of the genus *Rosa.*"

Likewise, the advertising writer who described a sweater as a "classic crew neck sweater for active sportswear" and added that it is "hand-loomed of fine, soft, pure wool Shetland" was playing on the readers' emotions far more than their intellect. That writer knew well the connotations associated with *classic, active, hand-loomed, fine, soft, pure,* and *Shetland.* As is said of successful restaurant menu writers, the successful ad writer sells the sizzle and not the steak.

Being unaware of connotations can lead to embarrassing blunders and wrong tone. The use of either *gay* or *queer* in a scientific paper on homosexuality would lead the readers to doubt the objectivity of the writer. The scientific terms for our various bodily functions have very different connotations than do their Anglo-Saxon, four-letter equivalents. Both have their place, but usually not in the same paper. An engineer acquaintance of ours failed to make his case with a town board because he emphasized the *progress* his company's project would bring to the town. In many quarters, *progress* is a good word. However, the members of this particular town board were proud of the unchanged character of their centuries-old town. To them, *progress* was a dirty word full of unpleasant connotations.

Choosing the right word with the right connotation is always worth the effort. We can *drink* a drink, or we can *drain, swallow, swig,* or *take a pull at* that drink. All choices will get the drink inside the drinker, but only one of them will have the right connotation. Which choice you make will depend upon your purpose, audience, and situation. (See also pages 104–105.)

Avoid Clichés (Cliché)

Clichés are tired, trite expressions. They have been worn out by overuse, either because they have been around for many years, or because they were yesterday's fad expressions. They are tempting to use because they are ready made and familiar to us. When the President evades a question at a press conference, the reporter can glibly write, "The President *stonewalled* the issue." Once *stonewall* was a vivid image. Now the term is exhausted. The student writer trying to condense nature into an understandable image may write of "Mother Nature." It would be better to say simply "nature" or, perhaps, to refer to some element of nature specifically: wind, rain, fire, ice, and so on.

The sportscaster who says, "The Giants came to play today," speaks as emptily as the interviewee who solemnly tells the interviewer, "The bottom line is that there are no problems, only opportunities."

Some clichés are simply old expressions that owe their longevity to a tricky or pleasant turn of phrase: *bag and baggage; first and foremost; high, wide, and handsome; lock, stock and barrel;* and *in no way, shape or manner.* Such expressions are so unobtrusive that the use of one on occasion probably causes little harm. But should you fill an essay with such expressions, you run the risk of appearing dull.

If you are tempted by a cliché because it is so apt, at least see if you can use it in an imaginative way, as in this paragraph:

> If all the world's a stage, our house was a thriving repertory theater with a large resident company of relatives, servants, dogs, cats, and

chickens. Father was financial angel, producer, business manager, and leading man. As a small child, my role was not, as you might think, the Infant Phenomenon or junior spear-carrier, but Banquo's ghost—that is a character outside the main action but ever present in spirit, looking on wide-eyed at what I see now was an extraordinary production.[21]

Avoid Euphemisms (Euphemism)

Euphemism, as we explain on pages 115–116, is an attempt to gloss over with inoffensive language things we consider to be distasteful, unpleasant, or taboo. Military language is full of such terms: a nuclear weapon called *The Peacekeeper,* a drive to kill and capture the remainder of an enemy force termed a *mopping up*. Scientists write euphemistically about how they "decapitated and subsequently ensanguinated" frogs instead of baldly stating that "We cut off their heads and then let the blood drain out."[22] Sellers of pornographic books call their establishments *adult* bookstores. People don't admit to being broke; they have *cash flow* problems. The hostess asks her guest if she would like to "freshen up a bit."

For the most part, you should avoid using euphemisms. Their use can produce vague, dishonest, or unintentionally comical writing (or all three at once). However, we must, if we are to be honest, caution you against avoiding euphemisms all together. You must, as always, consider what is appropriate to the audience and the situation. Scientists who wrote of cutting off frogs' heads might not get their articles published. When you deal with the functions of the body in any piece of writing above the most colloquial level, the Latinate terms are usually more appropriate than the Anglo-Saxon ones. The grieving widow probably doesn't need too much straight talk about how her husband died in an automobile accident.

Therefore, accept the conditions of your audience and situation and write what is appropriate. Within such restraints, write as honestly and specifically as you can, but do not mistake rudeness for either honesty or candor.

Correctness

Correctness in the mechanics of grammar has been stressed particularly in writing since the eighteenth century (see pages 127–131). A style that includes numerous errors in punctuation, sentence structure, and spelling will not be taken seriously by most readers. If you have not as yet learned to be correct in such matters, now is the time to master your skills. In Chapter 12, "Conventions," we describe the major rules that govern punctuation and other aspects of writing. In Chapter 13, "Glossary of Grammatical Terms," we define most of the terms you must know. (Remember that such terms used in this chapter are italicized and marked with an asterisk.) In the next few pages, we isolate, describe, and tell you how to correct twelve major mechanical errors. If you master the points we cover here, you will be on your way toward mastering a correct style.

Write in Complete Sentences (Frag)

Sometimes, in the heat of composition, we may fail to realize that something we have written is an incomplete sentence, often called a *fragment*. Such incomplete sentences are often *phrases** left unfinished or standing by themselves:

> The beginning of fall, a season of misty mornings, bright afternoons, colorful leaves, and football.

The example conveys a good deal of information, but because it nowhere contains a complete *verb**—only the *gerund* beginning*—it never completes the writer's thought. It can be completed if the writer furnishes a complete verb:

> Fall began, a season of misty mornings, bright afternoons, colorful leaves, and football.

Or

> The beginning of fall—a season of misty mornings, bright afternoons, colorful leaves, and football—has always been my favorite time of year.

In a similar way, *dependent clauses** left standing alone do not complete the writer's thought:

> Although assistance to our friends is appropriate.

The dependent clause must be linked to an *independent clause*:*

> Although assistance to our friends is appropriate, we must not ignore the nonaligned nations.

Fragments may be used as stylistic devices:

> Happy in his work. Happy in his marriage. He was the envy of all his friends.

If you choose to use fragments, be sure your use is so obviously stylistic that no one can mistake them for errors.

See also pages 132–135 and 247.

Separate Sentences Correctly (RO)

In general, two *independent clauses** should not be linked together without punctuation or with only a comma between them. When punctuation is totally lacking, the result is called a *fused sentence*. When a comma alone is used, the error is known as a *comma splice*. The term *run-on sentence* is also used for either construction. Normally, independent clauses are separated with a period, a semicolon, or a colon. Sometimes, two independent clauses may be joined with a comma and a *coordinating conjunction**. See the entries for these types of punctuation in Chapter 12, "Conventions," for advice on how best to use them with sentences.

In our experience, most run-on sentences occur when the writer uses one of the *conjunctive adverbs** (such as *however* and *therefore*) as though it were a coordinating conjunction (such as *and* and *but*). This error results in a comma splice like this one:

> The second half of the century has been a time of small wars and great uneasiness, however, it has been a time unmarked by world-wide conflicts.

The two independent clauses of the sample could be punctuated with either a period or a semicolon. Because the ideas of the two are closely related, the semicolon is typically used:

> The second half of the century has been a time of small wars and great uneasiness; however, it has been a time unmarked by world-wide conflicts.

Link Sentence Elements in Parallel Ways (Paral)

When you link sentence elements together in a pair or a series, make sure they have parallel grammatical constructions. If you shift constructions on your readers, you make things needlessly difficult for them. Here are a few samples of shifted constructions and their suggested revisions:

> *Walking* to work or *to jog* are increasingly popular among city dwellers.
> *Walking* to work or *jogging* are increasingly popular among city dwellers.
> My father likes *golf* and *to swim.*
> My father likes *to golf* and *to swim.*

Or, because a *gerund** is a noun, you could also achieve parallel structure with "My father likes *golf* and *swimming*.

They were dictatorial and authoritarian, and we were constantly bullied by them.

Here an *active voice** clause is linked with a *passive voice** clause. Although this is not grammatically incorrect, the result is awkward. Putting both clauses in the same voice often resolves the awkwardness:

They were dictatorial and authoritarian, and they constantly bullied us.

As you can see in the discussion on tone (see pages 214–215), conscious, correct parallelism is often powerful and elegant. Be sure to construct your parallel structures correctly.

Place Your Modifiers Carefully (Mod)

As we explain in Chapter 7, "Grammar," (see pages 120–122) English is heavily dependent on word order for meaning. Merely moving a *modifier** around in a sentence can change the meaning of the sentence. For example, "I insist *only* on my rights" says something quite different from "*Only* I insist on my rights." "He *almost* completed every pass he threw" (he came close on every pass) indicates less success than "He completed *almost* every pass he threw" (he completed quite a few).

"Coming out of the hall, he met his brother" is clear. "He met his brother coming out of the hall" is ambiguous. One of the following would be a better sentence:

He met his brother, who was coming out of the hall.

Or

Coming out of the hall, he met his brother.

The choice depends on which brother is coming out of the hall.

Be sure your modifier has something to modify, or else the result may be ludicrous, misleading, or both:

Flying over New England, many areas of downed trees were seen.

Because whoever did the flying is left out of the sentence, the modifier, "Flying over New England," just dangles in the sentence. Rewritten, the sentence makes better sense:

Flying over New England, we observed many areas of downed trees.

Dangling modifiers sometimes result from the modifier being placed before a *genitive** construction:

> *Twenty-two years old and already a millionaire,* Bill Bruce's pitching prowess delights his manager.

It is, of course, Bill Bruce and not his pitching prowess who is twenty-two and a millionaire. Here is a possible revision:

> *Twenty-two years old and already a millionaire, Bill Bruce* possesses a pitching prowess that delights his manager.

Use the Correct Verb Form (Vb)

If in doubt about the correctness of a *verb** form, consult your dictionary. There you will find the principal parts of the verb listed after the entry for the verb: for example, *lie* (in the sense of recline)—*lay, lain, lying, lies*. With this entry, you are provided all the information you need to construct such sentences as the following:

> He *lay* in bed last night.
> He *has lain* in bed for over a week.
> He *is lying* there, sick at heart.
> He *lies* there, day after day.

Make Your Verb Agree with Its Subject (V/Ag)

Except for a few special situations, we normally have little difficulty in getting proper *agreement** between *subject** and *verb**. We write or speak *she* and follow it with a singular verb like *is* or *has*. However, we do have trouble sometimes with words like *each, everyone, either, neither, anybody, and somebody*. These words are all singular, but in certain constructions they may take on a plural feel.

You likely experience no difficulty with "Everyone is coming home for the holidays." But when you separate your singular subject from its verb with a prepositional *phrase** that has a plural *object** you may be tempted to make the verb plural. If you do you'll mistakenly write "Everyone of the children *are* coming home for the holidays."

You may also be uncertain about what to do when you join a plural noun and singular noun with *or*. The rule is to choose your verb according to which noun is closest to the verb. Thus:

> Either John *or* his *brothers are* coming to the wedding.

But

Either his brothers *or John is* coming to the wedding.

Finally, when you work with *collective nouns** like *groups, team, commission, committee, and company,* you will have to decide whether you want to treat them as plural or singular. Either of the following is correct:

The *committee is* meeting in the conference room.
The *committee are* meeting in the conference room.

Be consistent in your use, at least within the same context. Make sure any pronouns you use agree with the verb chosen.

Write
The *committee is* meeting in *its* conference room.

Don't write
The *committee is* meeting in *their* conference room.

Make Your Pronouns Agree with Their Antecedents (P/Ag)

Any *pronouns** you use have to be in *agreement** with their *antecedents**

John insisted upon *his* rights.
Mary didn't care for her dessert.
John and Mary bought *their* new *house* after *they* negotiated a mortgage for *it.*
The *jury* is in the jury room. *It* should be coming out soon with *its* verdict.

Or

The *jury are* in the jury room. *They* should be coming out soon with *their* verdict.

Traditionally, when an indefinite pronoun, such as *anyone,* is the antecedent we have used a male pronoun. For example:

Everyone in our class had *his* picture taken.

Today, given our sensitivity to women's rights, we may be uncomfortable with such constructions. We may say instead, "*Everyone* in our class had *their* picture taken," which, unfortunately, is grammatically incorrect. (However, if enough people switch to such a usage it may become acceptable.) We may also say,

"*Everyone* in our class had *his or her* picture taken," which is correct but awkward. Perhaps the best solution for now is to rewrite the sentence to allow for a plural pronoun.

> *All* the students in our class had *their* pictures taken.

Use the Correct Pronoun Form (Pron)

At one time (as we discuss in Chapter 7, "Grammar"; see pages 125–127), English had an elaborate system of *cases** for its *nouns** and *pronouns**. Today, with the exception of the *genitive case**, case is found only in the pronouns. Case in pronouns is more important than you may think. It is not needed for understanding: sentences like "John and *me* went to the movies" or "He bought candy for John and *I*" are perfectly understandable. But such constructions mark the user as a person who doesn't use language properly. Such constructions stand out and may cause the people who use them to lose opportunities they might otherwise have. Follow these rules:

Use *nominative case** pronouns for *subjects**:

> John and *I* went to the movies.
> *We* women are dissatisfied with our pay.

Use *accusative case** pronouns for *objects** of *verbs** and *prepositions**:

> He bought candy for John and *me.*
> She drove *us* hard, but she was a fair boss.

Use *nominative case** after *linking verbs**:

> My mother influenced me greatly.
> It was *she* who convinced me to go to medical school.

Make Pronoun Reference Clear and Obvious (Ref)

Our writing is full of *pronouns**, so much so that we can lose track of which word or phrase is the *antecedent** of the pronoun. In this passage, the references are clear:

> My mother, a teacher, enjoyed working with children. *She* found *them* to be creative and funny.

Mother is female and singular. *Children* is plural. Therefore, the reference of *she* and *them* is clear and obvious. In this next sentence the reader cannot clearly identify the antecedent for *he:*

When my father left my brother at college, *he* was teary-eyed.

The *he* could refer to either *father* or *brother*. The sentence needs rewriting:

My father was teary-eyed when *he* left my brother at college.

Or

My brother was teary-eyed when my father left him at college.

In the following passage, the *this* is ambiguous:

In the commercial world, you do what you must to stay ahead of your competitors. I must tell you our firm is fiercely competitive. *This* may disturb some of my readers.

The *this* could refer to either the fact of the business competition or to the writer's statement that "our firm is fiercely competitive," or even to the notion of "I must tell you." To make such sentences clear, repeat enough of the antecedent to clarify the reference:

This competitive aspect of business may disturb some of my readers.

Watch out for Double Negatives (DN)

Expressions like "He doesn't want nobody to help" or "I don't want nothing" are termed double negatives. They have been considered grammatically incorrect since the eighteenth century. Use of the double negative will brand its user as an illiterate to many people. The combination of the double negative with an *agreement** error—"He don't want none"—is particularly deadly. If you are in the habit of using double negatives and expect to take your place as an educated person, you really have no choice but to break the habit.

There is also another type of double negative that is not considered ungrammatical. In the first type, "I don't want nothing," the intent of the speaker is to make a negative statement, but, at least by eighteenth-century logic, the two negatives cancel out and *inadvertently* make a positive statement. In the second type, the speaker *intends* to make a positive statement, as in this example:

The Internal Revenue Service will *not* bring criminal action *unless* there has been a deliberate attempt to defraud the government.

Although not ungrammatical, such constructions are troublesome. The reader has to sort out the two negatives to arrive at a positive statement:

The Internal Revenue Service will bring criminal action only when there has been a deliberate attempt to defraud the government.

An instruction might read, "Do *not* press button A *unless* the red light is on," which the reader has to translate to "Press button A only when the red light is on." Spare your readers the need to translate; they don't always do it successfully.

Use the Right Word (Word)

We once heard a television newsreader speak of an accident that *decapitated* a man's leg at the knee. A moment with your dictionary will convince you of the impossibility of that. Be sure of a word's meaning when you are using it, particularly when you are experimenting with new and strange words.

English has many close pairs of words that are particularly troublesome. *Flaunt* and *flout* are examples. *Flaunt* means to be ostentatious in your use of something, as in "He *flaunted* his money shamelessly." *Flout* means to treat with contempt, as in "The President *flouted* the Congress, to its great dismay."

Lie and *lay, fewer* and *less, compose* and *comprise, imply* and *infer*—all are examples of words that people frequently confuse. If in doubt, spend a moment with your dictionary. (See also the entry for *connotation,* pages 216–217.)

Spell that Word Correctly (Sp)

Before the sixteenth century, no one worried very much about consistency in English spelling. Within the same document words would be spelled several different ways; for example, *fellow, felow, felowe, fallow,* and *fallowe.*[23] But by the end of the seventeenth century, scholars and writers had standardized English spelling to a point close to where it is today. In the eighteenth century, Samuel Johnson's dictionary, published in 1755, provided most people who cared with a source for checking correct spelling. The standardization of spelling was part of the whole movement toward authority we discuss in Chapter 7, "Grammar" (see pages 127–131).

Incorrect spelling is today considered a serious error. Like it or not, you must give the matter some attention. Your dictionary is your prime source for checking spelling. However, you can find in your bookstore small pocket-sized books that spell correctly 20,000 words or so without definition. Such books can be very handy and much less cumbersome to use than a dictionary. We recommend that you buy one.

Exercises

1. Find a piece of writing that is well organized and that displays its organization well. In a short essay, analyze the piece, discussing both its organization and the ways in which the organization is displayed. Accompany your essay with a reprint of the piece analyzed.

2. Divide the class into four groups. Each group will take as its responsibility the teaching of one of the followings aspects of a clear style to the rest of the class:

- organization, including choice of organization and display of organization
- sentence structure, including sentence extension, avoidance of nounspeak, and choice of voice and mood
- the use of people in writing
- expression, including appropriate tone, precise word choice, and the avoidance of pomposity, clichés, euphemism, and the undue use of abstraction

Each group should use samples, of both good and bad writing, to illustrate its points.

3. Find a well-written paragraph, about one hundred words long, that is approximately in the middle between informal and formal style. Rewrite the paragraph four times as follows:

- unacceptably and ludicrously informal
- acceptably informal
- unacceptably and pompously formal
- acceptably formal

Be prepared to read your rewrites in class and to explain why you made the choices you did.

4. Create example sentences to illustrate each of the errors listed. Following each example, rewrite the sentence correctly. Be prepared to discuss the incorrect sentences in class:

- fragmentary sentence
- run-on sentence
- nonparallel structure
- misplaced or dangling modifier
- incorrect verb form
- faulty verb agreement
- faulty pronoun agreement
- incorrect pronoun form
- unclear pronoun reference
- ungrammatical double negative
- a double negative that is correct grammatically but poor stylistically

12

Conventions

Conventions are agreements between writers and readers that enable readers to read and understand what someone has written. Except for historical records and inventories, most writing before the invention of the printing press was not to be read but to be heard. A scribe copied a text, and someone recited it to listeners. As long as there were more reciters and listeners than readers and manuscripts, the conventions of spelling, punctuation, mechanics, and format remained rudimentary. But with the advent of printing, writers and readers were forced to pay attention to the look of writing on the page. Workable conventions were needed, and standardization became important.

Almost every convention of writing since the printing press has made reading easier. Conventions include punctuation and such things as abbreviations, symbols, and the use of capital letters.

Punctuation counts. When we speak we help our listeners follow our intended grouping and emphasis of words by pausing, gesturing, and by changing the tone and stress of our voice. When we write we show readers our intended grouping and emphasis by punctuation. Without punctuation, our writing would be worse than if we were talking in a deadpan, monotone voice.

In the following passage, we have removed the author's capitalization and punctuation:

> why has darwin been so hard to grasp within a decade he convinced the thinking world that evolution had occurred but his own theory of natural selection never achieved much popularity in his own time it did not prevail until the 1940s and even today though it forms the core of our evolutionary theory it is evidently misunderstood misquoted and misapplied

Going slowly, you probably figured out what the passage is saying. But you are working harder than you would have to if the proper conventions were used.

Here is the passage as it was originally capitalized and punctuated:

Why has Darwin been so hard to grasp? Within a decade, he convinced the thinking world that evolution had occurred, but his own theory of natural selection never achieved much popularity during his own lifetime. It did not prevail until the 1940s, and even today, though it forms the core of our evolutionary theory, it is widely misunderstood, misquoted, and misapplied.[1]

Although some other variations are possible (no comma after *decade,* a period or semicolon instead of a comma after *occurred,* an apostrophe between *1940* and *s,* and no comma after *misquoted,* for instance), you probably pretty much could determine the author's punctuation. That's how well you have already developed a sense that punctuation is an extension of speech for grouping words and that periods and commas do most of the work.

In addition to serving the ear, punctuation helps the eye by providing visual clues to the structure and meaning of a passage. For instance, the quotation mark and the apostrophe do not correspond with natural pauses or tones of voice in speaking. They depend on grammatical and logical relationships. *Utah's scenic Bryce Canyon* sounds like it could be written as *Utahs scenic Bryce Canyon*. Or *"The beach is our major attraction," said Mary Jayne, Menifee County naturalist. "And its undeveloped state is a major lure."* sounds like *The beach is our major attraction, said Mary Jayne, Menifee County naturalist. And its undeveloped state is a major lure*.

Although the missing apostrophe is distracting, most readers would have no difficulty knowing that *Utahs scenic Bryce Canyon* should be written as *Utah's scenic Bryce Canyon*. But the quotation marks of the second example are more important—they tell the reader who is saying what. Without the quotation marks, the reader would have to guess whether the writer of the passage or the person quoted is saying *And its undeveloped state is a major lure*. Thus, some types of punctuation have little relationship to recreating pauses and stresses, but they make the structure of the sentence more visible, and therefore easier to understand.

This use of punctuation to visualize structure has created an interesting "back formation" in the use of quotation marks. It is fairly common to see a speaker signal a direct quotation by raising both hands and making "quotation signs" by wiggling the index and middle fingers of both hands.

It seems, then, that punctuation stems from two traditions. In one tradition, the writer supplies the absent pauses and stresses of speech with punctuation marks. In the other, the writer uses punctuation to indicate logical relationships that do not relate to sound. Both traditions save readers time and effort in figuring out the meaning of a passage.

If the writer is lax about punctuation, it is sometimes impossible to reconstruct the intended punctuation. In such instances, the best that readers can hope for is a slight delay while working out the puzzle. Take, for example, this short sentence, which cries out for punctuation to clarify its meaning:

Mrs. Simmons our next door neighbor has two sons in college.

Which way is the sentence to be understood? As

> Mrs. Simmons, our next door neighbor has two sons in college. (The comma after *Mrs. Simmons* separates it from the rest of the sentence and shows that Mrs. Simmons is the name of the person being addressed.)

Or as

> Mrs. Simmons, our next door neighbor, has two sons in college. (The pair of commas sets off *our next door neighbor* from the rest of the sentence and shows that the four words are an *appositive**—a phrase that explains who Mrs. Simmons is.)

(In this chapter, the first time in each entry we use a grammatical term that we have defined in Chapter 13, "Glossary of Grammatical Terms," we note that term by italicizing it and marking it with an asterisk.)

When a *sentence** like *Mrs. Simmons our next door neighbor has two sons in college* has no comma or commas, no amount of struggling is going to help readers work out the intended punctuation, unless additional information gathered from the larger context of the sentence or paragraph helps.

Just as bad as no punctuation is incorrect or awkward punctuation. Assume that the writer intended to write *Mrs. Simmons, our next door neighbor, has two sons in college,* but wrote *Mrs. Simmons, our next door neighbor has two sons in college.* Again, unless information from the larger context tells readers something different, they will at first take the writer's punctuation at face value. For the reader's sake we should learn to punctuate to make our meaning clear—on first reading.

As we mentioned earlier, you punctuate as you write. But regardless of how much care you lavish on your writing, you should carefully proofread for punctuation. Those little marks, which are so important to the reader, are easy for you to overlook. According to a recent study of the most frequent errors found by professional copyeditors and proofreaders, omitted or incorrect punctuation accounts for 10.5 percent of the errors: that ranks fourth on the list of the ten top errors.[2] If you think incorrect punctuation causes only minor inconveniences, consider the two million dollar comma reported in *The Book of Lists:*

> An unidentified congressional clerk was instructed to write: "All foreign fruit-plants are free from duty." Instead, he wrote: "All foreign fruit, plants are free from duty." It cost the U.S. Government $2 million before a new session of Congress could rectify the error.[3]

Fortunately, most punctuation errors are not as expensive as that one.

However, there is more at stake than clarity. A punctuation error can rile many persons. There are readers who, if they cannot fault your thinking, will attack your writing on the grounds of erroneous punctuation. They will charge that you are careless or lazy or something worse. Don't leave yourself open to attack because of your punctuation errors.

Before we look in earnest at the uses of specific punctuation marks and mechanics, let us sum up what you may already know about them.

- You know that punctuation and mechanics are convenient for the reader. They show the reader how to follow words without having to reread and reform sentences to catch the meaning. When we read, our eyes move forward three or four words before our mind grasps the meaning of what we read. Our eyes are looking for punctuation and mechanics, so we can get more information about the written signal we are decoding.
- You sense that although some punctuation usage and mechanics may vary with individual writers, they must be consistent. There are fairly rigid rules about punctuation and mechanics because inconsistent punctuation and mechanics—like most other inconsistencies—can cause confusion. In early writing, conventions were rare and inconsistent. Some early manuscripts have almost no punctuation or mechanics; those that have use many conventions that are meaningless to us. Today, punctuation has been refined to the point that variations are limited. When there is divided usage, as in punctuating or not punctuating plural numerals (*three 7's* or *three 7s; 1940's* or *1940s*), the punctuated form (*three 7's* or *1940's*) is generally the older form used by more conservative writers. However, as with spelling and pronunciation, there is a tendency in punctuation to choose the simplest form and to phase out the more complicated.
- You know that some punctuation and mechanics are sometimes based only on personal preference and do not affect meaning—*1940's* versus *1940s,* for example. Within the limits set by custom, writers may choose to enclose an interrupting element in a sentence with parentheses, commas, or dashes—depending upon the effect desired. There is less freedom with mechanics.
- You know that it is easy to overlook needed punctuation and mechanics when proofreading.

Learning what else you need to know about punctuation and mechanics is a doable task. It is now time to make yourself at home with writing conventions so you won't have to be hindered by questions about them when you are writing. You will need to think about a great many other things. You should therefore be able to use almost by reflex (yet with intention) the following conventions:

abbreviations and acronyms
apostrophe
brackets
capitalization
colon
comma
dash
ellipsis marks
exclamation mark
hyphen

italicization
numbers
parentheses
period
question mark
quotation marks
semicolon
slash mark
symbols

Abbreviations and Acronyms

An abbreviation is a shortened form of a word or group of words: Mr. (Mister), vol. (volume), avg. (average), mph (miles per hour), CRT (cathode-ray tube), UFO (unidentified flying object).

An acronym is a coined word formed from the initial letters or other parts of a group of words: WATS (Wide Area Telecommunications Service), UNICEF (United Nations International Children's Emergency Fund, AIDS (Aquired Immune Deficiency Syndrome). An acronym is pronounced like a word: NOW (National Organization of Women) is pronounced like the word *now*. Acronyms formed in part by syllables of words are usually not written in full capitals: radar (*ra*dio *di*recting *a*nd *r*anging), centrex (*centr*alized *ex*change), and Nazi (*Na*tionalso*zi*alist). Such acronyms are sometimes called "hidden" or "forgotten" acronyms, because we do not recognize them as acronyms.

Abbreviations and acronyms are created mostly as shortcuts to pronouncing or spelling out long words or *phrases**. When overused, they make a passage look like a code to outwit enemy cryptographers. The following is part of an order one of your authors once received while in the service. It announced his transfer to another station:

> 3 Fol EM YN-3 (E-4) unoindic PMOSTOS ETS BPED PROFILE ind rel asg USNAVPERS Indc 11 NAVDIS (1361) this sta for mvmt to CE, SDiego. Pers ROB PA no ltr thn 0700 Aug. . . .

And so on for a dozen lines. We don't want to imitate the Pentagon in our writing, but used with care, abbreviations and acronyms are acceptable.

Abbreviations

Although abbreviations can save time and space, don't use them if they are likely to inconvenience readers. Abbreviations that are so obvious to us may be far from clear to others. The following six general points will help you use abbreviations in a way that will not confuse your readers.

- In general, do not begin a sentence with an abbreviation.
- Do not use a lot of abbreviations in your prose, although many abbrevi-

ations may be suitable in lists, tables, illustrations, and addresses, where space may be limited.

- If you are not absolutely certain that your reader will understand the abbreviation, spell out the full expression the first time and follow it with the abbreviation in parentheses. The abbreviation may be used alone in later references.

  Scientists at Yale University have put a gene for an enzyme called thymidine kinase (TK) into fertilized mouse eggs. . . . Of the first 180 mice that developed from injected eggs, three incorporated the TK gene.

- Be sure always to define an abbreviation that could have multiple meanings. For example, *ERA* represents the Equal Rights Amendment and Earned Run Average, and *NFL* stands for both the National Football League and the National Forensic League.
- Make your abbreviations consistent, as the writer has in this explanation of CPU:

  The Central Processing Unit (CPU) controls all computer functions, sends commands to the peripheral devices, and controls access to the memory. The CPU is the "brain" of the microcomputer that performs the arithmetic and logical functions. The CPU controls . . .

- When possible, use standard abbreviations that are sanctioned by professional organizations or college-level dictionaries.

Here are some negative and positive examples to illustrate these suggestions.

Not this:	RR cars will move the coal to the company siding.
But this:	Railroad cars will move the coal to the company siding.
Not this:	Jan. 15 is the deadline for applications.
But this:	January 15 is the deadline for applications.
Not this:	Prof. Chas. Warton became Dept. Chairman.
But this:	Professor Charles Warton became Department Chairman.
Not this:	Uniform corrosion is the form of metal deterioration for which corrosion rate is expressed as ipy or mpy.
But this:	Uniform corrosion is the form of metal deterioration for which corrosion rate is expressed as inches penetration per year (ipy) or mils penetration per year (mpy).
Not this:	The base is 4 inches by 4 in.
But this:	The base is 4 inches by 4 inches.
Not this:	Last February had 28 days, but next Feb. will have 29.

But this:	Last February had 28 days, but next February will have 29.
Not this:	The plane flew 2500 m. at speeds of from 450 to 550 m. per hr.
But this:	The plane flew 2500 miles at speeds of from 450 to 550 mph.

Some abbreviations are customary, even preferred. Here is a representative list:

- Titles before names—Dr., Mrs., Mr., Ms.
- Designations after names—Harry T. Street, Jr., Sen. Robert Dole (R-Kansas), Sir Anthony Firth, M.P.
- Academic degrees: A.A., M.A., M.D., M.F.A., Ed.D., B.A., M.S., M.B.A., Ph.D., LL.D.
- Long names of organizations and countries—

AFL-CIO	American Federation of Labor and Congress of Industrial Organizations
NCAA	National Collegiate Athletic Association
RCA	Radio Corporation of America
U.S.S.R	Union of Soviet Socialist Republics

- Commonly known units of measure—mph, rpm, mpg, amp
- Abbreviations used in bibliographical notations—p. (page), pp. (pages), ch. (chapter), col. (column), no. (number), nos. (numbers), sec. (section), supp. (supplement), n.d. (not dated)
- Postal service two-letter abbreviations for states and outlying regions—

Alabama	AL	Iowa	IA
Alaska	AK	Kansas	KS
Arizona	AZ	Kentucky	KY
Arkansas	AR	Louisiana	LA
California	CA	Maine	ME
Colorado	CO	Maryland	MD
Connecticut	CT	Massachusetts	MA
Delaware	DE	Michigan	MI
District of Columbia	DC	Minnesota	MN
Florida	FL	Mississippi	MS
Georgia	GA	Missouri	MO
Guam	GU	Montana	MT
Hawaii	HI	Nebraska	NE
Idaho	ID	Nevada	NV
Illinois	IL	New Hampshire	NH
Indiana	IN	New Jersey	NJ

New Mexico	NM	South Dakota	SD
New York	NY	Tennessee	TN
North Carolina	NC	Texas	TX
North Dakota	ND	Utah	UT
Ohio	OH	Vermont	VT
Oklahoma	OK	Virginia	VA
Oregon	OR	Virgin Islands	VI
Pennsylvania	PA	Washington	WA
Puerto Rico	PR	West Virginia	WV
Rhode Island	RI	Wisconsin	WI
South Carolina	SC	Wyoming	WY

Acronyms

The influence of scientific and technical terminology on our language has caused acronyms to sprout like mushrooms—practically overnight. Many of these acronyms are colorful, but unless readers know them they should be avoided. For instance, WYSIWYG (pronounced "wizzee wig") is the acronym for "What You See Is What You Get"—a term that describes computer capability to show on the screen exactly the format you will produce on a printer. However, few persons other than computer operators know the term.

Because many acronyms are not universally recognized and because they sometimes have more than one meaning, you should write out the group of words the first time and follow it with the acronym in parentheses. Then you may use the acronym in later references.

Apostrophe

The apostrophe has three major uses: (1) to form the possessive of *nouns** and *indefinite pronouns** (somebody, someone, anybody, others, and so on), (2) to form contractions (showing that letters and numerals have been omitted from words and figures), and (3) to form the plurals of numbers, letters, symbols, and words referred to as words.

Forming the Possessive

Add an apostrophe and an *s* to form the *possessive** of nouns and indefinite pronouns not already ending in *s*.

the *man's* jacket
Harold's airplane
women's attache cases

the *children's* trip
no one's fault
everybody's business
another's responsibility
either's choice

The apostrophe is not used to form the possessive of *personal pronouns**, even when they end in *s*: *your/yours, our/ours, his, her/hers, it/its, whose, their/theirs*. Do not confuse contractions with possessives. Note that *it's* is not the possessive of *it* but a contraction of *it is*, that *you're* is not the possessive of *you* but a contradiction of *you are,* and that *who's* is not the possessive of *who* but a contraction of *who is*. Writing *they're schedule* (= *they are schedule*) or *who's car?* (= *who is car?*) is a confusion of contractions and possessives.

Add an apostrophe alone to form the possessive of plural nouns already ending in *s*.

The *employees'* benefits include free dental care.
The three *soldiers'* rations have arrived.

When ownership is joint, add an apostrophe and an *s* to the last name: *Harold and Barney's* farm, *Cheech and Chong's* movies. When ownership is individual, add an apostrophe and *s* to each name: *Tammy's and Rita's* books.

To form the possessive of most inanimate objects, drop the *'s*, or use an *of* or *in* phrase. There is no grammatical rule about this, but stylistically the prepositional phrase is often better.

awkward	**better**
desk's top	desk top or top of the desk
book's cover	book cover or cover of the book
utility room's sink	utility room sink or sink in the utility room
"A Rose for Emily"'s setting	the setting of "A Rose for Emily"

Forming Contractions

Use an apostrophe to indicate the omitted letters or numbers in contractions.

I *don't* like to cook on electric stoves.
She's looking forward to her vacation.
We moved here in *'72*.

The more contractions you use, the more your writing will resemble spoken English. Sometimes you want to avoid sounding too formal. Here are two examples:

Let's get right to the point.
Why *isn't* the band playing in the parade?

This doesn't mean that you should use a contraction every time the opportunity comes up. Avoid such awkward-looking and sounding contractions as *it'll, should've, who've, that'll,* and *there'll,* unless used in dialogue.

Writers have long used contractions to represent the speech of characters who drop certain sounds. Mary N. Murfree attempted to recreate East Tennessee mountain dialect in "The 'Harnt' that Walks Chilhowee" this way:

> An' it air a toler'ble for'ard season. Yer wheat looks likely; an' yer gyarden truck air thrivin' powerful. Even that cold spell weuns hed about the full o' the moon in May ain't done sot it back none, it 'pears to me. (p. 283)

But we suggest that you keep this many 'postrophes out'n yer writ'n. Any overused technique becomes tedious for the reader to follow. A more fruitful approach to recreating the sound of the voice on the page is to work on diction, rhythm, and point of view.

Forming Certain Plurals

Add an apostrophe and an *s* to form the plurals of numbers, letters, symbols, and words referred to as words.

Dot your *i's* and cross your *t's.*
Hows many *Ph.D.'s* are on the faculty?
Our enrollment increased every year during the *1970's.*
My social security number contains four *7's.*
How many +*'s* does the equation have?
The mayor's proclamations are full of *whereas's* and *wherefore's.*

This use of the apostrophe is for clarity. Without the apostrophe, *four a's* becomes *four as*. Many writers, though, don't use the apostrophe with plural numbers. They apparently believe that plural numbers are easily recognized and do not need an apostrophe to denote plurality.

Two Additional Comments

1. When you use quotation marks within quotation marks, use single quotes for the inside marks. When typing, use the apostrophes for the single quotes (see page 267).

Garrett Mattingly in *The Armada* describes the importance of England's victory over Spain this way: "It raised men's hearts in dark hours, and led them to say to one another, 'What we have done once, we can do again.' In so far as it did this, the legend of the defeat of the Spanish Armada became as important as the actual event—perhaps even more important."

2. Never use *'s* to form plural nouns or verbs ending in *s*.

incorrect	**correct**
Six *award's* were presented at the banquet.	Six *awards* were presented at the banquet.
The hot weather *help's* me loosen up quicker.	The hot weather *helps* me loosen up quicker.

Brackets

Brackets are not used much, but when they are needed they are needed. Brackets enclose material that you insert in someone else's writing. Brackets *always* come in pairs—one at the beginning and one at the end of the enclosed material—so check for unescorted ones. In handwriting, make sure your brackets look like brackets [ ] not parentheses ( ). In typing, if your keyboard doesn't have bracket keys, either insert the marks by hand (remember to leave the spaces for them) or by using the slash mark and two underlines /‾ _7. The upper horizontal lines are made by striking the underline key on the line *above* that on which the bracket is being formed.

Brackets tell the reader that the inserted material is your comment, not the original author's. Such insertions may be to clarify a reference or to show by use of *sic* that there is an error in the quoted material. Do not use parentheses as a substitute for brackets, or your reader will think the inserted material is the original author's parenthetical statement. This example indicates that the writer has inserted material to clarify the references to Macaulay's use of *he* and *them:*

> A passage from his essay on Bacon illustrates Macaulay's belief that literature is an antidote to what Matthew Arnold was later to call the "sick hurry" and the "divided aim" of the Victorian age:
>
> > "The debt which he [the liberally educated person] owes to them [the great minds of the past] is incalculable. They have guided him toward truth. . . ."

The Latin word *sic* (meaning *thus* or *so*) is sometimes inserted in brackets within quoted material to identify an error in the original passage (in the following example, *pot* for *post*):

> The headline read "Martin Liedermann Appointed Pot [*sic*] Master."

Capitalization

Rules for capitalization vary, but it is fairly standard to use capital letters to mark (1) beginnings, (2) *proper nouns**, and (3) words derived from proper nouns. There is also a great deal of freedom in using capital letters for special purposes, such as using full capitals (FULL CAPITALS) to label settings on control panels and knobs and levers. But however you use capital letters, be sure to use them consistently in the same piece of writing.

Beginnings

We all know to capitalize the first word of every sentence. It is also general practice to capitalize the first word of a quoted sentence, a direct quotation, and a statement that follows a colon if the statement is a complete sentence:

The rain saved the garden.

1st Lt. Kathie J. Hightower replied, "At summer camp some of the troops referred to me as 'Mama.' I guess that's better than 'The Old Man.'"

"How's daddy's old boy?" he said loudly, giving a poke at the baby's chin.

A wise supervisor knows this: Don't be overly concerned with the origin of the complaint; be concerned with the merits of the complaint.

Capitalize the first word of a salutation or complimentary close in a letter.

Dear Professor Sanchez:
Dear Mr. and Mrs. Jones:
Sincerely yours,

Capitalize the first and last word of a title and heading. Capitalize all other words except *articles**, *conjunctions**, and *prepositions** with fewer than five letters. Note that the first letter of a subtitle is capitalized.

The Art of the Film
Sinclair Lewis: An American Life
"Music to Read By"
Conclusions and Recommendations
Chapter Five: Sources of Knowledge
Figure 4. Interior View of a High-Speed Pump

Capitalize the first word of a line of conventional poetry.

By the rude bridge that arched the flood,
    Their flag to April's breeze unfurled,
Here once the embattled farmers stood
    And fired the shot heard round the world.
        —*Ralph Waldo Emerson*

Much modern poetry is written without capital letters at the beginning of lines. Always use the capitalization of the passage you are quoting, even when some of the capitals would not be used by today's standards.

I heard a Fly buzz—when I died—
The Stillness in the Room
Was like the Stillness in the Air—
Between the Heaves of Storm—
        —*Emily Dickinson*[4]

The same holds true of prose. Take, for instance, this passage from Jonathan Swift's *A Modest Proposal,* first published in 1729:

> I profess, in the Sincerity of my Heart, that I have not the least personal Interest, in endeavoring to promote this necessary Work, having no other Motive than the *publick Good of my Country, by advancing our Trade, providing for Infants, relieving the Poor, and giving some Pleasure to the Rich.* I have no children, by which I can propose to get a single penny; the youngest being nine Years Old and my Wife past Child-bearing.

Proper Nouns and Words Derived from Them

Capitalize certain words to show you are referring to a particular or special person or thing. These words are called proper nouns. It is sometimes difficult to decide when a word is to be considered a proper noun or when a word is derived from a proper noun. Make certain that the word refers to a particular person or thing rather than to a general class of things before capitalizing. Here are some typical examples of proper nouns and derivatives.

People—William Shakespeare, Shakespearean sonnet, Jesus Christ, Christianity, Christian, Charles Darwin, Darwinism, James A. Van Allen, Van Allen Belts

Days of the Week and Months of the Year—Sunday, Monday, Tuesday, January, February, March (but not the names of the seasons: winter, spring, summer, fall, autumn)

Holidays and Holy days—Christmas, Easter, Mother's Day, Independence Day, Yom Kippur, St. Agnes' Eve

Geographical Entities—Switzerland, Swiss, the South, Southerner, the Eastern Seaboard, Missouri, Missourians, Mount St. Helens, the Mississippi River, Caney Creek, Lake Michigan, the Pacific Ocean, the Bay of Bengal, Appalachia, the Appalachian Trail, Yellowstone Park, Arctic Circle

Languages and Racial and Ethnic Groups—English, Russian, Yiddish, Vulgar Latin, Indo-European, Indian, Chicano

Religious Terms—God, the Bible, the New Testament, the Koran, Catholic, Mormon, Judaism, Muslem

Buildings and other Facilities—John Hancock Building, the Golden Gate Bridge, Tri-Cities Airport, Baird Music Hall, Boone County Hospital

Companies, Organizations, and Institutions—Ford Motor Company, the Republican Party, United States Senate, United States Navy (USN), the British Embassy, the Nuclear Regulatory Commission, the National Science Foundation, National Organization of Women, Future Farmers of America, Hickman High School, University of Pennsylvania, Zeta Tau Alpha

Brand Names—Chevrolet, Gleem, Pennzoil, Timex, Xerox, Compaq, Sanka, Coca-Cola

Historical Documents, Events, and Eras—Constitution, Treaty of Versailles, the Civil War, World War II, Romanticism, the Victorian Age, the Depression, the Johnstown Flood, the Golden Age of Greece, the Chia-Ching Period

Special Events—the World Series, the Olympic Games, the World Cup Series, The Kentucky Derby, The Rose Bowl Parade

Official Titles Before Names—General Omar Bradley, Sgt. Dorothy MacKenzie, Professor Lee Maloney, Senator Tucker, Officer Keller, Mayor Alfredo Ruiz, Rabbi Isadore Keyfetz, Pope John Paul II, the Rev. Alex Conyers

Course Titles—Economics II (but *My economics class meets from 10 to 11 MWF*), the Modern Novel, Foundations of Education

Full Capitals

Use full capitals to name controls and settings when they are panel or equipment markings.

Make sure the SQUELCH switch is in the ON position.
The malfunction seems to be in the R4 LEVEL ADJ switch.
When READY appears, remove diskette DC0007.

Colon

The colon, that odd-looking mark of punctuation consisting of two dots placed one above the other, has three important uses: (1) to introduce quotations, (2) to introduce lists, and (3) to introduce explanations. It says, in effect, to readers "Slow up: something important is coming."

Introducing a Quotation

Use a colon to introduce a quotation that you want to emphasize or one that is four or more lines long.

Machievelli had a rule:

> Get a reputation for truth-telling and promise-making by being scrupulous about both when there isn't much at stake. Then, having established that reputation, you can take advantage of it when a really important piece of treachery is in the making.

As this example illustrates, quotations indented and single spaced do not need to be enclosed in quotation marks.

Introducing a List

Use a colon to introduce a list.

There are four distinct systems for lacing boots: grommeted eyelets, swivel eyelets, open hooks, and "tunnel-like" hooks.

There were three important stages in drafting the Declaration of Independence: the Declaration as originally written by Thomas Jefferson; the Declaration as submitted by the Committee of Five; and the Declaration as it was finally adopted.

The topics to be discussed include the following:
—sense of place in Flannery O'Connor's fiction
—humor in Jesse Stuart's fiction
—dialect in James Still's fiction
—myth in Eudora Welty's fiction

Do not interrupt a *verb** or *preposition** and its *complements** with a colon. Don't write *Today is: Wednesday* or *I would like to travel to: Idaho, Utah, and New Mexico*. More desirable is *Today is Wednesday* and *I would like to travel to Idaho, Utah, and New Mexico*.

Undesired:	The three factors essential to using a microscope are: an object to be observed, light to observe it by, and an eye to observe it with.
Desired:	Three factors are essential to using a microscope: an object to be observed, light to observe it by, and an eye to observe it with.

Introducing an Explanation

Use a colon to introduce a statement that explains, amplifies, or summarizes another statement. As in introducing a quotation or list, the colon tells the reader to watch what comes next.

> All books fit into one of two classes: the books of the hour and the books of all time.
>
> The following question came up for discussion: What is the best method to prevent employee absenteeism?
>
> Success, in this instance, can be summed up in a single word: *teamwork.*

Capitalization after the Colon

In some of the examples given, the first word after the colon is capitalized. In others it is not. Capitalize when the information following the colon is a complete sentence or is a list of formal topics that serve as titles or subtitles.

The Colon with Other Punctuation

If an introductory statement ends with words closed in parentheses, the colon immediately follows the closing parenthesis:

> The following ingredients go into Souffle Humber (a mousse-like chocolate Bavarian):
>
> 1½ envelopes unflavored gelatin
> ½ cup milk
> 4 medium eggs, separated
> ½ cup strong coffee
> ⅓ cup sugar
> 3 tablespoons dark rum
> 1 cup heavy cream

If an introductory statement ends with words enclosed in quotation marks, always place the colon outside the final quotation mark:

> Here are a few characteristics of a "growth job": it involves risk-taking; it causes anxiety because you don't necessarily know what you are doing; it bases pay on productivity; and it instills a sense of mission and desire.

Other Uses of the Colon

The colon is also used in these ways:

- To follow the salutation of a business letter
  Dear Dr. Pennington:
- To separate hours from minutes
  8:15 A.M.
- To express a ratio or proportion
  4:1 or 3:5:3
- To separate a title from a subtitle
  "Changes in Children and Youth over Two Decades: The Perception of Teachers"
  The Rise and Fall of the Third Reich: A History of Nazi Germany
- To separate chapter from verse
  John 3:3
- In some forms of bibliography to separate the place of publication from the publisher
  Colin Fletcher, *The New Complete Walker,* Second Edition (New York: Alfred A. Knopf, 1975).

Comma

The comma is the most frequently used mark of punctuation. Because the comma serves so many purposes, many of us belong to the "pause and punctuate" school of thought. If we are unsure of when to use it, we tend to drop in a comma wherever we suppose the reader pauses. But the comma is not all that difficult to handle. If you learn the following applications, you will master its major uses.

Setting Off Items in a Series

Use a comma to separate words, *phrases**, or *clauses** in a series.

My roomate's clothes were strewn on the desk, on the bed, and on the floor.
Motels, restaurants, bars, souvenir shops, gasoline stations, clothing stores, and mountaineering and ski shops lined the main street of Mountain Center.

Usage is divided over whether to punctuate a series *a, b, c, and d* or *a, b, c and d,* as an authoritative guide states:

> Everybody favors the use of commas between all members up to the last two; but there the shooting begins. A large body of opinion that includes nearly all newspapers insists on *a, b and c*—that is, they omit the last comma. A smaller body, numbering many of the most respectable book publishers, stick to *a, b, and c:* they demand a comma before the cadence signaled by *and, or,* or *but*. Schools that teach composition are divided; so is the counsel of rhetorics, manuals, and teachers of freshman English.[5]

Our advice is to use a comma to separate the next to last and last items of a series. It is *never* incorrect, although newspaper editors don't prefer it.

Separating Independent Clauses Joined by a Coordinating Conjunction

Use a comma to separate two *independent clauses** joined by *and, but, for, nor, or, yet*. Put the comma *before* the *conjunction**.

At last Christmas vacation came, *and* I looked forward to going home.

Mark and Eric arrived at six o'clock, *but* Jerry and I arrived at seven o'clock.

Is it better to aim at a spot on the lane, *or* is it better to aim directly at the pins?

This rule covers only independent clauses joined by a *coordinating conjunction**. Other kinds of elements joined by a coordinating conjunction are not separated by commas. The following sentences are punctuated correctly:

We anticipated a pass and were ready for it.
(The coordinating conjunction *and* connects two verbs; no comma is necessary.)

Your advisor helps you decide where your interests lie and will counsel you about a course of study.
(The coordinating conjunction *and* connects two verbs—*helps* and *will counsel;* no comma is necessary.)

When my heart rate decreased and my endurance increased, I was thankful that I had started jogging.
(*And* connects two *subordinate clauses**; no comma is necessary.)

If the independent clauses are short and parallel in structure, the comma may be omitted, even though the coordinating conjunction is present:

She laughed and I cried.

The engine roared *and* the frame shook.
I tried *but* I could never dunk the ball.

Separating Elements from the Main Clause of a Sentence

We add information to the main clause of a sentence by adding words before or after the main clause or by inserting words that interrupt the main clause.

In a study of twenty recent or contemporary American writers—ten fiction and ten nonfiction—Francis Christensen found that they began about a fourth (24.47 percent) of their sentences with a word, phrase, or subordinate clause before the *subject** of their sentences.[6] Using a comma after such sentence openers is *never* wrong.

However, I would be exaggerating if I said your problems will disappear over night.

On a cold afternoon in October, Gene and Sherry were huddled on his dock shucking and eating oysters.

When we next saw Monica, she was working as an upholsterer for an antique dealer.

Sometimes, when the introductory element is short (say two or three words), you may omit the comma. These sentences are punctuated correctly:

By 1988 the coal liquification plant will be fully operational.
Last night the dorm staff had a picnic at Rodburn Wells.
In this chapter you will find a good explanation of cloning.

However, if you want to emphasize the introductory element, you should place a comma after it:

By 1988, the coal liquification plant will be fully operational.
Last night, the dorm staff had a picnic at Rodburn Wells.
In this chapter, you will find a good explanation of cloning.

Also keep an eye out for short sentence openers that should be followed by a comma to prevent awkwardness or misreading:

awkward omission of comma	**comma to prevent awkwardness**
Below Paul was painting the stair railing.	Below, Paul was painting the stair railing.
As we anticipated the package arrived on Saturday.	As we anticipated, the package arrived on Saturday.

The missing comma allows the reader to misread the first part of the sentence. The commas after *Below* and after *As we anticipated* make the structure of the sentence instantly clear.

Unless we are careful, we may make two other errors in setting off introductory elements. One is to mistake a long introductory element for a sentence. If the introductory element is long and rhetorically strong, it might seem like an independent clause, and you might incorrectly use a period where a comma is called for, thus creating a sentence fragment instead of a sentence opener.

incorrect	**correct**
In reprisal for rough treatment of British traders illegally operating in Spanish Colonial areas. England went to war against Spain in 1739.	In reprisal for rough treatment of British traders illegally operating in Spanish Colonial areas, England went to war against Spain in 1739.

The second error is to confuse a long, complete subject for an introductory element. This confusion could cause you to put a comma incorrectly between the subject and verb:

incorrect	**correct**
The rise in the cost of living, makes it difficult to maintain our previous standard of living.	The rise in the cost of living makes it difficult to maintain our previous standard of living.
The thirty mile stretch of beach to the east of the island, runs north from Cape Canaveral to just south of New Smyrna Beach.	The thirty-mile stretch of beach to the east of the island runs north from Cape Canaveral to just south of New Smyrna Beach.

We also can add information after the sentence core. But it is not always easy to tell when to place a comma before a subordinate phrase or clause that follows a main clause. Generally, you should use a comma in the following situations: before the final element if you want to emphasize the final element; if the final element presents a turn of thought; or if the final element completes a logical cause-effect relationship.

> Macauley took his seat in the House of Commons early in 1830, *at a moment of great significance in British history.*
>
> We were entertained by the Mulhollands on their yacht, *where we spent a most pleasant evening.*
>
> Utilitarians claim that we must evaluate the consequences of an action in light of how much good the action will produce for everyone, *not just ourselves.*

Occasionally you will add an opener and a closer to the core of a sentence. Use commas to set them off:

> *If you're going to have a threshold (or "saddle") on your new door jamb,* use something like yellow pine, *because it will receive a lot of wear.*

> *Comparing figures obtained in 1959 with those gathered twenty years later,* researchers have found that the average man in his fifties was two-and-a-half pounds heavier than his counterpart of two decades ago, *while the average man in his twenties was a full nine pounds heavier.*

We also use commas before and after a word, phrase, or clause that is parenthetical to the main thought of the sentence or that interrupts the flow of the sentence.

> The wolverine, *at fifty pounds,* is perhaps the strongest of all mammals for its size.

> "Throw it overboard," *Jessie shouted,* "and I'll climb up there and belt you one."

> Barite, *known locally as Tiff,* is chiefly mined in Washington and Crawford counties.

Forgetting to insert the closing comma is a common error. Usually the omitted comma (indicated in the following example by brackets) causes only minor inconvenience for the reader, but occasionally it can result in a confused sentence:

> If they supported the incumbent governor, *the delegates were told this week [ ] they would get better roads and more jobs.*

Enclosing Appositives and Nouns of Address

An *appositive** follows a word or group of words and serves to identify or explain them. It is always set off by a comma or commas. When the appositive is embedded in the sentence, enclose it with paired commas. When the appositive comes at the beginning or the end of the sentence, set it off with a comma.

> The nearest star, *or sun,* is a mere 93 million miles away.
> Jefferson City, *the state capital,* is on the Missouri River.
> Let's check with Turner Beckman, *our nutritionist.*

A noun of address is a pronoun, noun, or noun phrase used in direct address to indicate the person being spoken to or written to:

John, do you eat spaghetti?
Do you eat spaghetti, *John*?
Thank you, *ladies and gentlemen,* for your kind welcome.
Hey, you! What are you doing here?

Additional Conventional Uses of the Comma

The comma is the conventional mark of punctuation in several expressions.

Informal Saluation	Dear Betty,
Complimentary Close	Sincerely,
Names with Titles and Degrees	Ralph R. Dysart, DVM, has been appointed to the zoning commision.
Dates	August 4, 1955 is my birthdate. (Optional is *August 4, 1955, is my birthdate*. Notice that *4 August 1955* and *August 1955* are written without commas.)
Addresses Written in Sentence Form	Jason's address is 1808 Beaufort Road, Haldeman, OH 43911. (Note that no comma separates state and zip code.) Place a comma before and after names of states preceded by names of cities: The coal liquification plant will be built in *Louisa, Kentucky,* near Ashland.
Figures	The lowest bid was $21,000. The tax delinquent roll contained 1,738 names. (Note that certain numbers omit commas: *Engine No. 1853291* and *page 1173.)*

Dash

The dash may be used singly or in pairs. It has several uses—all emphatic. It can substitute for a colon in introducing a list, and it can replace commas or parentheses in enclosing additional information in a sentence. When substituted for these, it gives greater emphasis to the set-off passage. Its force comes apparently from the amount of room it takes up on the line—double that of other punctuation. Unlike paired parentheses, the dash makes a point forcefully.

The dash has additional uses; these are illustrated at the end of this entry. However, be cautioned that overusing either dashes or parentheses may be regarded as a sign of stylistic laziness.

To form a handwritten dash, make a line about twice as long as a hyphen. To form a dash on a typewriter, strike the hyphen twice, with no space between strikes or on either side of the dash. It should look like this:

```
She was rich, polished, and happy--at the expense of

others.
```

Introducing a List or Emphasizing Items in a List

Use a dash occasionally to introduce a list or to highlight items in a tabulated list:

> At Stalingrad the Russians relied on their ancient allies—space, time, and winter.
>
> I want to know all about the animals—foxes, possums, coons, rabbits, skunks, mink, groundhogs, and all others.
>
> Did you know that
> —the first king of England was Egbert?
> —part of Richard I's body was buried in one place and part in another?
> —the young Henry VIII was an accomplished scholar, musician, and athlete?
> —Queen Victoria was related, either directly or by marriage, to the royal houses of Germany, Russia, Greece, Romania, Sweden, Denmark, Norway, and Belgium? And that she ruled her own, and this wider family, despotically?

If the sequence of a list is unimportant, random, or obvious, use bullets (•) or dashes (—) to highlight items. If the order is important, use arabic numerals (1, 2, 3, 4, . . .).

Introducing an Explanation

Use a dash to place special emphasis on that which follows the opening of the sentence:

There he goes—the urban cowboy.

Women have a larger natural supply of fat—about 10 percent more than an equally conditioned man.

Enclosing Parenthetical Information

In a sentence that is already heavily punctuated, use a dash for special emphasis:

Within an hour's drive of campus, four state parks—Grayson Lake, Carter Caves, Greenbo Lake, and Natural Bridge—offer sights that bring visitors from all over the nation.

As this sentence illustrates, when the parenthetical statement interrupts rather than follows a clause, it must be set off by paired dashes—one at the opening and one at the close. Watch out for singles.

Adding aspirins and copper pennies to the water is a popular—and totally useless—practice of modern flower arrangers.

The portraits—grave, even somber—indicate that Holbein follows the Italian portrait tradition, which gives the face a neutral expression, rather than Dürer's practice of giving it an expression of keen intensity.

Other Uses of the Dash

Use a dash or dashes to indicate an interruption in thought or speech:

Once when I was in Manila—first let me tell you how I got there.

Judd yelled, "Oh, Amanda—come quickly—It is Sarah. She is sick—come quick!"

Use a dash to separate a direct quotation from its author or source:

"If people are at all peculiar in character they have to suffer from the very rules that produce comfort in others."

. —*Thomas Hardy*

He draweth out the thread of his verbosity finer than the staple of his argument.

—*Love's Labour Lost,* Act 5, Scene I

Ellipsis Points

Ellipsis points indicate (1) an omission of part of a quoted passage or (2) an emphatic pause in a passage.

Indicating an Omission from Quoted Material

When you want to shorten quoted material, use ellipsis points to indicate where you have omitted a word or words. When the omitted material contains no period, use three ellipsis points (three spaced dots).

original passage
It was government, as someone has said, that was not intolerably bad, but that was also never vigorously good.

passage as quoted
The political system was "not intolerably bad, but . . . was also never vigorously good."

The admiral was a well-built man of more than medium stature, long visaged with high cheeks, but neither fat nor thin. He had an aquiline nose and his eyes were light in color; his complexion too was light, but kindling to a vivid red. In his youth his hair was blond, but when he came to his thirtieth year it all turned white. In eating and drinking and the adornment of his person he was always continent and modest.

Columbus' son described his father as

> A well-built man of more than medium stature . . . but neither fat nor thin. He had an aquiline nose and his eyes were light in color; his complexion too was light, but kindling to a vivid red. In youth his hair was blond, but in his thirtieth year it all turned white. In . . . the adornment of his person he was always . . . modest.

When the omitted material comes at the end of a *sentence**, use four ellipsis (four spaced periods).

original passage
God is my witness how much against my will it was that Pope Paul forced me into this work on St. Peter's ten years

passage as quoted
Michelangelo regarded his work on St. Peter's as an act of dedication, thankless and without pay. Writing in 1557 to

ago. If the work had been continued from that time forward as it had begun, it would now have been as far advanced as I had reason to hope, and I should have been able to come to you in Florence.

his friend Vasari, he complained:

> God is my witness how much against my will it was that Pope Paul forced me into this work on St. Peter's ten years ago. If the work had been continued from that time forward as it had begun, it would now have been as far as I had reason to hope. . . . .

When deleting material from a direct quotation, take care not to change its meaning.

Indicating an Emphatic Pause

Use ellipsis points as an emphatic mark of separation between statements. Normally we would separate these figures by commas, as follows:

> 10,000,000 known dead soldiers, 3,000,000 presumed dead soldiers, 13,000,000 dead civilians, 20,000,000 wounded soldiers, 3,000,000 prisoners, 9,000,000 war orphans, 5,000,000 war widows, 10,000,000 refugees—this was the human cost in rough figures of World War I.

Ellipsis points would not only visually break up a long list, but they would also allow the text to reflect the thinking of the writer:

> 10,000,000 known dead soldiers . . . 3,000,000 presumed dead soldiers . . . 13,000,000 dead civilians . . . 20,000,000 wounded soldiers . . . 3,000,000 prisoners . . . 9,000,000 war orphans . . . 5,000,000 war widows . . . 10,000,000 refugees—This was the human cost in rough figures of World War I.

The ellipsis points also enable the writer to avoid the necessity of using *etc.* as an unemphatic ending to such a list. Work for this effect with caution. Overused, ellipsis points exasperate the reader.

Exclamation Point

The exclamation point is usually, but not always, a terminal mark of punctuation.

If your keyboard does not have an exclamation key, form it by striking a period, backspace, and apostrophe.

The only punctuation marks that may be used to end a sentence are the period, the ellipsis marks, the question mark, and the exclamation mark. Like the question mark, the exclamation mark explains itself. An exclamation is an abrupt, forceful outcry of surprise, emphasis, or emotion. Make sure that an expression of unusual force comes before any exclamation mark you use. If you use the exclamation mark too often, your writing will sound too shrill or over-excited. Use it sparingly—usually after a short interjection or sentence. Make it earn its way onto the page. Only then will it have the force you want it to have.
Here are three examples:

> Help!
>
> There is a teacher shortage(!) in Texas.
>
> "For God's sake, be quiet!" came cries from the back of the plane. "You're no worse off than anybody else."

When an exclamation mark and a quotation mark fall together (as in the last example), place the exclamation mark according to the logic of the sentence. If the exclamation is part of the quotation, it goes inside the quotation mark like this:

> You're a monster. You're a detestable, abominable, criminal fraud. If you come near—I'll scream out the window. Get back!"

If the exclamation is part of the sentence, the exclamation mark goes outside the quotation mark:

> "Calf rope"? What a curious way to say "I surrender"!

Hyphen

The Greeks had a name for it—*huphen*, which was a sign written below two consecutive letters to show they belonged to the same word. The Greek *hupen* is our hyphen. And although it seems to be used in a dozen different ways, the hyphen still works the Greek way in its two primary functions: (1) to link two or more words to make compound nouns or compound adjectives and (2) to divide parts of a word at the end of a line and the beginning of the next. In addition to remembering the Greek use of *huphen*, it is helpful to classify hyphens as combining hyphens and dividing hyphens.

Combining Hyphens

Use a hyphen to combine two or more words that are ordinarily separate so that they function temporarily as one word. Combined, they will be either a compound noun or a compound adjective. Compound nouns, however, don't always remain hyphenated. Newly formed compound nouns are often formed with a hyphen, but once they have been used awhile they tend to be written as either one word (*house-keeper* becomes *housekeeper*) or as two words (*copy-editor* becomes *copy editor*). However, some compound nouns retain their hyphen even after long use (I'm serving as a *go-between*). Because usage has not developed consistently, we get such compound nouns as *first-nighter* (He was a veteran *first-nighter* at the theater), *shootout* (I just read an account of the *shootout* at the OK Corral), and *carving knife* (Please hand me the *carving knife*). Other examples? How about *dog-ear, dogcatcher,* and *dog days.*

Before wringing our hands, we can make a few generalizations and say that the following types of compound nouns are usually hyphenated.

- Spelled-out numbers from twenty-one through ninety-nine *(forty-nine, sixty-six);* by contrast, spelled-out numbers lower than twenty-one are single words that are not hyphenated *(fourteen, eighteenth).*
- Family relationships *(mother-in-law, great-grandfather, great-aunt;* but not *grandson* or *granddaughter, grandfather* or *grandmother,* or *step-child).*
- Componds beginning with *-ex* or *self-* (*ex-husband, ex-governor, self-denial, self-government).*
- Compounds ending in *-elect* or *-designate (president-elect, senator-elect, bishop-designate, ambassador-designate).*
- Coordinate compounds (*player-manager, secretary-treasurer, catcher-firstbaseman, radio-phonograph, Mercedes-Benz).*
- Compounds of three or more words (*free-for-all, snake-in-the-grass, jack-of-all-trades).*
- Compounds of capital letter or letters with a following numeral or numerals (*DC-9, B-12, B-52, PT-106, Brother HR-15 printer).*
- Single capital letter with following noun (*A-frame, J-stroke, T-square, U-turn, X-ray, H-bomb*).
- Compounds of a prefix and proper noun (*un-American, anti-Semiticism, pro-Russian, trans-Canada, pan-American, all-Big Eight).*

Beyond these nine categories, it is not really necessary to memorize whether compound nouns are hyphenated or spelled as one word or two. Look up the spelling of compound words in an up-to-date dictionary.

Hyphens are also used to form compound adjectives. Here is the correct form for linking compound adjectives that come before a word or words they modify:

I am looking for a part-time job.
The club members approved the long-needed reforms.
My absent-minded sister forgot where she parked her truck.

Although these phrases would be clear even without the hyphen, you should link the compound adjectives to avoid confusion. Unless compound adjectives coming before the words they modify are hyphenated, thay may cause ambiguity—that is, be open to more than one interpretation:

The bureau issued a bad weather forecast. (Did the bureau issue a weather forecast that missed its prediction? If so, it should read as is. If the bureau issued a forecast for bad weather, then it should read *bad-weather forecast.*)

Hyphenating compound adjectives helps readers understand what words go together, what modifies what. The structure of *bad weather forecast* states that *bad* modifies the *weather forecast*. The structure *bad-weather forecast* indicates that *bad* modifies *weather*. The hyphen helps the reader make the correct link. Don't use a comma in the place of a hyphen to combine adjectives. An *olive-skinned woman* is likely to be lovely. An *olive, skinned woman* is too horrible to contemplate.

When compound adjectives follow the word or words they modify they are written as separate words.

before the word	**after the word**
the paper-thin cover	the cover is paper thin
a coast-to-coast flight	the flight was coast to coast
the lighter-than-air device	the device was lighter than air

The last two examples show that some compound adjectives consist of more than two words, so be sure to hyphenate all the way through:

the 35-year-old woman
a winner-take-all game
a get-it-while-you-can attitude

Two or more compounds with the same base are hyphenated as follows:

a three- or four-bedroom home (not three or four-bedroom home)
4-, 6-, 8-cylinder engines (not 4, 6, 8-cylinder engines)

Dividing Hyphens

Use the hyphens at the end of a line when part of a word is carried over to the next line. Divide between syllables, but keep these three practices in mind: (1) don't divide a word of one syllable (*moved*); (2) don't divide a word if the split will result in one letter standing alone (*cit-y, a-way*); (3) divide hyphenated compounds on the hyphen (or on one of the hyphens if there are two or more).

If you are unsure of where to hyphenate a word, look the word up in a dictionary to determine its syllables. Here is an example: *fore • cast • ing*. The dots mark syllable division. Hyphenate at one of the syllable breaks.

In addition to dividing words between syllables at the end of a line, the dividing hyphen has these uses:

- To indicate spelling—*Is it true that some kids spell "relief" R-O-L-A-I-D-S?*
- To suggest stammering or hesitation—*Wh-what d-d-d-id you s-say?*
- To represent dialect—*I'm a-going to town.*
- To designate political party affiliation and geographical area—*Thomas B. Sublett (D-N.Y.) sponsored the bill.*
- To separate parts of a telephone number—*783-2136.*
- To indicate a span of time, sums, or page numbers—*The gear is expensive ($100-175), but we can save weight.*
  —Plutarch described the troubles Marcellus encountered in laying seige to the city of Syracuse (213-211 B.C.)
- To avoid confusing of certain words—*We re-formed the organization.* (*Re-formed* means that the organization has been reorganized, restructured, or formed again. *Reformed* would mean that the organization has certain defective or undesirable practices that have been ended.

Italicization

Italics is a certain kind of typeface, like this sample: *National Geographic*. When you type or write, you indicate italics by underlining, like this: `National Geographic.`

Italics are used to indicate titles, foreign words and phrases, and to designate words, letters, and numbers referred to as such.

- Titles of books, magazines, newspapers, ships, and artistic works:
  John Irving's *The Cider House Rules*

Scientific American
Wall Street Journal
U.S.S. John F. Kennedy
Michaelangelo's *Pieta*

- Foreign words and phrases that have not become a part of the English language:

  Shakespeare's Falstaff was a Renaissance example of the *miles gloriosus,* a braggart soldier who is fundamentally a coward yet boasts of valorous deeds.

  Sturm und Drang was a revolutionary German literary movement that influenced Goethe, Schiller, Herde, and Lenz.

- Also italicize Latin scientific terms:

  detritus (rotting plant debris)
  Aurelia flavidula (North Atlantic jellyfish)
  Hedera helix (English ivy)

- But do not italicize Latin abbreviations and foreign words and phrases that have become part of the language:

etc.	alma mater
vs.	boutique
ibid.	camouflage

- Italicize words, letters, and numbers when referring to them as such:

  The word should be *personnel,* not *personal.*
  Your *h*'s look like *k*'s.
  A typing error put an extra *3* in the equation.

Numbers

Numbers can be expressed as a word *(fifty)* or a figure *(50)*. The following guidelines will help you decide which form to use.

Numbers in Figure Form

Writing a number as a figure is almost always done in the following instances.

Addresses—2012 Woodriver Drive, Apartment 3, Carbondale, IL 62901
Dates—August 4, 1986 or 4 August 1986 (Don't use 1st, 2nd, 3rd, 4th, and so on.)
Decimals—4.2 liter engine, 1.069 kilometers (It's customary to furnish a zero before the decimal point of decimal fractions, 0.025 meters, 0.453 kilograms.)

Exact Sums of Money with $ or ¢—$14.99, 29¢
Fractions Connected to Whole Numbers—33-1/3
Identifying Numbers — Engine Number H-396381245D
Her telephone number is (505) 291-4841.
His social security number is 041-36-1188.
Percentages—12 percent, 12%
References to Pages, Figures, and so on—page 25, Figure 9, Footnote 2
Time (with A.M. or P.M.)—8:30 P.M. (but *12 noon, 12 midnite,* and *eight o'clock*)
Units of Measure—15 gallons, 1000 lbs., 22 miles, 350 rpm, 12 minutes, 500 cc

Numbers in Word Form

The general trend is to use figures more often than words. However, the following are instances in which a word is preferred as an option in text.

Numbers at the Beginning of a Sentence: Spell out all numbers when they occur at the beginning of a sentence, or rewrite the sentence to avoid beginning with a figure.

Sixteen rebuilt pumps will be ordered.
The order will include 16 rebuilt pumps.

Numbers Over 10: Most style and usage books call for spelling out only numbers under 10 and use figures for everything beyond.

We edited four reports in one day.
Measure the distance between the two holes.
The smallest of the whales was 30 feet long.
The National Orienteering Championship in Buffalo is expected to draw 500 entries.

However, there is an exception. When a series of numbers contains a number greater than 10, each number should be expressed in figure form:

The class enrolled 3 freshman, 16 sophomores, 7 juniors, and 1 senior.
The 8 crews flew 127 sorties for a total of 466 hours.

Large round numbers are usually spelled out: 65 million (not 65,000,000).

Fractions: Small fractions are usually spelled out.

Two-thirds of the group were still working after dark.
A third of the group worked until midnight.

Time (with o'clock): Write 11 A.M., but eleven o'clock.

Adjoining Numbers: Spell out numbers when they immediately precede units of measure:

She ran four 2-minute laps.
In the corner were three 12-volt batteries.
Bill Miller readied two 10-speed bikes for the cross country trip.

Parentheses

Parentheses are used mainly for two purposes: (1) to enclose words, phrases, and sentences inserted as additional information, and (2) to enclose numbers or letters of lists run into the text (as in this sentence). In certain bibliography and footnote forms, parentheses enclose publication information:

Charles Berlitz, "UFO Update," *Omni* 2 (June 1980): 32.

John Irving, *The World According to Garp* (New York: Simon & Schuster, 1978) 132–133.

Parentheses come in pairs, so check for unescorted ones. The only exception to this rule is to use a closing parenthesis with numbers in an enumerated list—1), 2), 3). . . .

Enclosing Additional Information

As the following examples show, you can use parentheses to make additional points to your readers as they read the main statement of the passage. The additional points may be brief explanations, definitions, translations, references to other sources, and so on. Parentheses enable you to make two comments at once. Just don't overdo it.

Gluon (the particles that bind apparently indivisible pieces of matter together) sounds like it was named by a third grader rather than by a physicist.

The United States Information Service (USIS) is an important arm of the United States State Department.

During a visit to Bavaria in 1891, Wilhelm wrote *"Regis voluntas, suprema lex"* (The King's will is the highest law) in the golden-book of Munich's city hall.

Blue mold is found in 14 counties in southeast Kentucky (see map on page 5).

The parenthetical information can be omitted without destroying the grammatical completeness of the sentence. Commas and dashes often can be used instead of parentheses, as these versions of the first example show:

> Gluon (the particles that bind apparently indivisible pieces of matter together) sounds like it was named by a third grader rather than a physicist.
>
> Gluon, the particles that bind apparently indivisible pieces of matter together, sounds like it was named by a third grader rather than a physicist.
>
> Gluon—the particles that bind apparently indivisible pieces of matter together—sounds like it was named by a third grader rather than a physicist.

You may set off almost all parenthetical information by using any of these marks, and the ultimate choice is usually your own. About the only exception is a series of items within a parenthetical statement, where using commas to separate the items and also the parenthetical statement from the rest of the sentence could be confusing.

Possibly confusing:

> The ushers, John, Becky, Ricardo, and Lee, should be at the auditorium by three o'clock.

Clearer:

> The ushers—John, Becky, Ricardo, and Lee—should be at the auditorium by three o'clock.

Other than this, there are no hard and fast rules. The very people we might reasonably look to for guidance—successful writers—are as subjective as the rest of us. Just as some people are Ford owners, some writers are dash users. Others swear by Chevrolets and parentheses. Still, many people distinguish between the three marks. Commas are used to enclose short phrases that are closely related to the thought in the sentence. Dashes or parentheses are used to set off longer expressions or short phrases that make an abrupt break in the sentence.

Brackets ([ ]), of course, are a different matter. They are used to enclose corrections or explanations inserted in a direct quotation or to enclose parenthetical information already inside a parenthetical statement.

When a parenthetical sentence is inside another sentence, the first letter of the first word is capitalized, but there is no end punctuation:

> Two (Some say three) tornadoes cut a swath between Clarksville and the Red River.

When the parenthetical sentence stands by itself, its closing punctuation is inside the parenthesis:

> Farmers are not wanted and the young people go elsewhere. (The farm population is now less than 5 percent of the total population.) Building, on the contrary, is immensely needed.

Enclosing Numbers or Letters in Lists

To highlight items in a list, you may separate the items by numbers or letters enclosed in parentheses.

> Every aspirant to success in public speaking should have these qualifications: (1) determination to succeed, (2) desire to practice, (3) sincerity, (4) knowledge of facts about the subject, and (5) a broad vocabulary.

Some writers use only the closing parenthesis:

> Every aspirant to success in public speaking should have these qualifications: 1) determination to succeed, 2) desire to practice, 3) sincerity, 4) knowledge of facts about the subject, and 5) a broad vocabulary.

Period

Use a period for the uses illustrated in the following sections.

Abbreviations

> Mr. Dwight Barker, Jr.
> Dorothy Reynolds, M.D.
> Col. Joan Hutchinson

(Certain abbreviations are written without periods: HBO—Home Box Office. For more information about particular abbreviations, consult a college-level dictionary.)

Decimal Points

.05, $14.98

End Stop

It is no longer unusual to see a woman finish ahead of many men in a marathon.

(If a sentence ends with an abbreviation followed by a period, a second period is not needed: My mother works for A. Stimmons, Inc.)

Initials

James S. Robertson, Mary B. Bradshaw

Leaders

Leaders are spaced dots that lead the eye; they are sometimes used in tables and tables of contents.

How Is It We Know Something to Communicate 4
How Do We Create Symbols 15
The Silent Languages 20
In Search of Meaning 26
Bibliography 32

Run-in Sidehead

If a run-in sidehead is on the same line as the first line of text, it is often followed by a period.

Types of Stars. Stars are classified according to their photospheric ("surface") temperatures or according to color, which is a direct consequence of those temperatures. Some red supergiant stars are. . . .

With Quotation Marks

Always put the period inside the closing quotation mark, even when it doesn't seem logical, as in the second example:

Edwin Bayrd's book *The Thin Game: Dietary Scams and Common Sense* was extolled by a major consumer magazine as containing "the soundest commonsense diet to come along for a long time."

All of Yoshiaki's friends called him "Yoshi."

With Parentheses

When a period and a parentheses fall together, place the period according to the logic of the sentence. If the parenthetical expression is *part* of the sentence, the period goes outside the closing parenthesis.

One of the new director's suggestions is to reduce the number of plays per season from six to five (a change that has already been effected for next year).

Sure enough, a blackboard showed oranges down from 22 drachmas a kilo to 15 (about 40 cents).

If the entire sentence is parenthetical, the period goes inside the closing parenthesis.

In Arab homes Americans are apt to rattle around, feeling exposed and often somewhat inadequate because of too much space. (The Arab houses and apartments of the middle and upper classes which Americans stationed abroad commonly occupy are much larger than the dwellings such Americans usually inhabit.)

There is a lot to get used to. I miss the privilege of working whenever I feel like it. (This is my first eight-to-five job.)

Question Mark

The question mark is the end punctuation for all forms of interrogative sentences (sentences that ask a direct question). It may also be enclosed in parentheses to suggest uncertainty.

Ending Direct Questions

Place a question mark at the end of a direct question.

When does your flight leave?
Are the Eagles still in last place?
I like ragtime, don't you?

Polite requests may be punctuated with a question mark or a period.

May I call you for a personal interview.
May I call you for a personal interview?

Do not use a question mark after an indirect question.

Professor Glasser asked what the vote was.

When asking a series of questions in the same sentence, you may place a question mark after each query or at the end of the series, depending on how you want to emphasize the questions.

Who will be in the playoffs against the Padres? Will it be the Cardinals or the Mets?

Who will be in the playoffs against the Padres?
The Cardinals? the Mets?

When a question mark and a quotation mark fall together, place the question mark according to the logic of the sentence. If the question is part of the quotation, the question mark goes inside the quotation mark.

"When is graduation?" Art asked.
Art asked, "When is graduation?"

If the entire sentence is a question, the question mark goes outside the quotation mark.

When will we read "The Waste Land"?

What do you mean when you say the program is "viable"?

If the question mark belongs to the quotation, put it inside the quotation mark. That suffices for each mark.

Did you understand about the baby in "Who's Afraid of Virginia Woolf?"

She exclaimed, "Why me?"

Expressing Uncertainty

Use a parenthetical question mark to suggest uncertainty. If the uncertainty is expressed in a parenthetical statement, the question mark can stand alone.

Ambrose Bierce was born in 1842 and died in 1914 (?).

Ambrose Bierce (born Meigs County, Ohio, June 24, 1842–died 1914?) was a journalist, short story writer, poet, and satirist.

Quotation Mark

Quotation marks are used (1) to enclose direct quotations, (2) to set off words referred to as words, (3) to draw attention to words used in a special way, and (4) to designate titles of articles, essays, poems, and songs, and subordinate parts of longer works.

Enclosing a Direct Quotation

Enclose all quoted matter—writing or speech—in quotation marks.

As William James said, "We may philosophize well or ill, but philosophize we must."

"The information that consumers supply to the FDA often leads to detection and correction," says a bulletin published by the agency. "Many products have been recalled from the market because of the action taken by consumers."

In typed or printed material, extended direct quotations are indented without quotation marks.

Recent research has shown that the newborn is considerably more competent than had previously been thought. According to a recent study at a major medical center:

> The newborn child is a remarkably capable organism from the moment he begins to breathe. He can see, hear, smell, and is sensitive to pain, touch, and change in position. . . . The new born's behavioral equipment is also remarkably well developed. When only two hours old, he will follow a rapidly moving light with his eyes; his pupils will dilate in darkness and constrict in light; he will suck a finger or nipple inserted into his mouth. He can cry, cough, turn away, vomit, lift his chin from a prone position, and grasp an object placed in his palm.

Distinguish between the direct words of a writer or speaker (a direct quotation) and the indirect statement of what a writer or speaker says (an indirect quotation). An indirect quotation is not enclosed in quotation marks.

direct:	**indirect:**
She said, "Write your name and address on this card."	She said to write my name and address on this card.

In writing dialogue, begin a new paragraph with every change of speaker.

He finished rolling his cigarette and slipped his tongue across the paper, then sealed it. Then he held a string of paper over the lamp waiting for the fire.

"Last night. . . . "

Blue smoke rose up around, drifting first toward the lamp and rising suddenly upward.

"What about last night?" Leona asked.

"Where'd you go?"

"I didn't go."

"You did. I woke up, I called for you. You didn't answer."

Use a single quotation mark (apostrophe) to enclose a quotation within a quotation.

The woman at the desk said, "The policy states specifically, 'Seats cannot be reserved for Saturday performances.'"

Setting Off Words Referred to as Words

Writers are divided about using quotation marks or underlining (to indicate italics) to set off words referred to as words. Be consistent in your practice.

My handwriting is so poor that my lab instructor can't tell whether I am writing "value" or "valve."

My handwriting is so poor that my lab instructor can't tell whether I am writing *value* or *valve.*

Drawing Attention to a Word or Phrase

Quotation marks are sometimes used to mark nicknames, slang expressions, and satirical expressions. Although no general agreement exists about when to emphasize a word by enclosing it in quotation marks, it would seem to be overdoing it to place quotation marks around words that are generally accepted:

She was the brains of the outfit. (Not "brains.")

Landing on a pitching and rolling aircraft carrier often resembles a controlled crash. (Not "controlled crash.")

However, enclosing words in quotation marks to call attention to ironic or satiric intent is acceptable:

"Adult movies" are not necessarily designated for mature audiences, and "Magazines for men" are not necessarily designed for all men.

Designating Titles of Published Works

Titles of articles in periodicals, essays, short stories, poems, songs, and subordinate parts of longer works are enclosed in quotation marks.

> Have you read Irene Cortinovis' "China at the St. Louis World's Fair" in the *Missouri Historical Review?*
>
> Matthew Arnold's "Dover Beach" is a dramatic monologue.
>
> Gene Autry made a fortune singing "Rudolph, the Red-Nosed Reindeer."
>
> I want you to read the chapter titled "Seeing" in Annie Dillard's *Pilgrim at Tinker's Creek.*
>
> Some of the humorous—but a bit humiliating—physical and psychological examinations that prospective astronauts were subject to are described in Chapter 4, "The Lab Rat," of Tom Wolfe's *The Right Stuff.*

The Quotation Mark with Other Punctuation

The most common situations in which quotation marks are used with other marks of punctuation are illustrated below. (For further information, see entries on comma, dash, exclamation point, period, question mark, semicolon, and colon.)

When a comma or a period falls with the end quotation mark, always place the comma or period inside the quotation mark, even when it doesn't seem logical:

> The words "master" and "mistress," from which "Mr." and "Mrs." evolved, have meant different things in different periods of history.
>
> Thomas Jefferson's faith in education and the American people is best summarized in his own words: "Educate and inform the whole mass of people. . . . They are the only sure reliance for the preservation of our liberty."

When a question mark, exclamation point, or dash is part of the quotation, place it *inside* the quotation mark. When it is part of the entire sentence, place it *outside* the quotation mark.

> The debunkers ask a question that is far too general to be helpful—"Where did the Victorians go wrong?"
>
> Are you certain that Virchow's principle is stated as "every cell must come from another cell"?

Even before we removed our gear from the back of the truck, Dad and I could hear Mark yelling, "I've caught a fish!"

We could see the sign flickering in the light of the match. It read "Exit Trail by Nightfall"!

Place a semicolon or colon *outside* the quotation marks:

Conference presentations will include Eliseo Torres, "Supplemental Funding Sources for Bilingual Education"; Gracelia Orozco, "Exposicion de Materiales para Refuerzo Cultural"; Thomas Carter, "Implications of Recent Research in Findings on Bilingual Education"; and Alba Moesser, "Instructional Patterns for Bilingual Education."

"Advertising makes people buy things they don't need": this is a frequent charge made against advertising.

Semicolon

Do not confuse the semicolon with the colon. The semicolon has two uses: (1) to link the clauses of a *compound sentence**, and (2) to separate items in a series when commas would not make the separation clear.

Linking the Clauses of a Compound Sentence

Use a semicolon to link clauses in a compound sentence when no coordinating conjunction *(and, but, for, or, nor)* is used. The semicolon indicates a sharper break in the sentence than that provided by a comma but not as sharp a break as that provided by a period. As these examples show, the semicolon is especially good for emphasizing closely parallel thoughts between sentences.

A good car is a joy; a bad one is misery.

Oil sparked every invasion drive. It heated tents and billets; it powered mobile laundries; it was used to purify water; it was used in medicines and bug killers; in the form of jellied gas it fueled the deadly flame throwers. At least 60,000 gallons of gasoline were needed every day to keep a single armored division fighting.

When linking clauses with such *adverbs** as *however, moreover, also, so, accordingly,* or *nevertheless,* place a semicolon before the adverb:

Archeologists have not found so much as a scraper in the sites; therefore, we do not know what kinds of tools the first Americans had.

We wanted to finish the cabinets by the weekend; however, John didn't return the sander until late Sunday.

Separating Items in a Series

Use a semicolon to separate items in a series when one of the items itself contains a comma.

Contact between Europeans of different languages has increased exponentially in the 1970's. Trade contributes. In my uncle's home in London I found clothes and drugs with washing and administration instructions in English and French; a dishwasher with operating instructions in Dutch, English, French, and German; children's toys with instructions in English, French, and German; a tuner-amplifier with instructions in English, French, and German; a radio with instructions in English, French, German, Italian, and Spanish. All were made in Britain, Germany, and Italy for the European market.

The Semicolon with Other Punctuation

Place the semicolon outside quotation marks or parentheses.

The legislators were not locked into "positions"; they were quite open to, even sought, new information and innovative ideas.

A professional gambler bets aggressively (to win); an amateur gambler bets defensively (not to lose).

Slash Mark

You will write a long time before you use a slash mark, one of the more obscure marks of punctuation. But it does have its uses. If you have ever written *and/or* or addressed a letter to somebody "in care of" somebody else and used the informal abbreviation *c/o,* you have used the slash mark. To go along with its miscellaneous uses, the slash mark goes by a variety of names. Some persons call it a *bar;* others call it a *diagonal;* still others call it a *slant sign*. Some call it a *slash*. Dictionaries refer to it as a *virgule*. You might even call it a *slash/slant/bar/diagonal/virgule*. The slash mark, by whatever name you call it, is a sign of separation.

The address is Sgt. Mary Newland/APO 716/New York, NY 10009. (To separate the elements of an address.)

Tennyson's mariners, under the soporific influence of the Lotus, decide not to continue their journey home: "Then some one said, 'We will return no more;'/And all at once they sang, 'Our island home/Is far beyond the wave; we will no longer roam.'" (To separate lines of short passages of poetry quoted directly and written into a sentence. When quoting longer excerpts, present the lines as the poet expresses them.)

3/4, 5/8, 33-1/2 (To separate the numerator from the denominator in a fraction.)

5/21/86 (In informal writing, to separate the month from the day and the day from the year in dates.)

Symbols

A symbol is a written sign (certain letters or other marks) that represents something else by resemblance or convention. Readers are used to seeing only a few standard symbols, so we advise you to write out names of most symbols. Readers who know words like *liter, micro, angstrom,* or *ohm* do not necessarily recognize the symbols ℓ, μ, Å, and Ω.

It may be convenient for you to summarize the procedure for making common table salt with $2Na + C12 \rightarrow 2NaC1$. But if your reader doesn't understand the symbols, you will have to use other language, such as "When two atoms of sodium are reacted with one molecule of chlorine, two molecules of sodium chloride are formed." Or instead of writing $C_6H^1{}_2O_6 \rightarrow 6CO_2O$, you might write "The complete metabolism of glucose (blood sugar) in the human body requires six molecules of oxygen (O_2) to produce six molecules of carbon dioxide (CO_2) and six molecules of water (H_2O)."

A symbol represents the sound of speech: Fe, the symbol for iron, is pronounced as *iron*.

Be certain that your readers understand the meaning of a symbol you use, or explain it in parentheses the first time it appears.

13

Glossary of Grammatical Terms

Absolute An absolute is a *phrase** that modifies an entire *sentence**. It offers an economical way of adding detail. You may have more than one in a sentence:

> *Our research completed,* we began the task of writing our results.
> He adjusted to speaking French slowly, *the accent seeming strange to him, the shapes of the words coming reluctantly to his lips.*

See also *Modifier**.

Accusative Case See *Case**.

Active Voice See *Voice**.

Adjectival See *Adjective**.

Adjective an adjective is a word that modifies a *noun** or *pronoun*:*

> a *unique* endeavor
> an *effective* technique

Attributive an adjective placed next to the word it modifies, usually in front of it, is an attributive adjective:

> *wide* knowledge
> *intimate* style

Predicate An adjective joined to its noun or pronoun by a *linking verb** is a *predicate** adjective:

He is *tall.*
The earth smelled *fresh.*
She sounded *angry.*

Adjectival Words or groups of words other than adjectives, such as nouns and prepositional *phrases**, serving to modify nouns and pronouns are adjectivals:

cable television
wrist watch
A woman *on the go*

Adjective clause A *clause** containing a *subject** and *predicate** may function to modify a noun and thus be an adjective clause, sometimes also called an adjectival or adjectival clause:

People *who live in glass houses* shouldn't throw stones.

See also *Degree**, *Verb**, *Modifier**, *Preposition**, and *Verbal**.

Adjective Clause See Adjective*.

Adverb An adverb belongs to a class of words that modify *verbs**, *adjectives**, other *adverbs**, and even *phrases** and *clauses*:*

verb	The antenna turned *rapidly.*
adjective	He had *radiantly* black hair.
adverb	She walked *extremely* quietly.
phrase	He was *almost* out of the room before I called him back.
clause	*Unhappily,* his father died when he was very young.

Adverbial Phrases and clauses and words other than adverbs can serve as adverbs. When they do, they are called adverbials:

phrase	He always played golf *on Saturday mornings.*
clause	*When students succeed,* they gain confidence in their work.
noun	*Weekdays,* he worked in an office.

Conjunctive Adverb Words that serve as both adverbs and connectives are known as conjunctive adverbs. Common conjunctive adverbs are *consequently, furthermore, however, moreover, nevertheless,* and *therefore:*

Last Year we traveled in Mexico; *however,* this year we are going to France.

See also *Degree** and *Modifier**.
Adverbial See *Adverb**.

Agreement *Nouns** and *pronouns** have number; they can be singular (*girl, she*) or plural (*girls, they*). *Collective nouns** may be either singular or plural, depending on how you use them. Nouns and pronouns have gender; they can be masculine (*boy, he*), feminine (*girl, she*), or neuter (*chair, it*).

When pronouns are substituted for nouns, they must agree with them in number and gender:

> *Susan* lost *her wallet,* but *it* was returned to her.
> The *boys* enjoyed *their* classes, but *they* looked forward to *their* afternoon games.
> The judge gave the *jury its* instructions.
> The *jury* returned to *their* rooms at the hotel for the night.

Likewise, a *verb** must agree with its *subject** in *person** and number:

> *I play* hard.
> *John plays* hard.
> *He was* a short man.
> *They were* short men.
> The *squadron moves* to its new airfield today.
> The *squadron receive* their new assignments today.

See also *Antecedent** and *Case**.

Antecedent The thing or person for which a *pronoun** substitutes is the antecedent of that pronoun:

> Wherever *Rebecca* traveled, *she* took photographs of *children. Their* gaiety and freshness delighted *her.*

Rebecca is the antecedent of *she* and *her; children* is the antecedent of *their.*
See also *Agreement**.

Appositive An appositive is a *noun** or noun expression placed next to a noun or *pronoun** to modify it. Appositives must agree in number and *case** with what they modify:

> Let *us, you and me* discuss this issue.
> *We, you and I,* should discuss this issue.
> My *uncle, John McGinty*, was a state senator.

See also *Agreement** and *Modifier**.

Article The three articles, *a, an,* and *the,* are used with *nouns**. The definite article, *the,* sets a limit on the noun specified: *The box* singles out a specific box. The indefinite articles, *a* and *an*, set no limit: *A box* does not single out a specific box. *An* is used before words that are pronounced with a beginning vowel sound: *An informative visitor,* but *a visitor.*

Auxiliary An auxiliary *verb** (or simply an auxiliary) is a helping verb. It is combined with a base verb to construct a *tense** or *voice*:* for example, "He *has* gone to work" and "The grass *was* cut by my son." Some of the major auxiliaries are *can, do, does, had, has, may, might, ought, shall, should,* and forms of *to be.*

Case Case is a way of showing the relationship of *nouns** or *pronouns** in a *sentence**. In our pronouns we still show case by *inflection*;* that is, by altering the form of the word. In the nominative case for pronouns used as *subjects** in a sentence, we have, for example, *he* and *she*. In the accusative case, for pronouns used as *objects** of *verbs** and *prepositions**, we change the words to *him* and *her*. With both nouns and pronouns we use the genitive (possessive) case, as in *John's, Mary's, his,* and *hers*. With the exception of the genitive, nouns show relationship not by inflection but by placement in the sentence. Thus, as in the old joke, "The dog bit the man," does not make news, but "The man bit the dog" does.

See also pages 125–127.

Clause A clause consists of a *subject** and a *predicate**.

Independent A clause that can stand by itself as a complete *sentence** is an independent clause:

The status of the two offices remained unchanged.

Dependent A dependent clause cannot stand alone. It must be connected to an independent clause:

Although additional people were hired, the status of the two offices remained unchanged.

See also *Conjunction*, Noun Clause*, Phrase*,* and *Relative Clause**.

Collective Noun See *Noun**.

Comparative Degree See *Degree**.

Complement The word or words used to complete a *predicate** are called a complement:

The government released *a study.*
The federal government sent *the states a tax plan.*

The true reward is *job satisfaction.*
The candidate's answer seemed *vague*.

See also *Adjective**, *Adverb**, and *Object**.

Complex Sentence See *Sentence**.

Compound Sentence See *Sentence**.

Compound-Complex Sentence See *Sentence*.*

Conjunction Conjunctions are connectives used to join together other *sentence** elements such as words and *clauses**.

Coordinating *And, but, for, nor, or, so,* and *yet* are the coordinating conjunctions. They are used to join sentence elements of equal grammatical rank:

His assets included stocks, bonds, *and* real estate.
We can have a complete library on a silcon chip *or* the controls for an entire factory on a silicon wafer.
We had health and good fortune, *yet* we were restless.

Subordinating Subordinating conjunctions such as the following join a dependent clause to an independent one: *although, as, because, before, if, though, until, when, whereas* and *while*.

Matching the right computer software to a procedure is no easy task, *as* the problems in our office make clear.

Conjunctive Adverb See *Adverb**.

Coordinating Conjunction See *Conjunction**.

Degree We have three degrees for our *adjectives** and *adverbs*: positive, comparative,* and *superlative*. Here are a few samples:

Positive	Comparative	Superlative
good	better	best
slow	slower	slowest
thick	thicker	thickest
late	later	latest
fearful	more fearful	most fearful
delicious	more delicious	most delicious

Positive The positive is the root adverb or adjective:

He is an *early* riser.

Comparative The comparative is used to compare two people or things. It can also be used to indicate a change in degree:

John is *sicker* than Mary.
Now that he is *older*, he is *slower* of foot than he used to be.

Superlative The superlative is used to indicate that something or someone has achieved the greatest degree of some quality among three or more people or things:

He had the *shiniest* shoes in the platoon.

Demonstrative The demonstrative *pronouns*, this, that, these,* and *those*, may also serve as demonstrative *adjectives**. They are words that point to things:

I'll have *those shirts*.

Or, simply,

I'll have *those.* (pronoun)

Dependent Clause See *Clause**.

Direct Object See *Object**.

Expletive *There* and *it* are termed expletives when used at the beginning of an *it is, there is, there are* sentence:

There is a lovely moon tonight.
It is a chair my father left me.

Genitive Case See *Case**.

Gerund See *Verbal**.

Imperative Mood See *Mood**.

Independent Clause See *Clause**.

Indicative Mood See *Mood**.

Indirect Object See *Object**.

Infinitive See *Verbal**.

Inflection Inflection is an important part of our grammatical system. With it we alter words to show their role or relationship in a *sentence**. Thus we show the past tense of *speak* by changing it to *spoke*, change *girl* to the plural by adding an *s, girls,* and so on. Don't confuse this specialized grammatical meaning of *inflection* with its more common meaning, which is to change the volume or tone of the voice.

See also pages 121–122.

Intensifier An *adverb** used as a *modifier** to add emphasis to the word modified is called an intensifier:

He was *very happy* the dance was over.
She was *certainly relieved* to have him off her feet.

See also *Intensive**.

Intensive Intensives are among the *-self pronouns** used in a *sentence** to draw attention to, to emphasize or intensify, a *noun** or *pronoun**:

Senator Weaver herself voted against the bill.
I myself have never cared much for fudge.

See also *Intensifier**.

Intransitive Verb See *Verb**.

Linking Verb See *Verb**.

Mass Noun See *Noun**.

Modifier A modifier is a word, *phrase**, or *clause** that qualifies, limits, or provides additional information about another word, phrase, or clause.

He drank from a *pewter* mug.
Situation TV comedies, *through the use of canned laughter,* are made to seem funnier than they are.
Weathered and creased, his face revealed a lifetime of hard work.

See also *Absolute**, *Adjective**, *Adverb**, and *Appositive**.

Mood *Verbs** have three possible moods, two, *indicative* and *imperative*, commonly used, and one, *subjunctive,* rarely used.

Indicative In the indicative mood, the most used form, the verb makes a factual statement or asks a factual question:

He *is coming* for dinner tonight.
Is he *coming* for dinner tonight?

Imperative The imperative mood expresses a direct command or request:

Turn right at the corner.
Please *come* for dinner tonight.
Dress informally.

Subjunctive The subjunctive mood is little used in modern English, although it is still in wide use in other European languages, such as French. When it is used, usually in somewhat formal English, it is identifiable chiefly by the use of *be* for *is, were* for *was,* and the use of the third-person singular form of the verb without the customary s-ending (*speak* for *speaks*). *Sentences** constructed with *auxiliaries** such as *may, would,* and *should* are also considered subjunctive by some grammarians, though there is not universal agreement on this point. The subjunctive is most used in resolutions and recommendations and in the expression of situations considered conditional, that is, situations that may or may not occur.

> *Were* he to come to dinner tonight, he *would find* us all informally dressed.
> Therefore, I recommend that he *be* dressed informally if he *come* for dinner tonight.
> He *may come* for dinner tonight. If so, he *should bring* dessert.

Earlier, more widespread, use of the subjunctive in English survives in such expressions as "If I were you" and "Be that as it may." If you feel uncomfortable using the subjunctive, few people will notice your substitution of the indicative.

See also *Person**, *Voice**, and pages 135–138 and 208–209.

Morpheme A morpheme is a linguistic unit with a definite meaning or grammatical function that cannot be further divided without losing its meaning or function. *Man* and *woman* are morphemes. *Walked* has two morphemes, *walk* and *ed*, as does *books, book* and *s*.

See also *Case**, *Inflection**, *Phoneme**, and pages 120–122.

Nominative Case See *Case**.

Noun Nouns name things: people, places, concepts, animals, and things in general. In the sentence "John cooked the dinner while Mary, being good at arithmetic, paid the monthly bills," *John, dinner, Mary, arithmetic,* and *bills* are all nouns.

Proper nouns name specific persons and things and are normally capitalized: *Ronald Reagan,* the *Eiffel Tower,* the *Hudson River.*

Collective nouns name entire groups of things or people: *committee, company, squadron, school, gaggle.*

Mass nouns, such as *money, milk, aluminum,* and *bravery,* are normally only expressed in the singular and, in most instances, do not take the indefinite *article**. We speak of *the money* but not of *a money.*

See also *Case**, *Noun Clause**, *Object**, *Pronoun**, and *Subject**.

Noun Clause A noun clause is a dependent *clause** used as a *noun**:

> *That white-collar crime is so prevalent* shocks many people.

Object An object is a *noun** or noun substitute, such as a *pronoun**, *phrase**, or *noun clause**, that receives the action of a transitive *verb** or is otherwise governed by a transitive verb or *preposition**. In some grammars direct objects and indirect objects are called *complements** in the sense that they complete the *predicate**.

Direct Object A direct object receives the direct action of a transitive verb:

He kissed his *bride.*

Indirect Object An indirect object is that *for whom* or *to whom* the action is done:

He bought *Mary* a fur coat.
Father gave *John* a good scolding.

Object of Preposition The object of a preposition completes the *phrase** begun by a preposition:

The waiter brought the pie *for John.*

Indirect objects can always be expressed as objects of prepositions.

He bought a fur coat *for Mary.*
Father gave a good scolding *to John.*

Participle See *Verbal**.

Passive Voice See *Voice**.

Person In *pronouns** we speak of three persons:

First person, the person(s) speaking: I, my, mine, me, we, our, ours, us.

Second person, the person(s) spoken to: you, your, yours.

Third person, the person(s) or thing(s) spoken about: he, his, him, she, her, hers, it, its, they, their, them.

In *verbs**, English has distinct endings for the verb *to be* in all three persons and for the third person singular in the present and perfect *tenses** of all other verbs:

to be	I am, you are, he is, we are, they are.
present	I speak, you speak, he *speaks,* we speak, they speak.
perfect	I have spoken, you have spoken, he *has* spoken, we have spoken, they have spoken.

See also *Agreement* and pages 125–127.

Phoneme Phonemes are the speech sounds we make that allow us to distinguish one word from another. They are the smallest units of language. Notice how changes in phonemes distinguish the following words: ma*p,* ma*t,* *t*at, ta*p,* t*o*p.

In written English, we attempt to represent the phonemes with letters of the alphabet. The letters for the consonants represent the phonemes fairly well, but the letters for the vowels *(a, e, i, o, u,* sometimes *y)* work rather imperfectly. For instance, compare *tap* with *tape* and *dine* with *dinner*. To overcome this difficulty, linguists work with a more complete set of symbols known as the

International Phonetic Alphabet, which can be found in linguistic dictionaries.
See also *Morpheme**.

Phrase Phrases are words grouped together into units to serve some grammatical function in a *sentence**. Unlike *clauses**, they do not contain both a *subject** and a finite *verb**. Phrases are classified according to the part of speech they are formed around, such as

prepositional	at the boat race
gerund	sailing his boat
infinitive	*to sail a boat*
noun	the sailboat

Phrases are the basic building blocks of sentences and can function in many ways, for example, as

Subject	*Sailing his boat* made Bob a happy man.
Adjective	The day *at the boat race* was a delightful one.
Adverb	He quit his job *to sail a boat.*
Object	He bought *the sailboat.*

See also *Absolute**, *Adjective**, *Adverb**, *Appositive**, *Complement**, *Modifier**, *Object**, *Preposition**, and *Verbal**.

Positive Degree See *Degree**.

Possessive Case See *Case**.

Predicate The predicate is one of the two basic components of a *sentence** or *clause**. (The *subject** is the other.) The predicate makes a statement about the subject. In "Sally hit the ball well," "hit the ball well" tells us what Sally did and how she did it. We speak of the *simple predicate,* which consists of the *verb** and any *auxiliaries** it may have *(hit* or *has hit).* But often when we use the term *predicate* we refer to the *complete predicate,* which is the simple predicate plus all *complements**, *modifiers**, and *objects** *(hit the ball well).*

Preposition Prepositions are relationship words. They introduce a *noun**, *pronoun**, *clause**, or *phrase** and relate it to some other unit in the *sentence**:

We camped *at the beach.*
We pitched the tent *for them.*
The success of your camping will depend *upon how well your equipment functions.*
Lying in the tent, I heard the murmur *of falling rain.*

Proper Noun See *Noun**.

Pronoun Pronouns substitute for *nouns** and function like nouns:

Susan came home late.
She came home late.

Pronouns are classified in various ways. Examples of the use of the more common classifications follow.

Personal	*I* gave up *my* seat in the train for *your* grandfather.
Interrogative	*Who* asked you to do so?
Relative	I enjoy books *that* make me laugh.
Reflexive	She looked at *herself* in the mirror.
Demonstrative	I'll have two of *those* and three of *these.*
Indefinite	*Anyone* can play this simple game.

See also *Agreement**, *Antecedent**, *Case**, *Demonstrative**, and *Relative Clause**.

Relative Clause A relative *clause** is a dependent clause connected to its independent clause by a relative *pronoun** *(who, whose, whom, which,* and *that):*

I have a dog *whose name is Orion.*

Sentence A sentence is an independent *clause** that contains a *subject** (S) and a *predicate** (P):

Morgan slept.
S P

The complete subject may contain various *modifiers**, and the complete predicate may contain modifiers, *objects**, and *complements**:

Little, 10-year old Morgan
S
played baseball as well as boys 15 years old.
P

When using the imperative *mood**, we may have sentences in which the subject (you) is understood:

Close the door.

Simple A simple sentence consists of one independent clause:

Mary Ellen graduated from college in 1985.

Compound A compound sentence consists of two or more independent clauses:

Mary Ellen graduated from college in 1985, and she went to work the following year.

Complex A complex sentence consists of one independent clause and one or more dependent clauses:

Although Mary Ellen graduated from college in 1985, she did not go to work immediately.

Compound-Complex A compound-complex sentence consists of a compound sentence plus at least one dependent clause:

After Mary Ellen graduated from college in 1985, she looked for work near home, but, not finding any, she moved to New York in 1986.

Simple Sentence See *Sentence**.

Subject The subject (S) is one of the two basic components of a *sentence** or *clause**. [The *predicate** (P) is the other.] The subject is a *noun** or noun substitute (such as a *pronoun** or *phrase**) about which the predicate makes a statement:

The boy who was late	*is my brother.*
S	P

In this sentence, *boy* is the simple subject, and *The boy who was late* is the complete subject.

In the imperative *mood**, the subject (you) will be understood rather than stated:

Please pass the salt.

Subjunctive see *Mood**.

Subordinating Conjunction See *Conjunction**.

Superlative Degree See *Degree**.

Tense Tense is the way—through the use of *inflection** and *auxiliaries**, such as *will* and *had*—we show time relationships in our *verbs**.

Present	I speak
Past	I spoke
Future	I will (shall) speak
Perfect	I have spoken
Past Perfect	I had spoken
Future Perfect	I will (shall) have spoken

See also pages 120–127.

Transitive Verb See *Verb**.

Verb Verbs show action, occurrence, existence or condition. The verb's chief function is, in a *predicate**, to make a statement about the *subject** of a *clause** or *sentence*:*

Mark *drove* the ball into the net.
Susan *swam* across the pool.
Morgan *is* with us in Chicago.
David *seems* much better today.

When a verb takes a direct *object**, we call it a *transitive verb:*

Penny *set her cup* down.

When a verb does not take a direct object, we call it an *intransitive verb:*

Brittany *appeared* at last.

Many verbs can be either transitive or intransitive, depending upon how they are used:

Jan *read the book.*
Rita *read* well.

When a verb is used not to show an action but rather to connect the subject to another *noun** or a *modifier**, we call it a *linking verb. To be* is the chief linking verb, but many verbs, such as *seem, feel,* and *appear* can function as linking verbs:

He *is* a professor.
Her act *seemed* impossible to duplicate.
I *am* sick; I *feel* bad.
His story *appears* true.

Note that *adjectives*, not adverbs**, are used to complete linking verbs. We say "I feel *good*" not "I feel well." It's "I feel *bad*" not "I feel *badly.*"

See also *Agreement**, *Mood**, *Tense**, *Verbal**, and *Voice*.

Verbal Verbals are forms of the *verb** used as *nouns**, *modifiers**, or parts of verbs. They may be used alone or in *phrases**. The three kinds of verbals are *gerunds, participles,* and *infinitives*.

Gerund The gerund is the *-ing* form of the verb used as a noun:

Flying was her chief recreation.
Flying light airplanes was her chief recreation.

Participle The present participle is the *-ing* form of the verb. The past participle is either the *-ed* form of the regular verb or an irregular form such as *spoken*. Participles can be used as *adjectives**:*

The *speeding* car turned the corner.
The car, *speeding around the corner,* overturned.
The *spoken* word is older than the *written.*
His words, *spoken in anger,* inflamed his audience.

Participles, present and past, are also used as parts of verbs:

I *am speaking* to you.
I *have spoken* to you.

Infinitive The infinite form of the verb is the present *tense** form of the verb (speak) usually with a *to* before it *(to speak)*. Infinitives are used as nouns, adjectives, and *adverbs**:*

To fly was her dream. (noun)
To fly a commercial jet was her dream. (noun)
The golf professional is the right person *to ask for golf lessons.* (adjective)
He pulled off the road *to see the view.* (adverb)

See also *Absolute**.

Voice Transitive *verbs** can be used either in the *active voice* or the *passive voice*. In the active voice, the *subject** of the *sentence** does the action, and the *object** of the sentence receives the action:

Anne locked the door.

In passive voice, the object is changed to a subject and is acted upon. The original subject, if it appears at all, is in a prepositional *phrase** following the verb:

The door was locked by Anne.
The door was locked.

Other Examples:

Active	The rangers quelled the riot.
Passive	The riot was quelled by the rangers.
Active	The janitor washed the blackboard.
Passive	The blackboard was washed.

See also pages 138–140 and 207–208.

Chapter Notes

Preface

1. Richard Young, "Arts, Crafts, Gifts, and Knacks: Some Disharmonies in the New Rhetoric," *Reinventing the Rhetorical Tradition,* ed. Aviva Freedman and Ian Pringle (Conway, AR: L&S Books, 1980) 55–56.

2. Young 55.

3. As quoted by Young from *The Basic Works of Aristotle,* ed. Richard McKeon (New York: Random House, 1941) 690.

4. For a description of how Britton uses the terms *expressive, poetic,* and *transactional,* see his "Writing to Learn and Learning to Write," *Prospect and Retrospect: Selected Essays of James Britton,* ed. Gordon M. Pradl (Montclair, NJ: Boynton/Cook Publishers, Inc., 1982) 94–110.

5. Frederick L. Gwynn and Joseph L. Blotner, eds., *Faulkner at the University* (New York: Vintage Books, 1965) 1.

6. For a discussion of these purposes, see Caroline D. Eckhardt and David H. Stewart, "Towards a Functional Taxonomy of Composition," *College Composition and Communication* 30 (1979): 338–42.

7. For a summary of the goals of a liberal education, see David G. Winter, David C. McClelland, and Abigail J. Stewart, *A New Case for the Liberal Arts* (San Francisco: Jossey-Bass Inc., Publishers, 1981) 12–13.

Chapter 1 Discovery: The Beginning of the Writing Process

1. Interviews conducted with writers by *The Paris Review* and published in a series of books called *Writers at Work* provide excellent source material concerning the writing process. The series has been published by Viking and by Penguin, and most of the volumes in the series have been edited by George Plimpton. In another book, Malcolm Cowley sums up the process described in *The Paris Review* interviews as follows: "There would seem to be four stages in the composition of a story. First comes the germ of the story, then a period of more or less conscious meditation, then the first draft, and finally the revision, which may be simply 'pencil work,' as John O'Hara calls it—that is, minor changes in writing—or may lead to writing several drafts and what amounts to a new work." *And I Worked at the Writer's Trade* (New York: Penguin Books, 1979) 180.

2. For example, see Aviva Freedman and Ian Pringle, eds., *Reinventing the Rhetorical Tradition* (Conway, AR: L&S Books, 1980), particularly the essays therein by Ann E. Berthoff, Douglas R. Butturff and Nancy I. Sommers, Richard Young, and W. Ross Winterowd.

3. For these categories of purposes, we are indebted to Caroline D. Eckhardt and David H. Stewart, "Toward a Functional Taxonomy of Composition," *College Composition and Communication* 300 (1979): 338–42.

4. As quoted in Henry M. Boettinger, *Moving Mountains* (New York: Collier Books, 1969) 8.

Chapter 2 Discovery: Using the Library

1. For the questions used we have with some modification followed the suggestions in Anne K. Beaubien, Sharon A. Hogan, and Mary W. George, *Learning the Library: Concepts and Methods for Effective Bibliographic Instruction* (New York: R.R. Bowker Company, 1982) 75.

Chapter 3 Composing: Using Logic and Rhetoric

1. Harlan Cleveland, "Information as a Resource," *The Futurist* December 1982: 34.
2. For many of the concepts in this chapter regarding hierarchies we are indebted to Herbert A. Simon, *The Sciences of the Artificial,* 2nd ed. (Boston: The MIT Press, 1981) 192–229.
3. U.S. National Aeronautics and Space Administration, *The Mars Geoscience Climatology Orbiter* (Pasadena: CA: Jet Propulsion Laboratory, 1983) 8.
4. As quoted by Sir William Cecil Dampier, *A Shorter History of Science* (New York: Meridian Books, 1957) 120–121.
5. U.S. Bureau of the Census, *Statistical Abstract of the United States,* 104 ed. (Washington, DC. U.S. Government Printing Office, 1984) 162.
6. *Statistical Abstract of the United States* 420.
7. Louis Engel and Brendan Boyd, *How to Buy Stocks,* 7th ed. (Boston: Little, Brown and Company, 1982) xiii.
8. Stephan Wilkinson, "Building on a Bright Idea," *Raytheon Magazine* Winter 1983: 16.
9. U.S. National Aeronautics and Space Administration, *Voyager at Neptune and Triton: 1989* (Pasadena, CA: Jet Propulsion Laboratory, 1984) 2.
10. David F. Linowes, "Computers and the Learning Environment," *Vital Speeches of the Day* 50 (1984): 439.
11. James A. Perrelia, "Challenging the Hazards of International Business," *Vital Speeches of the Day* 50 (1984): 554.
12. This example is borrowed from Simon, *The Sciences of the Artificial* 217–218.
13. Richard Conniff, "X-rays from Another Dimension," *Raytheon Magazine* Fall 1983: 26.
14. Conniff 31.
15. Michael Padnos, "A Fish Story," *Raytheon Magazine* Fall 1983: 4.
16. John Yellen, "Bushmen," *Science 85* May 1985: 42.
17. Conniff 26.
18. Lynn Weaver, "The Outlook for Nuclear Power," *Vital Speeches of the Day* 50 (1984): 465.
19. *The Way Things Work: An Illustrated Encyclopedia of Man and Nature* (New York: Simon and Schuster, 1980) 294.
20. Joseph D. O'Connell, "Dangers of Cultural Isolationism in an Interdependent World," *Vital Speeches of the Day* 50 (1984): 570–73.

Chapter 4 Composing: Planning, Writing, and Revising

1. Used with permission of the student writer, Elizabeth Strickland.
2. David Quammen, "What the Spider Knows," *Natural Acts* (New York: Nick Lyons Books, 1985) 13.
3. Quammen, "A Republic of Cockroaches," *Natural Acts* 53.
4. Gregory A. Jackson, "Technology and Pedagogy: Making the Right Match is Vital," *Change* May/June 1986: 52.
5. Steven W. Gilbert and Kenneth C. Green, "New Computing in Higher Education," *Change* May/June 1986: 33.
6. Quammen, "What the Spider Knows" 17.
7. Quammen, "A Republic of Cockroaches" 58.
8. Jackson 57.

9. Peter F. Drucker, *The Effective Executive* (New York: Harper & Row, Publishers, 1967) 29.

10. From an unpublished student paper, used with permission of the author, Doug Wendell.

11. Lynn Weaver, "The Outlook for Nuclear Power," *Vital Speeches of the Day* 50 (1984): 465.

12. Stephen Jay Gould, "The Rule of Five," *The Flamingo's Smile: Reflections in Natural History* (New York: W.W. Norton & Company, 1985) 200.

13. John Kenneth Galbreath, "Writing, Typing, and Economics," *Atlantic* March 1978: 103.

Chapter 5 Editing

1. As reported in Bruce O. Boston, ed., *STET! Tricks of the Trade for Writers and Editors* (Alexandria, VA: Editorial Experts, Inc., 1985) 228.

Chapter 6 Words

1. © 1975 by Houghton Mifflin Company. Reprinted by permission from the *User's Guide to The American Heritage Dictionary of the English Language*.

Chapter 7 Grammar

1. Breyne Arlene Moskowitz, "The Acquisition of Language," *Scientific American* November 1978: 92.

2. Moskowitz 92–108.

3. Moskowitz 96.

4. "be," *The Oxford English Dictionary*.

5. "be," *The Oxford English Dictionary*.

6. Albert C. Baugh and Thomas Cable, *A History of the English Language*, 3rd ed. (Englewood Cliffs, NJ: Prentice-Hall, Inc., 1978) 293.

7. Baugh and Cable 276–77.

8. Baugh and Cable 278.

9. Baugh and Cable 283.

10. Baugh and Cable 283.

Chapter 8 Sentences

1. Francis Christensen, "Notes Toward a New Rhetoric," *College English* October 1963: 7–18.

2. Christopher Fahy, *Home Remedies* (New York: Charles Scribner's Sons, 1975) 21.

3. "The Original Tsukuba: Still an Experiment," *Science 85* July/August 1985: 55.

Chapter 9 Paragraphs

1. John McPhee, "Ranger," *Pieces of the Frame* (New York: Farrar, Strauss and Giroux, 1975) 242.

2. Charles Maechling, Jr., "Japan and the United States: the Brittle Alliance," *The Virginia Quarterly Review* 57 (Winter 1978): 16.

3. Eric Sevareid, *Not so Wild a Dream* (New York: Alfred A. Knopf, 1946) 33.

4. Gilbert Highet, *Talents and Geniuses* (New York: Oxford UP, 1957) 256–57.

5. Norman Cousins, *Anatomy of an Illness* (New York: Bantam Books, Inc., 1981) 92–93.

6. Eleanor Perenyi, *Green Thoughts: A Writer in the Garden* (New York: Vintage Books, 1983) 54.

7. Lewis Thomas, *The Youngest Science: Notes of a Medicine-Watcher* (Toronto: Bantam Books, Inc., 1983) 62–63.

8. Louis D. Giannetti, *Goddard and Others: Essays on Film Form* (Rutherford, NJ: Fairleigh Dickinson UP, 1979) 69.

9. Rene Dubos, *Man Adapting* (New York: Yale UP, 1980) 424.

10. George Greenstein, "Heavenly Fire," *Science 85* July/August 1985: 75.

11. John McPhee, "Travels in Georgia," *Pieces of the Frame* (New York: Farrar, Strauss and Giroux, 1975) 17–18.

12. James D. Watson and Francis H. D. Crick, "A Structure for Deoxyribose Nucleic Acid," *Nature* 15 April 1953: 737.

13. Charles T. Kuntzleman, *The Complete Book of Walking* (New York: Pocket Books, 1979) x.

14. Eldridge Cleaver, *Soul on Ice* (New York: Dell Publishing Co., Inc., 1968) 15.

15. Robert Pirsig, *Zen and the Art of Motorcycle Maintenance* (New York: Bantam Books, Inc., 1974) 143–44.

Chapter 10 Format

1. Figures 10-1, 10-2, 10-3, 10-4, 10-7, and 10-10 illustrate pages from an unpublished student paper, reprinted with permission of the author, Elizabeth Strickland.

2. Morris Kline, *Mathematics and the Search for Knowledge* (New York: Oxford UP, 1985) 97.

3. Kline 78.

4. Kline 104–5.

5. *The Manual of Style,* 13th ed. (Chicago: U of Chicago P, 1982).

6. Ellen Swansen, *Mathematics into Type* (Providence, RI: American Mathematical Society, 1979).

7. Walter S. Achtert and Joseph Gibaldi, *The MLA Style Manual* (New York: The Modern Language Association, 1985).

Chapter 11 Principles of Style

1. *Nounspeak* is a term taken from Bruce D. Wise, "Noun Overuse Phenomenon Article," *Verbatim* 2, no. 4 (1976): 1.

2. Daniel B. Felker et al., *Guidelines for Document Designers* (Washington, DC: American Institutes for Research, 1981) 63.

3. David Pierpont Gardner, "The Humanities and the Fine Arts," *Vital Speeches of the Day* 50 (1984): 664.

4. Gordon N. Gill, "The End of the Physician-Scientist?" *The American Scholar* 53 (1984): 355.

5. Christina Hoff Sommers, "Ethics Without Virtue: Moral Education in America," *The American Scholar* 53 (1984): 381.

6. Marcella Hazan, *The Classical Italian Cookbook* (New York: Alfred A. Knopf, 1977) 171.

7. U.S. Department of Commerce, *How Plain English Works for Business: Twelve Case Studies* (Washington, DC: U.S. Government Printing Office, 1984) 77.

8. *How Plain English Works for Business* 77.

9. Jeremy Bernstein, "Tom Lehrer: Having Fun," *The American Scholar* 53 (1984): 295.

10. Clifford Orwin, "Democracy and Distrust: A Lesson from Thucidides," *The American Scholar* 53 (1984): 313.

11. Gill 353.

12. Michael Rozek, "Our Town," *Raytheon Magazine* Spring 1985: 20.

13. "Quotation of the Day," *New York Times* 29 April 1986: 2.

14. Edward Le Comte, "Douglas Bush Remembered," *The American Scholar* 53 (1984): 390.

15. Gary Walther, "Dinosaur Rock," *Raytheon Magazine* 53 (1985): 10.

16. David Wetmore, "Yaz," *The American Scholar* 53 (1984): 396.

17. Michael Burns, "War and the Private Calendar," rev. of *French and Germans, Germans and French: A Personal Interpretation of France Under Two Occupations, 1914–1918, 1940–1944,* by Richard Cobb, *The American Scholar* 53 (1984): 425–26.

18. *Trained and Sculptured Plants* (Baltimore: Brooklyn Botanic Garden, 1961) 21.

19. Bruce L. Felknor, "Intelligencewise," *Simply Stated* April 1984: 3.

20. Felknor 3.

21. Virginia Wetherbee, "The Golden Age of Eccentricity," *The American Scholar* 55 (1986): 208.

22. Harry Cohen, "Down to Earth in a Low Country," *Verbatim* 10, no. 2 (1983): 3.

23. Albert C. Baugh and Thomas Cable, *A History of the English Language,* 3rd ed. (Englewood Cliffs, NJ: Prentice Hall, Inc., 1978) 208.

Chapter 12 Conventions

1. Stephen Jay Gould, *Ever Since Darwin: Reflections on Natural History* (New York: W.W. Norton & Company, Inc., 1977) 11.

2. Sheila Shulman, "The Case for Proofreading," *Modern Office Procedures* 24 (February 1979): 106.

3. David Wallenchinsky, Irving Wallace, and Amy Wallace, *The Book of Lists* (New York: William Morrow and Company, 1977) 470.

4. Reprinted by permission of the publishers and the Trustees of Amherst College from *The Poems of Emily Dickinson,* edited by Thomas H. Johnson, Cambridge, MA: The Belknap Press of Harvard University Press, Copyright 1951 © 1955, 1979, 1983 by The President and Fellows of Harvard College.

5. Wilson Follet, *Modern American Usage: A Guide* (New York: Hill and Wang, 1966) 398.

6. Francis Christensen, "Note Toward a New Rhetoric," *College English* October 1963: 7–18.

Index

D

H

I

J

L

M

N

O

P

Q

R

S

Y